SVALBARD

BARENTS SEA

Moffen I.

Bear I.

Nordkapp (North Cape)

FINLAND

Isfjord SPITSBERGEN

Hammerfest

30°

GREENLAND SEA

Tromsø

70°

80°

SWEDEN

Lofoten Islands

Bodø

NORWAY

Jan Mayen Land

20°

GREENLAND

ARCTIC CIRCLE

Scoresby Sund

60°

DENMARK STRAIT

Siglufjord

10°

Reykjavik

ICELAND

Faeroe Islands

Angmagssalik

Westmann Islands

0°

BRITISH ISLES

SCOTLAND

ENGLAND

50°

Prins Christians Sund

EIRE

Cape Farewell

ATLANTIC

C

0°

OCEAN

10°

0   100   500   1000
KILOMETERS
0   100   500   1000
STATUTE MILES

40°   30°   20°

Saml. H. Bryant

Down Denmark Strait

Books by E. Newbold Smith

American Naval Broadsides
Down Denmark Strait

Down Denmark Strait

E. NEWBOLD SMITH

Little, Brown and Company — Boston — Toronto

FIRST EDITION

The author is grateful to C. Hurst & Co. (Publishers) Ltd.,
London, and McGill-Queen's University Press, Montreal, for
permission to quote from *History of Greenland*, Volume I,
Earliest Times to 1700 by Finn Gad, translated from Danish
by Ernst Dupont.

LIBRARY OF CONGRESS CATALOGING IN PUBLICATION DATA
Smith, Edgar Newbold.
    Down Denmark Strait.
    Includes index.
    1. Reindeer (Yacht)   2. Smith, Edgar Newbold.
3. Arctic regions.   4. Travelers — United States —
Biography. I. Title.
G606.S54   910'.09163'2   80–10250
    ISBN 0–316–79958–0

MV

Designed by Susan Windheim
Published simultaneously in Canada
by Little, Brown & Company (Canada) Limited

PRINTED IN THE UNITED STATES OF AMERICA

For
Ellie, Stocky, Lewis, and Hank
and in Memory of
Henry B. duPont
Who Sailed His Last Voyage

Acknowledgments

THE AUTHOR WISHES TO THANK certain people who made special contributions to the preparation and the final production of this book. Most notably, I could not have put it together without the indefatigable Orlin Donaldson. His help included early study and research in libraries and in government offices. His enthusiasm for all aspects of the North was positively addictive, and his photography speaks for itself. Other photographers include Diana Russell, Lewis duP. Smith, and Stockton N. Smith. Those who labored on the manuscript include Susan Gyger Baker, Nancy C. Tucker, and Jan Tripp. A special debt is owed to Charles H. Vilas, editor of the *Cruising Club News*. He published my articles and gave me special help and encouragement to expand them into a full-length book. Lastly, I am most grateful for the untiring effort of Christina Potter of Little, Brown and Company, who winnowed out a lot of chaff and produced some wheat.

Foreword

THE AMAZING PROLIFERATION of yachts and yachtsmen in recent years has been matched only by the proliferation of yachting publications and books. From my perspective as a boat owner for more than half a century and an editor of one yachting publication myself, *Down Denmark Strait* ranks among the best of these.

Just as water cannot rise higher than its source, so authors cannot write beyond the depths of their own experience. Newbold Smith's seasoned qualifications as a sailor, the accommodations and limitations of his vessel, *Reindeer,* and the explorer's curiosity he brought to his northern cruises combine here in a splendid story of adventure.

Until recently, about the only type of small yacht considered suitable for cruising northern waters was one of heavy scantlings, such as the Colin Archer–designed *redningskoite,* or "rescue boat." The scorn with which such boats are regarded by the modern racing enthusiast is equaled by the knowledgeable cruising man's incredulity that anybody would be foolhardy enough to sail into the waters from which Newbold Smith and *Reindeer* have emerged unscathed. *Reindeer,* however, is a far cry from her heavy predecessors in northern waters. She is a Sparkman and Stephens–designed, Nautor-built Swan-43, one of the earliest boats designed to the International Ocean Racing Rule.

The name Sparkman and Stephens means but one thing to an experienced yachtsman: safe, strong, fast, and comfortable ocean-going yachts, whether they be for cruising or racing. The New York Yacht Club honored Rod and Olin Stephens in early 1979 with a testimonial dinner celebrating the fiftieth anniversary of the founding of their firm.

Reindeer is but one of some 2,300 designs to come from their drawing boards. She is not a "one-off" but a production boat with modifications insisted upon by a veteran sailor unwilling to compromise comfort and seaworthiness to the single aim of winning races.

Being a Colin Archer buff myself, I still get culture shock when I see a modern IOR type of yacht out of water; yes, and even a Sparkman and Stephens Nautor-built Swan-43! My generation was introduced to yachting at the tail end of a thousand-year tradition of seaworthiness built block upon block from experience and passed on from father to son from century to century, until a reasonable defense against Father Neptune had been established. After World War II, much of our accumulated wisdom was abandoned in the excitement of new and exotic materials combined with the pressures of competition among the racing crowd. My ingrained instinct causes me to shudder at the sight of unsupported spade rudders, fin keels, high-windage, light-displacement hulls — everything that seems to tempt Neptune to take a jab with his trident. The results can be perilous, as has been so tragically demonstrated in the 1979 Fastnet Race. *Reindeer*, however, survived a Greenland grounding that would have shaken the nerves of even the great maestro Colin Archer himself, had she been a boat of his design.

It is true that Smith strengthened the scantlings of *Reindeer* in preparation for his northern cruises, but the fact remains that after finishing first in his class in the 1974 Bermuda Race and placing second on corrected time, he blithely took off for the iceberg-ridden waters of the North. This is no small tribute to Smith's confidence in his vessel's durability, for, of the first three American yachts to visit Greenland, *Shanghai*, *Leiv Eriksson*, and *Direction*, all were wrecked and only *Direction* was salvaged. A continuing testament to *Reindeer's* enduring versatility is the happy news that *Reindeer* placed second in class in the 1979 Marblehead-Halifax Race with Newbold Smith in command.

Smith has not sacrificed his "all" in order to live a life afloat. He is no escapist from civilization. He has a home, a wife, and a family. He has interests other than yachting, although yachting may loom foremost in his affections. Former football player, horseman, historian, and businessman, and the author of *American Naval Broadsides* in 1974, Smith is a man whose many facets enhance the remarkable experiences recounted in these pages.

The primordial urge to live free from the restraints of civilization is so strong that many of us, at one time or another, long to renounce everything we own to break out of our Promethean chains. But not all such dreams are fulfilled. Witness the sad ranks of dreamers who have come to the end of the line in distant, exotic harbors. Lack of experience is the primary cause, though an unsound boat, unsound finances, or unsound health may also be contributing factors. Happily, however, there are some fortunates whose urge toward freedom combines with the experience and the means to achieve their goals. But they too make sacrifices and even, as in the case of Major H. W. Tilman, who is mentioned elsewhere in this book, make the ultimate sacrifice by paying with their lives. Newbold Smith and his crew were well aware of the imminence of that final payment. But, as *Down Denmark Strait* proves, the rewards lie in the doing. Is that not what living a full life is all about?

There is another, more tangible reward in Smith's case, though it is not one he anticipated when *Reindeer* set out for northern waters. Newbold Smith was awarded the coveted Blue Water Medal of the Cruising Club of America for his 1976 cruise to Spitsbergen.

For more than half a century, the Cruising Club has been meticulously selective in bestowing this award. In fact, very few of the club's own members have been recipients. The Blue Water Medal is awarded for, among other distinctions, "noteworthy voyages made in small boats" and "meritorious seamanship displayed by amateur sailors of all nationalities." Alain Gerbault, Marcel Bardiaux, Eric Tabarly, and Bernard Moitessier of France; Eric and Susan Hiscock, Sir Francis Chichester, Major H. W. Tilman, and Sir Alec Rose of England; John Guzzwell and Beryl and Miles Smeeton of Canada; Vito Dumas of Argentina; Harry Pidgeon, Roderick Stephens, Jr., and Hal Roth of the United States — these are but a few of the distinguished recipients from a list spanning more than fifty years. Newbold Smith is in good company — as the reader will be throughout this book.

Charles H. Vilas
On board *Direction*
Baddeck, Nova Scotia
August, 1979

Contents

Down Denmark Strait

Prologue:

Notions Northward

ON A COLD, CRISP DECEMBER DAY in 1968, I was at Mystic Seaport in Connecticut for the annual meeting of the Mystic Marine Museum. It was Friday evening and I was drinking beer and conversing with my friend Jack Parkinson, an old salt if ever there was one. I had known Jack through mutual participation in sailing events, both racing and cruising. He was a man who lived life to its fullest.

We compared notes that night and found amazing correlation in our lives, although he was nineteen years my senior. He had played guard for Harvard; I played tackle for the Navy. He had hunted the red fox in Massachusetts; I had done the same in Pennsylvania. He had ridden timber races, point-to-points; so had I. He had won the John Jorrocks Race, so had I — thirty-seven years later. He had raced and cruised his boat up and down the East Coast, to Bermuda, Halifax, and to Britain and Europe. So had I. But he had done one thing I hadn't done, and that was of crucial interest to me. He had crossed and recrossed the far North Atlantic in a four-piper World War I vintage destroyer, one of the type given by FDR to Churchill for antisubmarine work. Parky had chased U-boats and convoyed merchantmen in World War II, even before the United States entered the war. He had steamed north of Iceland and down Denmark Strait, summer and winter, fighting the enemy in the fiercest conditions. His enemy was not just Germans; it was also weather. (The only enemy I had ever fought was our own Army football team, and not too successfully at that, for four years at Annapolis. They had a backfield of Davis, Blanchard, and Tucker, against whom all we could throw was Faith, Hope, and Courage.)

It was Jack's North Atlantic experience that caught my rapt attention, for I was just in the process of negotiating the purchase of a new boat in Finland and I wondered if I could sail her back via the northern route. The monthly pilot charts of the North Atlantic, put out by the Navy's Hydrographic Office, revealed the greater prevalence of northerly winds the farther north on the chart one went. This seemed significant to me because it meant that a boat could avoid the prevailing sou'wester-lies, which would normally be on the nose on the return to the States, by steering a course well to the north of the traffic lanes and by passing close by Iceland and Greenland. Parkinson had never sailed his yawl up there, but his Navy experience in those waters was rare and invaluable. I was bent on tapping that font of knowledge.

"Jack, what do you think of my sailing the new *Reindeer* back home the northern route via Iceland and Cape Farewell, Greenland?" My question evoked silence and then gradually an avuncular smile. He had me like a child on his knee, and he was going to make the most of it.

"Newbold, my friend, you are just plain out of your mind," Jack said with finality. "Never — and I mean never — get your ass in those waters between Iceland and Greenland. If you do, and I know you're just apt to try it, you'll have your head handed to you!"

"But, Jack, I was just looking at the pilot charts," I said.

"Oh, the hell with those things," he interrupted. "Do you think they apply to a tissue-paper-thin racing machine Sparkman and Stephens have designed?"

"Well, gee, I don't know, Jack. Rod Stephens himself sailed back the northern route in *Dorade* in 1932," I said.

"Yes, I know, but he didn't go up where you're talking about. You can't take an ocean racer into those waters." Jack was adamant. "You hit a chunk of pack ice with that fiberglass hull and you'll have ice water at your crotch in no time flat. Besides, you're a fool to risk a new and untried boat in an ocean passage."

Even though they had been using fiberglass with polyester resin in hull construction for ten years, Parkinson didn't trust it. He knew it was ideal for ocean racing because of its high strength-to-weight ratio, but he couldn't accept it for the Far North, where ice and severe storm conditions prevail. I had to concede that he was correct about exposing a new boat to a trans-Atlantic crossing. I should have known that from my two earlier boats. There is always something wrong with a new boat in the beginning.

Somehow that evening, however, the message I got from Jack's lips was "Stay away from Denmark Strait," but the message I got from his eyes was "If I were only ten years younger I'd sign on with you." The whole idea of a challenge in the Far North was just his meat. It warmed him up to tell sea stories, not only of his own experience in that vintage tin can, USS *Bainbridge,* but also the saga of *Bismarck,* the crack German pocket battleship that went on a North Atlantic rampage in the spring of 1941. Together with the heavy cruiser *Prinz Eugen,* the 42,000-ton *Bismarck* took off from Norway on a northwestward course across the top of Iceland. The Royal Navy was quickly alerted to the sortie and immediately dispatched a good part of her Home Fleet to intercept the raiders. The worst possible weather, sea, and ice conditions were predicted for Denmark Strait, so of course that's just where the Germans headed. *Bismarck* and *Prinz Eugen* slipped down the strait between the pack ice on the Greenland side and minefields on the Iceland side. The weather was so bad the Germans went undetected for a long time. Britain sent her battleships *Hood, Prince of Wales, King George V,* several destroyers, and the aircraft carrier *Victorious* in pursuit. The latter steamed south of Iceland, not dreaming the Germans would sneak into Denmark Strait with the pack ice.

By dumb luck an American pilot in a patrol plane spotted *Bismarck* through a break in the cloud cover. She was steaming southwest near Cape Farewell, the southern tip of Greenland. We were not yet at war, but this sighting was reported quickly to the British, and their fleet went to the attack. The first casualty was HMS *Hood,* which was promptly sunk with all hands by the *Bismarck'*s deadly accurate gunnery. Finally, torpedo bombers from the carrier *Ark Royal,* together with salvos from HMS *Prince of Wales* sank the mighty *Bismarck* before she could escape to the coast of occupied France. *Prinz Eugen,* meanwhile, did escape to the port of Brest.

Clearly Parkinson was not exaggerating about the conditions that prevail in that body of water that separates Iceland from Greenland. For that reason, and his equally cogent point about the danger of a new and untested boat, I dropped the idea of sailing my new vessel home across the Atlantic. Instead, I planned to take delivery of the boat in June of 1969 at a Finnish port in the Gulf of Bothnia and thereafter take a six-week cruise across Sweden, the south coast of Norway and up the east coast as far as Søgne Fjord. Then we would sail south to Germany via the west coast of Denmark and ship *Reindeer* home from Bremen.

I signed the purchase contract in a January visit to Jakobstad (near the Arctic Circle), where the first few Swan-43 hulls were already on the assembly line. I'll never forget climbing in and around the fiberglass shells of those boats. The hull thickness was no greater than five-eighths of an inch and compression strength depended to a great extent on four transverse plywood bulkheads. I was able to point out some bad features of the interior design of those early boats and ordered special changes in my particular copy. The joiner work was superlative, but the builders were early in their learning curve. They had no idea of the stresses of ocean racing, so I insisted on much beefing up, which later became standard practice.

I returned in May for another check on the progress. All sorts of decisions had to be made. The electronics package had to be selected. The choice of engine, stove, and even deck configuration was optional. I made the best choices I could, and in this respect Rod Stephens, the famous naval architect, was a big help. He was over there to supervise the details of construction and to help the builder. Some say Rod is God, for good reason. In the sailboat business he comes pretty close to being the ultimate authority.

Even after all these preparations, when we finally took delivery in late June and set out on the cruise, many things went awry. The mess table in the main cabin was merely screwed to the deck, rather than through-bolted. During the first little blow someone fell against it and knocked it right off the cabin sole. There was no flexible steel hose in the exhaust line, so the line broke at the manifold under normal engine vibration, creating a mess. Our voltage regulator blew out. The freshwater tanks leaked. Our stove had the wrong brushes in the burners; they were soldered instead of brazed. They melted and started a conflagration that was a three-alarmer. Then the midship winches were in-

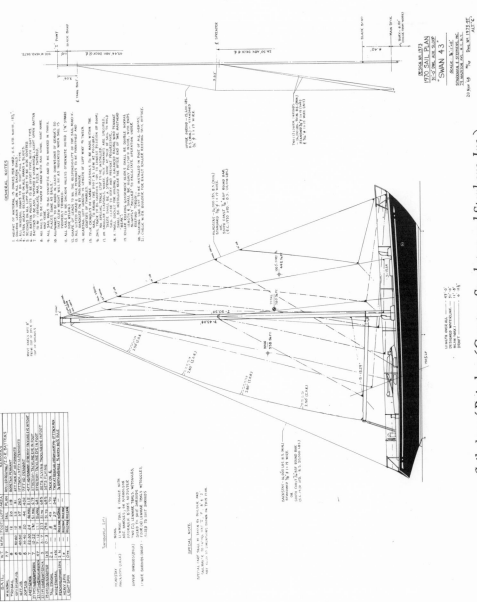

Sail plan of Reindeer (Courtesy Sparkman and Stephens, Inc.)

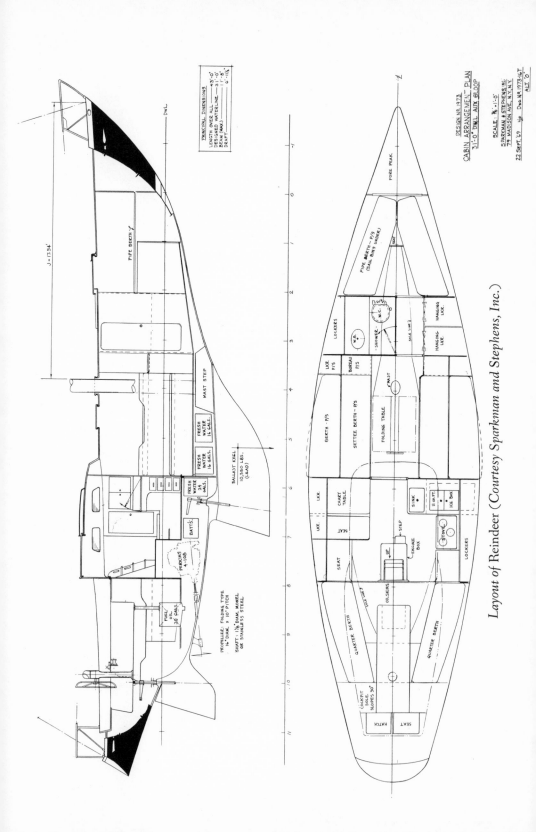

PRINCIPAL DIMENSIONS
LENGTH OVER ALL — 43'-0"
DESIGNED WATERLINE — 31'-0"
BEAM (MAX.) — 11'-6"
DRAFT — 6'-11¼"

PIPE BERTH

J = 17.54'

DWL

MAST STEP

FRESH WATER 16 GALS.

FRESH WATER 16 GALS.

BALLAST KEEL
10,380 LBS.
(LEAD)

FRESH WATER 24 GALS.

BATT'S.

PERKINS 4-108

FUEL OIL 20 GALS.

PROPELLER: FOLDING TYPE.
16" DIAM. X 10" PITCH.
SHAFT: 1⅛" DIAM. MONEL
OR STAINLESS STEEL.

0   1   2   3   4   5   6   7   8   9   10   11

DESIGN N.º 1973
CABIN ARRANGEMENT PLAN
31'-0" DWL AUX SLOOP

SCALE : ⅜" = 1'-0"

SPARKMAN & STEPHENS, INC.
79 MADISON AVE., N.Y., N.Y.

22 SEPT. '69   hp   DWG. N.º 1973-167
ALT. "0"

FORE PEAK

PIPE BERTH ~ P/S
(SAIL BINS UNDER)

SAIL

W.C.

SHOWER

SAIL LINE ?

HANGING LKR.

HANGING LKR.

LOCKERS

W.C.

LKR. P/S

BUREAU P/S

BERTH ~ P/S

SETTEE BERTH ~ P/S

FOLDING TABLE

MAST

LKR.

CHART TABLE

SINK

ICE BOX

SEAT

UP

STEP

STOVE

LKR.

SEAT

ENGINE BOX

LOCKERS

QUARTER BERTH

QUARTER BERTH

OILSKINS

LOCKER LINE ?

COCKPIT SOLE. SLOPES 50°

SEAT

HATCH

Layout of Reindeer (Courtesy Sparkman and Stephens, Inc.)

adequate in size. In total, a lot had to be corrected, so we stopped for three days at a shipyard in Sweden. We muddled through, but I shudder to think what would have happened had we sailed her back that first summer! Instead we got her to Germany, where she was carefully cradled and put on the deck of a ship of the North German Lloyd line. She arrived in Baltimore in early September without a scratch — typical German efficiency.

That winter I began to think about Jack Parkinson's stories about the North Atlantic. I had already read a considerable amount of material on the Arctic, beginning as far back as 1950 when I was buying books by great polar explorers. I read about the Norwegians: Nansen, Sverdrup, and Amundsen; the Britishers: Hudson, Phipps, Parry, and Franklin; the Danes, the Swedes, the Icelanders, the Canadians, and Americans, such as Kane, Peary, Hall, Greely, and Byrd. They all had one thing in common: love of the Arctic. Explorers were the astronauts of yesteryear and in their day they had a following who identified with them and celebrated their exploits. In earlier years it seemed to be a drive for a northern route to the Orient that inspired arctic exploration. Later it was the polar passion, the race to get there first. Whatever the stated objective that drove these men of the north, they all professed an excitement and love for their arctic environment, and those who returned wrote of it in awe. The spirit of their accounts was contagious. I began to wonder if I could go there on my own.

Not only the old polar explorers, but seafaring sorts of this century, like Captain Bob Bartlett and Commander MacMillan, caught my attention. Their many trips to Arctic Canada in schooners stirred the boyhood adrenalin of many readers of accounts of such adventure. Even today sailors of the Royal Cruising Club don't bat an eye at a 20,000-mile trip to Patagonia and back. Major H. W. Tilman's stories of his many forays into the ice off Greenland, Spitsbergen, and Jan Mayen Island are dangerously enticing. Another addict of the North, Paul Sheldon, M.D., of the Cruising Club of America, had sailed his beloved ketch *Seacrest* down the Labrador so often he was nearly as well known in that part of the world as Sir Wilfred Grenfell, the Labrador Doctor himself. Sheldon's logs were put together in a book by his friend Charles H. Vilas, a sailor and writer of the North, and the title they selected, *Lure of the Labrador,* was extremely apt.

The combination of adventure in the North and that on the high seas is truly mystical and powerful. I'm reminded of three stanzas of a favorite poem of mine by Longfellow, which neatly captures the feeling of those who venture far across the sea:

> *How he heard the ancient helmsman*
> *Chant a song so wild and clear,*
> *That the sailing sea-bird slowly*
> *Poised upon the mast to hear,*
>
> *Till his soul was full of longing,*
> *And he cried with impulse strong, —*
> *"Helmsman! for the love of heaven,*
> *Teach me, too, that wondrous song!"*
>
> *"Wouldst thou," — so the helmsman answered,*
> *"Learn the secret of the sea?*
> *Only those who brave its dangers*
> *Comprehend its mystery!"*

These verses ring especially true, it seems to me, for those seamen of the past and present who have had the good fortune to sail to the Arctic and return.

Sailing is an intricate sport, and sometimes a demanding one. The ocean plays no favorites except perhaps with those who are respectful and well prepared, and it provides endless change and challenge to those who answer its call. My means of answering has been the three ocean racing boats that I have owned and skippered since 1953. The last of these, *Reindeer*, was so well designed and crafted that I expected to keep her many years. Then came a new international handicap system for ocean racing, called the International Offshore Rule (IOR). This was the result of a long effort to amalgamate the various U.S. and foreign handicap systems under which boats of different dimensions and potential speed could race one another fairly. The new rule, very complex and arcane, encouraged development of ultralight displacement and a tall rig. *Reindeer* had neither. Newer boats, much lighter in construction, were designed to take advantage of this new rule (IOR), which was heavily influenced by the Royal Ocean Racing Club of Britain. As years passed, more and more boats were designed and produced as purely racing machines. They looked like something out of Cape Kennedy, not Cape Cod. Modern technology had combined with the influence of day racing enthusiasts to produce a monster that seemed to me to be out of control as to purpose and price. *Reindeer*'s disadvantage was particularly noticeable downwind, where her conventional displacement would not enable her to match the extreme-light-displacement, surfing types that were collaring all the cups in recent years. While *Reindeer* was designed and constructed to withstand any sea conditions, the new IOR types had become stripped-out machines with only one virtue: speed. Under normal racing conditions *Reindeer* could not compete with these newer boats. Since traditionalists have scorned this trend toward expensive, one-shot boats known as Grand Prix types, a corrective adjustment to the handicap system was to be expected, but meanwhile in races we were behind the eight ball. From a cruising standpoint, however, *Reindeer* was more than adequate, especially where performance meant something, like going to windward to beat the pack ice to a safe haven. In short, I felt that a fast boat designed for racing could, under tough circumstances, be an ideal vessel for cruising purposes.

In my case, cruising and racing have always been compatible, rather than mutually exclusive, sports. Like Burgundy and claret, both should be savored. Cruising provides the opportunity to expand one's understanding of nature, to observe oceanic flora and fauna and, depending on the time and facilities at one's disposal, to see parts of the world less adulterated by man. Racing, on the other hand, offers an enjoyable outlet for the urge to compete. It also is responsible for the rapid development of more efficient boat designs, better materials and technique.

By the time I bought *Reindeer*, racing had become even more important to me after an accident I'd had in 1972 that had left me partially paralyzed on my right side. I was thrown from a horse while jumping a small stake-and-bound fence on my farm. The horse was a fine hunter and had carried me in many hunts and races over timber. On that fateful morning in September, however, he decided suddenly to give me the heave-ho. I landed on my head and jammed a couple of disks into the cervical area of my spinal cord and became instantly quadriplegic — paralyzed from the neck down. I lay on the ground for three hours before some children found me. Conscious all the while, I could see turkey vultures licking their chops on the tree limbs overhead. These creatures worried me a bit, for I had no way to protect my eyes, my hands and feet being paralyzed. It was a helpless feeling, not being able to move.

Thank God the children came along! They summoned an ambulance and I was carefully taken to the hospital, where later a cervical laminectomy was performed. After two months of intensive care and physical therapy I got back on my feet, but my right leg and arm were left with neurological deficit, meaning that my choice of activities would be curtailed. Although I couldn't bounce around the deck as before, I could still sail (and shout orders), and this became essentially the only athletic activity in which I could compete.

Early in the seventies I began studying the charts of Labrador, and names popped out like Run-by-Guess, Smokey Tickle, and Battle Harbour. Interesting, I thought to myself. Most sportsmen I know respond viscerally to names such as the Galloping Ghost, the Fighting Irish, or the Army Mule. Some hold sacred the Sultan of Swat, Joltin' Joe, and the Gashouse Gang. On the greens maybe they talk of the eleventh at Merion or the eighteenth at Pebble Beach. But whoever heard of Run-by-Guess and Smokey Tickle? Or, for that matter, Fair Isle and Dungeness, Ushant and Scilly, and Fastnet Rock? Close to our shores: Kick 'em Jenny, Sambro Light, and Brenton Reef.

These names are all part of the lore of the deep-water sailor. They ring in the minds of generations of seafarers. The feel of rounding Fastnet Rock in the Irish Sea after a hard beat to windward in half a gale and the relief thereafter as the spinnaker goes up and the boat roars downwind at ten knots is something probably few people have experienced. In *Reindeer* I felt I had the means to enjoy some of these experiences and see some of these places.

By 1974 *Reindeer* had been well tested and improved, and I wasn't much in doubt about the vessel's ability to handle the ocean, any part of it. She was safe enough for us to undertake a long trip in parts of the ocean where hazard was not uncommon. After all, the Gulf Stream is seldom a picnic, and we had crossed it several times going to and returning from Bermuda.

So it was in the summer of 1974 that I decided to cruise to Labrador, after the finish of the Bermuda Race. There are other important international races, such as Britain's Fastnet and Australia's Sydney-Hobart, but none is equal in stature to the Bermuda Race. Also, none is more fun after the race is over. In short, I was hooked. Therefore, we had to make dual preparations for the race and for the cruise north after a little R and R in Bermuda. Actually this made good sense, for an arrival too early off Newfoundland and Labrador might be fraught with excessive problems with ice. While Bermuda would add some 1,300 miles to the trip, the race itself would be an excellent bench test for all the rigging and hull. If some stay or halyard were going to part, surely the race would be where it might happen. Likewise with the hull, if it could take the pounding of racing through the usually rough waters of the Gulf Stream, we could sail to the Canadian sub-Arctic with a lot more confidence.

In preparing for the Bermuda Race, most owners — at least those to whom a boat is something more than a vehicle to fame — must consider and plan for the trip home. Usually it's a passage to that part of the East Coast where the skipper plans to sail during the rest of the summer. Thus, even under ordinary circumstances, dual preparation is required, for the race and the subsequent cruise or passage. In our case the distance and the temperature change necessitated more than average planning for the entire summer.

The first phase of the cruise was from Bermuda to St. John's, Newfoundland, a distance of about 1,100 miles. After a crew change, the second phase would take us to the vicinity of Hopedale, Labrador, and the new crew could fly there or to wherever we were then located for a second crew change. Phase III would take us north to our turning point, which I did not dare predetermine for fear of tempting fate. How could I know what the ice situation would be months hence? The end of Phase III would find us back at Corner Brook, Newfoundland, where I planned to turn over the command to my son Stocky, who, with three college friends of his, was to take *Reindeer* down the coast to Connecticut.

Preparations for any expedition should begin with the advice of experts. In this respect, Dr. Paul Sheldon of Princeton was immensely helpful, as was his book *Lure of the Labrador*. The logs of his trips in the old ketch *Seacrest* were consulted regularly, even more than the *Coast Pilot*, a publication of the Canadian Hydrographic Office. Another valuable source of information was Jimmy Madden of Beverly Farms,

Massachusetts. Jimmy had been a young Harvard man on the 1931 expedition to map the northern Labrador, under the command of Dr. Alexander Forbes and the auspices of the American Geographic Society. They took the schooner *Ramah*, along with float planes, and mapped the whole Torngat mountain range for the first time. The hardbound report of that expedition was must reading, as well as a handy reference.

Equipment for the cruise was another major consideration. One of our principal additions was a radar set, the antenna of which was mounted on a pedestal on top of a special jigger mast. We sent all that paraphernalia to Bermuda to be installed after the race, along with a hot-water radiator for added cabin heat and odds and ends like Cutter insect repellent, mosquito netting, extra rubber tanks for spare diesel fuel on deck, special down-filled sleeping bags, gloves, and bags of charcoal. Even with all the careful planning, we did not have any excess of alcohol for the stove. The same could be said of large-scale, small-area charts. Extra anchor chain, anchor lines, and heavy plow anchors were important additions, as, of course, were medical supplies and safety equipment.

One surprise last-minute item that I thought might be handy was a telephone book for the Northeastern Territories. The names listed in this telephone book in some of the villages were unusual: Sydney Trapper and Philip Voyageur and Ronnie Loon of Mistassini Lake; Levi Nochasak of Makkovik; Koomangapik, Hyak, and Koonoo of Pond Inlet; Lizzie Okkuatsiajuak and E. Merkuratsuk of Nain, Attaguarjukuserk of Igloolik; Methusaleh Kunuk of Frobisher, and Simon Poker of Davis Inlet, just to name a few. The ethnic mix in these names reflects the meeting of the races and cultures in the north, revealing English, French, and Eskimo, and even Old Testament names typical of the eighteenth and nineteenth centuries.

While I was working on plans for this expedition, Tom Watson of IBM and Yacht *Palawan* was busy organizing a trip to West Greenland, with Jimmy Madden as navigator. His trip would make us look like pikers, as he intended to go north of Thule. That's getting up there! When Madden told me their plans and Norrie Hoyt showed his slides of an earlier trip he took to Greenland, I began to expand my dreams to include Greenland, Iceland, Jan Mayen, and perhaps even Spitsbergen someday. I tucked these thoughts away in the back of my mind.

Meanwhile, by happenstance I met Dean William Gaither of the

College of Marine Studies of the University of Delaware. Both Dean Gaither and Professor Franklin Daiber were interested in my Labrador project. Delaware was building a first-class school of oceanography and marine biology that might one day rank with Scripps Institute and Woods Hole. I agreed to take two young graduate students majoring in piscatory matters. At first I was apprehensive about the college guys. I had visions of seagoing Don Quixotes. Happily, they worked out well, and each of them made significant contributions, both to *Reindeer* and to my own store of knowledge. None of the scientists was part of the racing crew. The racers were more interested in knot count than plankton count, and for the first 650 miles, Newport to Bermuda, that's what mattered. The boys I invited to propel us to Bermuda were no tyros. They knew victory and defeat, and if in defeat one gained character, then, I figured, we would be a ready lot at Newport.

1

The Bermuda Race

MY RACING CREW ASSEMBLED at Newport on Thursday night, 20 June 1974. The race committee for the first time had changed the start to Friday instead of the normal Saturday. We welcomed this idea on the theory we'd get more beach life once we got to Bermuda. Arriving by plane from different places, we all became aware of the high-voltage excitement in the air. Nothing new, of course; that's always the way it is on the eve of this great biennial event. But one thing was different.

The year 1974 was a bummer for the bourses of the world, especially the one in Manhattan. The New York Stock Exchange was out to lunch. No help was coming from the White House; its occupants were in bunkers. Here we were at Newport, which once was the summer home of the Four Hundred. I reckoned it was now down to about four; yet out there on the water sat 150 glistening gold-platers, aggregating $30 million, give or take. All over the streets were well-scrubbed young men in blue blazers going about their business, last-minute errands on the eve of the race.

All seemed positively oblivious to what looked like the death rattle of the Western World. For Britons, this was old stuff: white tie and tails on the way to the poorhouse. But for us Philadelphia Quakers it was eye-popping. I couldn't help wondering how long we were going to be able to keep this show up! Get rid of the cleaning woman, take the bus to work, but for God's sake, don't sell the boat! That seemed to be the theme.

In any event, my gang, which numbered nine, finally made it to James-town, across Narragansett Bay from Newport, where *Reindeer* was riding at a mooring. Jamestown was quieter, and I preferred to stay there during the week before the race. Besides, one of my old shipmates, Bart Lippin-cott, had a summer home there, and he and his gracious family provided us with bunks and other perquisites that made life pleasant.

The rest of my crew were studies. The two watch captains had made this race with me since 1960; names of Madeira and Ballard, old names, been around awhile. Both lawyers, both peacocks, and not afraid to talk. Also, not afraid to tell me to go fly a kite. Ned Madeira doesn't know the difference between a Pauillac and a yarmulke, yet he got invited into the Commanderie de Bordeaux! As a seagoing chef, however, he's in a class by himself. One of his average concoctions is grapes flambés.

John Ballard made it to the top through memory. He memorized so many hymns they hired him as counsel to the Diocese of Pennsylvania. What they didn't know was Ballard's repertoire of dirty songs. He mixes both gracefully, such as "Now the Day Is Over" and "My Girl Mary Anne, Queen of all the Acrobats" — as ribald a number as they come.

The navigator, Edwin Gaynor from Southport, Connecticut, had one special quality: he could snow the watch captains. Not only that, he could stop them in midsentence by such deft prose as "Have you lawyers ever met a payroll?"

The other crewmen were equally talented. Terry Lloyd from Phila-delphia and Phil Parish, Bill Starkey, and Gary Robson, all from the Eastern Shore of Maryland. Each of them had special capabilities, and they all had raced on *Reindeer* many times.

As in past years Gaynor and I checked everyone out on the presumed position of the Gulf Stream, as observed by the Woods Hole oceanogra-phers. Weather is a capricious thing over 650 miles of open ocean, and it is even more pertinent in the area of the Gulf Stream, the dominant factor that makes the Bermuda Race unique. Stream behavior and the proper analysis thereof are the most important determinants of success. There are frequent meanders in the generally east-flowing Gulf Stream, and if one can catch a southeast meander, he can get a terrific lift. The variables are many, and of all of those one of the most important is luck. I announced my intentions of where to hit the Stream, so as to take maximum advantage of a southeasterly meander, occurring somewhere west of the rhumb line. The rhumb line and the rum line are indistinguishable; the former is the straight course on a Mercator projection, crossing all longitudes at the same angle; the latter is the course we think will get us to the bar at the Royal Bermuda Yacht Club the quickest. The strategy is to get the maximum kick out of the Stream in a direction roughly toward Bermuda and, alternatively, to avoid any kick from the Stream in the opposite direction. Both favorable and unfavorable sets by the Stream are usually available. If you hit it right, it's skill — if you don't, it's bad luck.

Gaynor was fiendish in his pursuit of the probabilities, both as to weather and Stream activity. We have never had a strategy difference, Gaynor and I, and luckily all the other Indian chiefs seem to defer to us on that. Tactics, however, are another matter. The watch captains keep a weather eye on both the navigator and the skipper, especially as we close the island. It's surprising how many assistant navigators come out of the woodwork when the horizons aren't so hot for sights or when Edwin and I have any facial contortions that might suggest we don't know where we are. We are then referred to as Fugawi Indians, who are noted for muttering in muffled tones, "Where the fugawi?"

"Okay, you guys," Ed said, as he had on so many races before, "please record your watch in the log every hour, and if you set half-hour wheel stints, make half-hour entries. Also, please don't figure a fudge factor for steering error or leeway or set. I'll take care of that."

Parish put in a plug for charging batteries on a regular schedule. Other comments were made by Terry, Gary, and the others — all constructive. It's no different from in the locker room before a game. We know the competition, his strengths and weaknesses, and we're just reminding each other of all the little things we already know.

Once all was covered to my satisfaction, to Ballard's satisfaction, to Neddy's satisfaction, and to Edwin's satisfaction, we relaxed for a round of nightcaps and a little repartee before some of us departed for our last night ashore.

The next day we were underway in plenty of time to reach the starting line area to get the feel of things. "How much time to the warning gun, Ned?" I asked as I steered *Reindeer*, maneuvering for the start of this twenty-ninth biennial race. Madeira was the tactician, and he had the stopwatch, or at least the one that I didn't have. I used one watch for timing certain distances, but Ned had the official one, so I wouldn't make the mistake of nervously stopping it. Steering at the start of a race is a full-time occupation, and as the pressure builds up I find it helpful to talk to someone and to hear from others, at least a few crisp words.

"Two minutes to the warning gun for our class," Madeira replied calmly.

I had already practiced a few runs upwind of the destroyer, which was the committee boat on the windward end of the line. That way we were clear of the first class to start, which was Class F. This year they were holding a reverse start, sending the little boats off first. Class F had started at 1300 hours, and we were in Class E, starting at 1330. The three-inch gun on the "tin can" boomed out our warning signal. Ten minutes to the start. In five minutes the propeller had to be locked. Visibility was fair, wind south sou'west, twelve knots.

Starting 160 boats, all the way from seventy-footers manned by eighteen men down to thirty-six-footers manned by six men, was no small task. The fleet was divided into six classes, all according to the vessels' handicap ratings. An effort is made to group boats of similar dimensions in each class, so that the real competition is among boats of roughly equivalent speed. There is an overall prize for first place on corrected time, but normally the overall winner is a matter of weather and timing. If the race is a fast one until the fleet hits a calm area north of Bermuda, then it would surely be a small-boat race. The smaller boats would catch up to bigger boats and close the gap in their time handicap. Conversely, if there were light air on the surface for a long period, particularly at the end of the race, probably the bigger boats would be favored, as they would have the tall rigs to pick up some wind aloft and there would be a longer interval between their finish and that of the little babies.

Tactics at the start of a long race are not as critical as that of an America's Cup match. A fantastic helmsman like Ted Turner has an advantage, but he can't stand watch for three or four days. Nor would his deft hand on the wheel make as much difference as, say, his navigator's accuracy. But his organization, on the other hand, would be vitally important. Here at the start, the skipper maneuvers about in order to decide where to cross the line and exactly what sail combination to use. He doesn't want to be late getting to the line at the gun; more important, he doesn't want to be early and get recalled for another start.

As we practiced for the start, I didn't like the way the spectator fleet was pushing out toward our path, but the Coast Guard saw the problem and got right on them. We jibed at about 250 yards past the line and headed back for our final reach to the start.

"Six minutes to the start, leader." Neddy's voice was a little more taut than before.

"Okay, Phil, cut the engine and lock the prop, please."

Parish had already anticipated me, and the two-bladed folding prop was locked in neutral, and off went the engine. Henceforth the engine would be used only to charge batteries, until after we crossed the finish line in Bermuda.

When the starting line includes a large vessel at the windward end and there are lots of starters, I usually prefer the middle or the leeward end. However, since the sturdy Brenton Reef Light Tower instead of a buoy was the leeward end, I didn't like that end either. It might be unforgiving in the event we misjudged it. The weather end usually is crowded, and a vessel as big as a destroyer blankets out the wind in the area immediately to leeward of it. Furthermore, gray paint off a warship wouldn't blend well with the dark blue of my topsides. A boat to leeward has the right of way, so at the weather end one can be forced right into the mark until the starting gun sounds and the leeward boat must fall off to her normal course. Fouling the starting mark would take place in full view of the committee, and even though its chairman was a former partner of mine in the brokerage business (prior to Armageddon), I knew his friendship would cut no ice in a matter of this kind. Therefore, considering all this, the middle of the line was the place for us to jockey for position. Just then I chose to go for it. "Jibe ho," I hollered, as I saw an opening in the middle of the line.

"Do you see *Dynamite*, Newbs?" Ballard sung out from his forward position with his head under the skirt of the number one genoa. *Reindeer* and *Dynamite* were on a collision course.

"Son of a bitch; she's barging," I said.

"Come off, Smythe, we'll be over the line," Terry Lloyd barked.

"Damn it, I've got *Vib* over here to leeward," I said. "I see you, Bill," a quick assurance to *Vib*'s skipper that I recognized her right of way.

Dynamite was the culprit, but if I put it to her I might go over the line myself and be recalled for a false start. It wasn't worth risking that, just to put the tag on *Dynamite*. This wasn't a team match. How we fought for the start even though we had 650 miles to go! A matter of pride, I guess.

"Boom," the gun sounded, and we fell off looking for free air. Tensions abated.

All during the first few hours after the start we seemed to be holding our own, maybe inching away from some. Our sister ships, *Dove* and *Tiger Too,* both very well sailed, were well up to weather and doing a little better, I feared. My strategy changes in every Bermuda Race, but this early in the race I decided not to keep her too close to the wind. I figured I could climb up to weather later if the wind hauled or let up. Of course I didn't know what the others were thinking, but my idea, after long consultation with Gaynor, was to hit the Stream about twenty to twenty-five miles west of the rhumb line, which is indeed where we hit it. As it later turned out, perhaps thirty or thirty-five miles might have been better.

For the most part on Friday we carried our number one heavy genoa, occasionally going to the big reacher. When the wind slackened we tried the flanker, which is a flat-cut reaching spinnaker, but it improved things only in light air. When the wind piped up, the flanker heeled us too much and we'd go back to the reacher. Later in the afternoon, the big boys started to parade by; they had started later. One such vessel, *Challenge*, belonging to Fenny Johnson, absolutely steamed past us. She was well crewed, and she looked fat at that point.

All Friday night and during the day Saturday the wind held steady, twelve to fifteen knots out of the southwest to west southwest. Gradually the fleet was spreading apart, so one had less to go on, in regard to competitors. Earlier we had been sighting the competitors regularly. *Gambler*, *Decibel*, *Caroline*, and *Ariel* were all near enough to give us comparative bearings. Before dark on Friday we were passing Class F boats, but some of them, like *Hot Canary* and *Privateer*, were hanging in there, not dropping back as they should have been doing. I was constantly bugged by the question of where was *Dove*? Where was *Tiger Too*? They were our sister ships that had been doing better than *Reindeer* in competition. Both were well up to weather in the early going. Another question was the whereabouts of *Harpoon*, Mark Ewing's Swan-44. She was always well sailed and her red and white striped chute was usually too far ahead. At one point late on Friday afternoon, I was sure we spotted her on our starboard hand, a little abaft the beam. She had started in Class D, which went off right after our class.

For some reason this was turning out to be a race with very few sightings of competitors. On the off watch on Saturday, for the hell of it, I decided to examine the crews, at least for those boats who got their crew lists in on time. Mentally I classified the hottest sailors in the categories of Larchmont dinghy sailors and Long Island Sound Internationals, Marbleheaders, the Pacific Coast, Britishers, and Chesapeake types, not necessarily in that order. There were all kinds of big names of the sailing world represented in that fleet, like, for example, Ted Hood, Bus Mosbacher, and Lowell North. The real key to a keen crew is not just big names, but a good balance in talent. In an ocean race you need the constant competitiveness of the day-racing, round-the-buoy type, but you also need the good judgment of a seaman: the man with plenty of experience who knows how much the rig will stand, who constantly looks for chafe or other signs of a dangerous problem, and who can tell by the look of the sky and the sea that it's time to reduce canvas and brace for a squall.

In the Bermuda Race the requirements are such that all the entrants have experienced crew. This, coupled with strictly enforced rules on equipment and seaworthiness, has prevented tragedy from striking. Certainly in my eleven races to the Onion Patch there had been many gales and high seas, which, in racing, as opposed to cruising, put the boats to the ultimate test. The parting of sails, shackles, and halyards is commonplace; even dismastings are not rare. Loss of life, however, has been avoided (with, I believe, one exception), and that is attributable to the extreme thoroughness of the sponsors.

By early Sunday we hit the Gulf Stream. There was a sudden rise in water temperature, and surface seaweed appeared in regular lines, indicating Stream activity. Another typical indicator of the Stream was the marked cloud formation that almost described a sky tracing of the path of this amazing ocean phenomenon. There are other ocean currents, but the Gulf Stream must have the highest value economically, because without it Great Britain, Scandinavia, and the rest of northern Europe would be mostly tundra. Indeed, the northeastern United States would have solid ice in all its rivers in winter.

The Stream, as we call it with some deference, is not in any way stationary. It moves. Its path has many offshoots and meanders, and they change. Fortunately for us, the Woods Hole oceanographic people are equipped to determine a probable path by flying over the Stream and studying temperature data that they collect with heat-sensing devices. Woods Hole renders such data to the entire fleet, and in return we are supposed to submit our temperature and navigation records for their data bank. Many times I've heard rumors that certain eager beavers have flown out over the Gulf Stream and compiled private data, but if true it hasn't especially helped them, judging from the winners.

We sliced through the Stream on Sunday, and the wind hardly ever exceeded force 7, unlike in so many previous races. Neither was it flat calm for us, and therein lies the key. I figure if you are becalmed for any great amount, you can forget it; you'll never win a damn thing, because sure as hell someone in some other part of the ocean has a breeze and he's legging it toward Bermuda. In the 1972 race, we had been in flat calm for fourteen hours as we watched even our own garbage get ahead of us. Needless to say, we were a very poor also-ran. This time our luck was better.

Well into the Stream, the wind piped up and of course the sea was noticeably rougher. We shortened sail to a working jib and a single reefed main for a brief time. The wind piped up briefly to force 8, or about 40 knots. All of a sudden, after sighting almost nothing, a large ketch appeared on our starboard hand, less than a mile away. Who was going in the opposite direction with a full press of canvas? I looked at Gaynor with a questioning eye. Then I looked at each compass. I was dumbfounded. She was without doubt the ketch *Barlovento*, belonging to Pete duPont. This shook me up. I knew that Pete's navigator was Hughie Sharp, superlative at navigation.

What in hell was she doing going the other way, not to mention the fact that she was a Class A yacht and should be out in front? I said little, but this sighting was puzzling me. I knew very well Pete knew what he was doing. Hughie, too. I concealed my apprehension and carried on. Since we had not been monitoring the radio, other than when it was our duty to do so, I didn't learn until after the race was over that *Barlovento* had gone to the rescue of *Arieto*, which had radioed she was in trouble. *Barlovento* stood by *Arieto* until the Coast Guard came to her assistance. First, Pete called one of the Pan Am planes (flying overhead) on single-side-band and got the latter to relay to the Coast Guard the position of the stricken vessel. Then *Barlovento* waited for the Coast Guard. For this unstinting effort Pete duPont was merely credited with some time allowance by the committee. He had done his duty, as most of the yachting fraternity would do instinctively.

Once through the Stream on Sunday, we settled down to a very steady close reach, usually under a reefed main and number three genoa. As we neared the Bermuda high the wind tended to abate; it usually does when one gets closer to the center of a high-pressure system. Of course, when in very close proximity to the island one normally finds a fresh sou'wester, caused in part by the thermal gradient between land and sea.

Monday was an overcast day, and we drove steadily through a light sea, averaging 6 to 7 knots. Around noon, radio reports from Bermuda stations commenced broadcasting bad news; we still had 130 miles to go and *Ondine* had finished. She was first across the finish line in the elapsed time of 2 days, 20 hours, and 8 minutes. Clearly we had to fly to save our handicap from her. Then a little over 4 hours later, another Class A boat, Lynn Williams's *Dora*, was reported a probable winner in Class A.

Ed Gaynor managed to snag a few sun lines, but star fixes were impossible, owing to cloud cover. Our dead reckoning position showed us to be comfortably to weather, and I urged the tactic of starting sheets and heading for the barn. Ballard wanted to keep some money in the bank by continuing to head above our course for Kitchen Shoals. He reasoned that we made too much leeway with our low-profile keel. The crew privately agreed with Ballard, and thus a conspiracy was set in motion to fudge our heading a few degrees to weather of what the skipper had in mind. They were right. Heading above course was a wise policy, for later, when our loran set (allowed for the first time within forty miles of the finish) was turned on, we found we had indeed made leeway and we were now hard on the wind, beating toward Northeast Breaker Buoy.

The wind held all Monday night, and on Tuesday morning sails started to appear on the horizon. As we got to the buoys at the eastern end of Bermuda, none of the boats in sight were small. They were

Swan-48's and some even bigger. We couldn't believe our eyes. Mathematically it was now impossible to win the whole race; according to radio reports *Scaramouche* and *Charisma* in Class B, and *Recluta* of the Argentine were already beyond reach. Our hopes focused on Class E.

We rounded Kitchen Shoals and headed for the finish line off St. David's, where we sighted *Bellatrix, Sitzmark,* and *Chasseur* in Class D — all bigger boats. Then we saw *Zest* and *Chee Chee* in Class C, even bigger. The crew's spirits soared. Nothing smaller had been sighted.

We crossed the line around 1045 on Tuesday in the fastest elapsed time that I had ever sailed there: three days, twenty-one hours, twenty-six minutes, thirty-five seconds. In eleven Bermuda races in three different boats, this was the best time. Twice in my Block Island 40 I had been a bridesmaid — second place in class. But now Bermuda Radio said we were first to finish in Class E, and we were well down in the handicap list; it was a comfortable feeling.

The trip up the channel to Hamilton Harbour, which takes about two and one-half hours because Hamilton is at the western end of the island, was as pleasant as any I can remember. We soon made it to our dock at Newstead, and the only boat there was Jimmy Madden's *Gesture*, a Swan-48. Nothing else. We certainly seemed fat. Not even *Challenge* in Class C had arrived. I went to sleep in our room at Newstead thinking we had won Class E. It was a darn good sleep. Surely few feelings in this world could be better. When wakened for supper I was told that *Cayenne*, an S and S 41-foot, had slipped in thirty minutes after us and saved her time allowance (due to rating difference) from *Reindeer*. Thus, again we were second, but no complaint, we had done our best and all hands were happy.

The round-the-clock open house at the Royal Bermuda Yacht Club was gathering momentum, as finishing times were being posted on the huge scoreboard. As always after this race, bleary-eyed shipmates would belly up to the bar, plunk down their chits, and receive their rum fizzes. Then the postmortems would begin.

Gradually as the fleet came in and crewmen spilled onto the lawn at the Yacht Club, the stories unfolded. The duel between *Scaramouche* and *Charisma* was a favorite topic. They were one, two in the fleet, and less than seven minutes separated them at the end of 650 miles. The first three boats in Class B were from the Great Lakes, and the pre-

Reindeer *after finishing the Bermuda Race,* 1974 (*Courtesy Bermuda
News Bureau*)

vious winner, *Noryema* from Britain, could manage only a seventeenth in that class. Eric Ridder, whose ketch *Tempest* was second to finish, reported winds of fifty knots on the second night out. We didn't experience any winds of that magnitude on *Reindeer*, which of course shows how variable conditions can be, even within a distance of a few miles at sea, especially in the area of the Gulf Stream. This is particularly pertinent when it comes to calms. There is no doubt in my mind that the most important tactic in the Bermuda Race is to avoid a flat calm, even if temporarily one has to steer perpendicular to his course to the finish.

Finishing so early was a blessing for us in that we were thus provided time to rerig the vessel for the cruise north to the Labrador. A lot of work had to be done. First, a good cleanup, then removal of racing sails and other paraphernalia pertinent only to racing. A huge box, which contained radar, cruising sails, and even emergency rations, was awaiting our arrival to clear through Customs. We used the same box to ship racing gear home. By Friday we had the boat ready to go to sea in cruising trim, and the man most responsible for this metamorphosis was Phil Parish, who, with his wife, Jeannette, was to take part in the passage to St. John's, Newfoundland.

The Cruising Club had its traditional raft-up at lunchtime on Saturday. All the members' boats tied together and hung on *Tempest*'s anchor rode. We dressed ship with signal flags and joined in a happy gam. When the raft broke up, *Reindeer* headed out to sea and by 1800 we signaled cheerio to Bermuda Harbour Radio and set sail on a north nor'east course for Newfoundland, 1,100 miles away.

2

North to Newfoundland and Labrador

THE TRIP NORTHEAST from Bermuda to St. John's, Newfoundland, North America's second oldest city and the easternmost point of the Western Hemisphere save for part of Brazil, was in 1974 a pleasant eight-day downwind slide. Until we reached the Grand Banks, the sighting of sea and bird life and even human life, in the form of shipping, was sparse. It was, in short, an easy reach and one in which even the Gulf Stream was remarkably passive. As compared with the indelibly etched path of the Stream at the point of our southward crossing in the Bermuda Race, the trip north took us through a Gulf Stream that seemed diffused and indefinable. Perhaps it was because we were cruising, not racing, and the crew's relaxed attitude tended to obscure our perception of Stream activity. Most probably, the Stream at a point three or four hundred miles east of the race course was not as narrow and not as fast. In any event, we experienced no special weather pattern and no unusual set, other than in a direction a little east of our course.

For most of the trip we sailed with a number two genoa and a single reefed mainsail or a full main. Sometimes in daylight we set a spinnaker, and at other times it was so calm we were obliged to use the engine. In the early going, not far off Bermuda, we were followed by magnificent frigate birds, one of which came down and ate bread out of Phil Parish's hand. We also were visited by some very large whales, which might

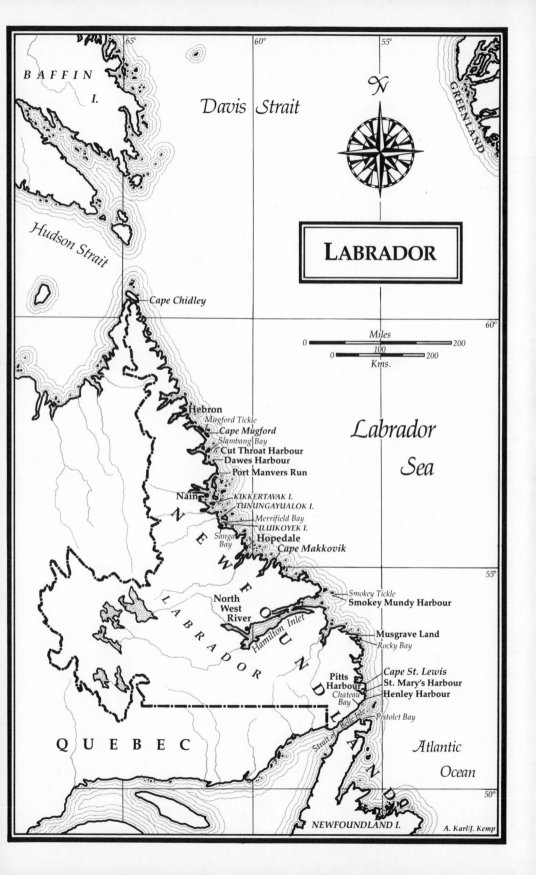

BAFFIN
I.

Davis Strait

Hudson Strait

GREENLAND

N

LABRADOR

Cape Chidley

Miles
0 _____ 100 _____ 200
0 _____ 100 _____ 200
Kms.

Labrador
Sea

Hebron
Mugford Tickle
Cape Mugford
Slambang Bay
Cut Throat Harbour
Dawes Harbour
Port Manvers Run
Nain
KIKKERTAVAK I.
TUNUNGAYUALOK I.
Merrifield Bay
ILUIKOYEK I.
Sanga **Hopedale**
Bay **Cape Makkovik**

N
E
W
F
O
U
N
D
L
A
B
R
A
D
O
R

**North
West
River**

Hamilton Inlet

Smokey Tickle
Smokey Mundy Harbour

Musgrave Land
Rocky Bay

**Pitts
Harbour**
*Chateau
Bay*

Cape St. Lewis
St. Mary's Harbour
Henley Harbour

Pistolet Bay

Strait of Belle Isle

QUEBEC

Atlantic

Ocean

NEWFOUNDLAND I.

A. Karl/J. Kemp

have been humpbacks. Frequently a whole school of porpoises would cavort about us as if to toy with our little hull.

By the fifth of July we were on the Grand Banks, and the environment changed sharply. The temperature had declined, and the air was filled with a sudden plethora of bird life — gulls, gannets, and guillemots — whereas during most of the trip our only feathered friends had been petrels and shearwaters. This was my fifth trip across the Grand Banks, but the first time with good visibility, due to the prevalence of northerly winds. Usually the prevailing southerlies and sou'westerlies bring warm, moist air from the Gulf Stream over the cold water of the Labrador Current that flows south along the Newfoundland coast — a mix that guarantees fog.

Visibility was excellent as we closed the coast. "Land ho!" my son Hank suddenly shouted from the foredeck. Sure enough, one point off our port bow was Cape Pine, a few miles to the west of Cape Race. It was Saturday evening, 6 July. The air temperature was 48°F. and the water 45.5°, a far cry from the warmth of the Gulf Stream, from which we had emerged a few nights before. It was cold and crisp and there was a full moon in the east and bright stars dancing in their galaxies all across the sky. The wind was a steady fifteen knots from the northwest, permitting us to reach along with a comfortable heel to starboard and at a speed of seven knots. The lights of the sky were augmented by an unusual amount of phosphorescence at the wave tops where our hull sliced through the water. Sighting land after a passage always warms the heart. It's like breaking through low cloud cover just before landing at the airport. You think you know where you are, but it is reassuring to see it for yourself.

I should have foreseen the happy event of sighting land. Only an hour earlier three big baleen whales had popped up before our eyes, one hundred yards abeam. The sight of these marvelous monsters never fails to stir the adrenalin. You get a feeling God is telling you something. No wonder over the centuries mariners have regarded such sightings as a good-luck omen. Now that land was in sight, maybe we could relax.

Just then Phil Parish, manning the radar screen, suddenly called out, "Two blips off the port bow!" I looked ahead in the dark, and a fishing vessel hove into view. Then further ahead I saw a fantastic sight. It

Iceberg in the Strait of Belle Isle, Labrador (Tom Campbell)

looked to be a huge white ketch, someone from Oyster Bay or Newport; pretty damned well heeled, I thought. What the hell was he doing up here? No, wait a sec, I thought; that's no boat — it's an iceberg!
Sure enough, there it was — our first iceberg. What a sight! All hands
rushed up from below for their first glimpse of a berg. It was magnificent: tall and, as we got closer, cathedral-like; an immense piece of
sculpture. It was underway, propelled mainly by the Labrador Current
and also, like ourselves, by the wind. It was worth coming 1,750 miles
to see, and it validated all that I had read about the ice off Labrador.

As we passed Cape Race in the early hours of the next day, the sev-
enth of July, the wind was fresh out of the northwest, and we just
steamed along on a broad reach as new sights appeared everywhere.
Whales surfaced, sometimes in schools. Our young oceanographers
identified one as a sperm whale. Another huge baleen whale had two
blowholes. Flights of seabirds were seemingly endless. Murres, puffins,
guillemots, fulmars, kittiwakes, and even the incomparable and strikingly beautiful gannets kept constant patrol of the coast.

Never having been on the east coast of Newfoundland, I was struck
by the contrast to the more protected south coast. There are no land

obstacles all the way to the Bay of Biscay, and eons of ocean waves have hammered this coast into a barren but unbowed fortress of rock. The history of this segment of Newfoundland is replete with struggle, that between the English and French and especially that of pirates versus the Royal Navy. The Avalon Peninsula is loaded with the names of pirate strongholds like Fermeuse, Cape Broyle, Bay Bulls, and Ferry Land. Since this corner of the island lies on the Great Circle route from the Spanish Main to the Old World, it was not too distant from the route of the pirates and the plate fleets of the seventeenth and eighteenth centuries. Moreover, the harbors have narrow entrances that form natural and impenetrable fortresses. There were no land access routes to afford an adversary attack from the rear. The terrain is so rough that even today few roads exist. One can readily understand why the pirates picked the caves in these harbors for parking their caches of gold and silver.

Unbeknown to us on that Sunday's unforgettable sail was a modern pirate adventure that had transpired a week before. It seems one Michael Carr, a British doctor who practiced in the village of Catalina just north of St. John's, had returned to England and bought himself a fifty-foot sailboat. He then sailed her to Colombia, South America, where he apparently took on about two million dollars' worth of marijuana. With this cargo and a few friends he sailed to Newfoundland, landing at Fermeuse Harbour. Here the cargo was unloaded into a cave. Somehow the RCMP got the word, and a detachment of Mounties caught the group red-handed. It was, of course, an instant news item that excited tremendous public interest and curiosity. Someone told the Mounties that if they thought this was a big haul, they ought to wait until the second boat arrived.

It so happened that the next sailboat to ply northward along this coast was the American sloop *Reindeer*, with the U.S. ensign at the taffrail and the blue and white burgee of the Cruising Club of America flying at the masthead. About halfway between Fermeuse Harbour and St. John's, a helicopter descended from the sky and circled us at masthead height. Its occupants scrutinized us through binoculars, and of course we waved to them. Strangely, they made no reciprocal gesture.

"Those guys don't seem too friendly," my wife, Peggy, noted.

"Oh, don't worry about that, Peggy, they're probably the Coast Guard and don't want us to get in trouble with the ice," I casually replied.

Soon we passed Cape Spear, the easternmost point of North America, and headed into the entrance of St. John's. We were now hard on the wind with a single reef in the main and the number three genoa. A patrol vessel with the letters RCMP on her topsides came out from the land and ordered us alongside in the outer harbor. These were the Mounties, and the voice over the bullhorn didn't sound like the usual Canadian friendliness. I tried to think what law I had violated. There were some wine bottles in the liquor locker, but not even duty-free. It was like the cop stopping your car and simply demanding your cards without saying what in hell was the violation.

One of the Mounties came aboard, looked at my papers, which were rattling nervously in my hands — and gave the boat a thorough inspection and interrogated me. Apparently he was satisfied that we were no threat to the peace of the Province and the laws of the Dominion, and then he related the story of the drug drop.

We cleared with the harbor master and were assigned a berth alongside an old fishing schooner at the head of the harbor. A Customs and Immigration Officer came aboard immediately, and we were soon cleared. This permitted us to step ashore and go about our business.

The Battery Motel was an ideal headquarters in St. John's, and it proved a convenient base for crew transfer. Here I parted with my entire Phase I crew after an appropriate farewell dinner. Their Phase II counterparts arrived on time, including my son Stockton Smith, Orlin Donaldson, Bill Van Alen, John Biddle, and Professor Daiber of the University of Delaware.

The new crew went to work immediately to put all in order for the trip to Labrador. It soon became quite apparent that our plan to sail north from St. John's along the outer coast of Newfoundland and thence to the Labrador coast was impossible. The northerlies that had brought such clear weather out on the banks had also brought the worst ice conditions in fifty years to the Province. No shipping could move on the northeast coast of Newfoundland and, needless to say, along the coast of Labrador.

The boys in the Ministry of Transport were emphatic: "You can't go north out of here and get back into any harbor. Our coastal boats aren't going out. We can't get supplies to Makkovik, much less to Hopedale and Nain. As a matter of fact, a Greek freighter has been sunk in the

radar went on the fritz, and every time we found a repairman with some electronics knowledge the condition got worse. Finally I decided to call the factory and have an expert sent up to fix it. In no way was I going to gamble on missing the bergs in fog or night, to say nothing of rocky shores and off-lying skerries. Meanwhile, since ice was not present on this part of the coast, we proceeded on schedule. We didn't want to arrive at the Strait of Belle Isle too soon, unless of course the wind were to shift to the west or sou'west and blow the pack ice offshore.

We put in at several harbors, bays, and inlets along the south coast, which is one of the most interesting stretches of land I had ever seen. Each inlet had some outstanding feature. At Avirons Bay it was the waterfall of nearly one thousand feet. At Rencontre it was the deserted village, a really spooky experience. At Grey River, it was the salmon at the head of the North Arm and of the East Arm, plus also the village of Jerts Cove, where intermarriage has had noticeable effect. At Harbour Le Cou it was total isolation, except eagles and gulls, in one of the world's most totally protected anchorages.

Of all the places that we visited along this coast, perhaps Rencontre Bay was the most fascinating, not for what was there but for what wasn't. We put in at what appeared to be a relatively tidy if not prosperous town. No one was there! We spooked around the houses, the church, the little Anglican school, and searched for clues as to what had happened. We found newspapers dated the previous August; there were schoolbooks, family Bibles, and other items that suggested a hasty departure.

Finally we found one old man with his grandson busily salvaging some siding, and he told us the incredible tale of how the government had ordered certain villages to close and resettle in other coastal towns. The purpose was to simplify the job of supply to these autonomous but dependent hamlets, which had only one path of transport — the sea. The old man was despondent over the forced removal from the only home he had ever known.

At Port aux Basques, which is the ferry terminus from Sydney, Nova Scotia, and a relatively modern town with roads, we took one last crack at the radar. No dice. Before departing I phoned the factory at Charlottesville, Virginia, to make final arrangements to meet at Bonne Bay the technician who was flying up to repair our radar. Our trip to that scenic indentation in the coast was a sleighride before winds that reached fifty knots. We covered 175 miles in twenty hours, which is flying.

In due course the expert arrived and put the radar straight. Donaldson left us to return to his job, and the remaining five got underway for Labrador. Again the wind was whistling out of the sou'west and we bombed northeastward on a coast altogether different from that of the south. There are very few harbors on the west coast, and since the Trans-Canada Highway runs along most of the coast, the villages, unlike those of the south coast, are quite modern and used to tourists. We reached the Strait of Belle Isle late the following morning, and there they were — iceberg after iceberg, but the pack had gone. No problem at all, excellent visibility. We were now on the Labrador!

Navigation had to be taken seriously, for buoys and lighthouses, beacons and foghorns became scarcer and then nonexistent. For really good coastal information Stockton and I relied heavily on the logs of Paul Sheldon.

Sheldon's book had on the cover a picture of his ketch *Seacrest*, high and dry out of the water on the rocks. That's a good warning for starters! He states quite accurately that "nowhere on the Atlantic coast of North America is there scenery to compare in grandeur with" the Labrador, from the Strait of Belle Isle eight hundred miles northwest to Cape Chidley and Hudson Strait. "But," he says, "any yachtsman who would see it during its all-too-brief summer will work for what he gets." He refers, of course, to the dangers: the ice, the sudden changes of weather, the uncharted passages, the total lack of navigational aids like lighthouses and buoys, and, most important of all, the absence of people and towns.

"Truly," Sheldon says, "one is on his own. . . . Winds blow hard and are from north and west much of the time. Radio weather broadcasts are not to be depended upon. The lowly barometer again becomes important, and, like the natives, one tends to venture cautiously once the glass starts up. It is in this phase that trouble most often strikes." That amazed me — warning against a rising barometer! In our part of the world, East Coast to West Coast, a falling barometer is a storm signal and a rising barometer a sign of clear weather ahead. But on the Labrador, Sheldon warned, look out for the opposite.

We also had U.S. Hydrographic Office publications and the Canadian *Coast Pilot* for reference. The latter is extensive and authoritative, but it contained many errors, owing in part, I guess, to its reliance on voyages of individuals who, like me, are fallible.

Time and distance dictated our choice of anchorage for our first night on the Labrador. It was Pitts Harbour, peaceful and uninhabited. There were some cottages there that later we found were used by summer fishermen from Newfoundland, who would move up for several weeks to fish in virgin territory. None was occupied when we were there. The next day, we sailed in good visibility past Henley Harbour and the very impressive lighthouse at Camp Island, and finally to St. Mary's Harbour and tied up at the Grenfell Mission, where we did our laundry, filled our fuel tanks, and fetched fresh water from the river by bucket brigade.

From St. Mary's Harbour we radioed Goose Bay to tell the incoming crew where to meet us. They then flew by float plane. Bill Maclay and his son Jim, Diana Russell, and Tom Campbell, together with a load of fresh food and canned goods, were landed safely at the dock where *Reindeer* was tied. The same plane returned Biddle, Van Alen, and Daiber to civilization, for better or worse.

On 25 July, the beginning of Phase III of our cruise, we got underway at 0500, traveled about fifty yards, and then went aground. It was not that we had been careless; we were right in the channel. The tide was at maximum ebb, and we just found a rocky spot. Because of the short length of our keel we were able to spin around and get off the bottom quickly. There was no wind, so we motored out past Cape St. Lewis, marveling at the flights of puffins, guillemots, and scoters. By suppertime we had made it to Domino Point just as fog closed in. We turned westward into Domino Run, where a Canadian Coast Guard cutter emerged out of the mist actively ferrying supplies ashore by helicopter. We surmised that the government was helping the fishing communities that had been shut off by the ice. By 2130 we were anchored safely in Rocky Bay between Isle of Ponds and Musgrave Land. For some reason there were no flies or mosquitoes, whereas the night before we had been forced to use every defense known to man to hold off Labrador's twin pests.

On the way north from St. Mary's Harbour the captain of a passing Esso tanker told me the pack ice was bad ahead and suggested we take the inside route where possible. Going across Hamilton Inlet, which is

Iceberg off Cape St. Lewis, Labrador (Stockton N. Smith)

a large bay that leads to North West River and the base at Goose Bay, we encountered drift ice, and up ahead we were confronted with what appeared to be a solid plateau. It turned out to be ice blink, which in the argot of the Arctic is a refraction phenomenon of ice on water. The effect is similar to a mirage.

Continuing northwestward, we headed for a passage called Run-by-Guess. Passing through this aptly named tickle, we were under constant surveillance by black-backed gulls and white-vested murres, looking like small penguins as they stood on rocky islets. Meanwhile, in the water on either side of the boat, if one merely looked at a puffin or a scoter, he would duck under the surface. Sometimes they would paddle furiously with their wings to a safe distance. Black guillemots get airborne more easily and usually fly in flights.

As we sailed through the northern end of Run-by-Guess, we were overtaken by a long-liner, a small diesel-powered fishing boat. We asked her skipper for advice on anchoring and he motioned to follow him. He led us to Smokey Mundy Harbour, a favorite summer base of the northern Newfoundlanders who fish on the Labrador. We dropped our anchor at around 2200 in total darkness and had a fine meal and a good sleep.

This tiny settlement was where Robert E. Peary, on his way south, informed the world by wireless that he had reached the North Pole in 1909!

For the next two days we worked along the coast, mostly in the inside passages. The first night was spent in an uncharted harbor on Kikkertavak Island. We somehow avoided the unmarked ledges, but the mosquitoes required a full court press. That meant netting, Cutter repellent, and at times a near-lethal spray — lethal to us. We made it to the Eskimo village of Makkovik on Sunday, 28 July. We toured the village, then got underway for Hopedale, which we reached after spending one night anchored in a fairway in fog, using a Bahamian moor to prevent the vessel from swinging into the shore. This is the technique of putting out a second anchor at right angles, so a wind shift won't blow the boat on shore.

The weather seemed to run in three- or four-day cycles, and leaving Hopedale it was cold and foggy. We sailed north through Windy Tickle and west through Shoal Tickle, where the only people we encountered were a team of Canadian hydrographic personnel taking soundings for chart making. We passed an abandoned Hudson Bay trading post, and thence to Sanga Bay, which the *Coast Pilot* indicated was the inside passage to Merrifield Bay and the "Bridges" to Nain. This turned out to be entirely too shallow for passage, so we retreated to Davis Inlet on Iluikoyek Island.

Taking the inboard passage to Nain, we skirted westward of Tunungayualok Island and narrowly escaped grounding on ledges again not shown on the chart. However, once past the ledges we found a superb uncharted harbor on the western shore of Tunungayualok. It was a perfect anchorage, and Tom Campbell and Diana Russell strung out our gill net at the head of the harbor where a stream tumbled down from the hills. The next morning we pulled in a full catch of arctic char, a fish that I consider superior to salmon and in fact to any other fish I've ever eaten. We feasted on it for breakfast, lunch, and dinner.

This harbor taught me a lesson that was to serve us well, one I was not to forget. Simply put, it is much better, when looking for a spot to drop anchor in bays surrounded by mountains or cliffs, to pick a break in the wall rather than a place in the lee of a steep hill or rocky promontory. There are two reasons for this. First, good holding ground is the most important requirement and is more apt to exist in a delta or where a stream enters the fjord or bay. Such a stream will most likely have deposited earth or gravel on the bottom. Otherwise, in these rocky areas of the north the anchor may just drag across the bottom. Second, despite what may seem to be more exposure to wind, the chance of a blow-me-down is greatly lessened. Blow-me-downs are notorious phenomena of the steep-sided harbors of Labrador and Newfoundland. Winds as high as one hundred knots have been known to swoosh down a cliff when the velocity of the wind in the general area was no more than thirty knots. According to the natives, one-hundred-foot schooners have been smashed to smithereens in these sudden and devastating outbursts.

The passage through the "Bridges" to Nain was quite spectacular, because of the way in which the glacier had carved out this narrow run. Nain is now the northernmost settlement in Labrador. Prior to 1953, the village of Hebron was the northernmost active community. In that year the government decided in its infinite wisdom to consolidate the settlements, and most of the residents of Hebron went to Makkovik, where they now form the ghetto there. Nain has a population of seven hundred people, all Eskimo except for the missionaries of the Moravian Church, who happen to be members of the Hettasch family, as noble an example of servants to mankind as I have ever seen.

It was cold, cloudy, and wet on the day we sailed into Nain. There at the dock was the hospital ship of the Grenfell Mission, *Strathcona III*, Captain Stoake commanding. The captain waved us alongside. He knew we were coming; he had heard by radio from the captain of *Marine Voyager*, with whom we had tied at the dock at Hopedale. Surprising how news travels on this sparsely populated coast. The captain was most cordial and informative. One thing I noticed when he showed me around the ship was the wheel in the pilothouse. This wheel had been on Sir Wilfred Grenfell's original *Strathcona* and was inscribed in brass, "Follow me and I will make you fishers of men." This immediately told me that the famous Labrador doctor was a spiritual missionary as well as medical. Indeed, the Grenfell Mission has always taught the spirit of God as well as the medical science of man. Furthermore, as the Moravians and the Anglican Church both know, the spirit is even more important than the body for withstanding the rigors of these remote and sometimes frigid regions, isolated as they are from the rest of the world.

Captain Stoake introduced me to Professor Tony Morse, who was

Wheel in the charthouse of Strathcona III, *Grenfell Mission boat at Nain, Labrador. "Follow me and I will make you fishers of men." (Diana Russell)*

heading a geological expedition investigating anorthosite, which is found in profusion in the rock around Nain. After giving me a primary course in geology, Tony entrusted to me a bundle of mail addressed to members of his team, then camped "somewhere near Hebron or Saglek Fjord."

"Dr. Morse," I said incredulously, "what happens if I can't find these guys?"

"Oh, don't give it a thought. You'll find 'em," said Tony.

"What about the pack ice?" I could not get that hazard out of my head.

"Well, I came down from Hebron last week in this bucket" — Tony motioned with his arm toward his motor boat tied at the dock — "and I didn't see much ice at all. You'll be okay."

While I was getting all the poop, my shipmates were busy taking on fuel, water, and groceries in preparation for the next day's sail north through Port Manvers Run, which would lead us out to sea again.

There are two narrow necks in Port Manvers Run where the current gets up to six knots. These are called the First Rattle and the Second Rattle. We started early in the morning in pea soup fog and no wind, navigating entirely by radar. Just as we reached the area of the First

Bishop's Mitre, Mugford Tickle, Labrador (Stockton N. Smith)

Rattle the radar antenna drive belt broke in two. We quickly anchored off to the side so we could assess our situation. As so often happens, while one is maneuvering to attack one problem, suddenly another one arises. The chain belt on the steering mechanism jumped out of its sprockets. We fixed the helm without difficulty, but since we did not have a spare rubber drive belt for the radar antenna, we had to swing it manually with a broomstick until Stockton could fashion a jury rig. Fortunately the fog lifted, but not until we had missed the best current opportunity. By the time we got to the Second Rattle, the flood current was all of six knots, so in order to fight through that, we had to go within one-half boat's length of the rocky shore. We crept along through the rattle, taking advantage of a little back eddy.

The next day was again cold and overcast. I hit the deck at 0620 to see how we looked; the night before we had made Dawes Harbour under IFR (instrument flight rules) conditions and had therefore seen little. Wow! The whole perimeter of this little harbor was covered with fresh snow. Also, we were quite close to some jetty-type ledges that we hadn't seen in the radar, and I wanted to get the hell out of there pronto. Just then Stocky riveted his eyes on something in the water.

"Hey, Dad, look over there," Stocky said, pointing toward the entrance to the harbor. I saw a black fin almost four feet tall slowly passing out the harbor entrance.

"Fisherman, get up here," I hollered to Tom Campbell, our piscatory expert from the University of Delaware. Tom sprang up just as the fin disappeared.

"Listen, fisherman, the aspect ratio on that fin was unreal," I told him. "Don't give me that look; Stocky saw it, too."

"Yeh, Tom," Stocky agreed. "That was no shark fin or anything else I've ever seen. What the hell could it be?" Tom dodged the question, but I saw him later consulting his fish book.

We got underway for Mugford Tickle with a light southeast wind and fair visibility. On the way north, we passed Okak Island, with its harbor called Slambang Bay, where once the Eskimos used to set up a summer fishing camp, but no activity was observed this time. Mugford Tickle, with its steep cliffs and mountains up to 4,300 feet on either side, was a sight none of us would forget. I prayed that on our trip back the weather would be better, so we could get good pictures of the Bishop's Mitre and other scenic promontories around Cape Mugford, said to be the greatest spectacle on the Labrador.

It soon became apparent that we couldn't make it to Hebron before dark, so I took a good look at the chart and the *Coast Pilot* and decided on Takatat Inlet as a decent spot to drop the hook. At about 1600 I spotted what looked like a black spar buoy up ahead. It disappeared; then it reappeared. Was something wrong with my eyes? I turned to Maclay.

"Hey, Bill, give me the binocs; I see something ahead. It looked like a buoy, but maybe it's a periscope," I said.

Maclay saw it with his own eyes. "That's no buoy," he said.

"It must be a whale or a blackfish; let's get the fisherman up here."

Tom Campbell came up the ladder. Meanwhile the object was now off to starboard and closer. "That's exactly what we saw this morning, Tom. It's a fish or whale, but I've never seen a fin that tall and thin," I said.

"That's a killer whale, skipper," Tom said calmly. A review of his fisheries book after the morning's sighting had put conviction in his voice.

The fin was now about seventy-five yards to starboard and slicing through the water parallel to our course. It was four feet in height and no more than a foot fore and aft at its base. It would disappear now and then, always straight down like a periscope being retracted. We all looked at each other. All of us had read stories of attacks on small boats by these denizens, although I never knew whether to believe them or not.

The killer whale disappeared, and we then concerned ourselves more with drift ice and unseen ledges. Takatat wasn't a bad anchorage as long as the resident iceberg stayed anchored. Here for the first time since New-foundland we saw bald eagles on guard on top of the cliffs. The next day we slid into Hebron and spent a morning spooking around the deserted village. No signs of the geologists, but animal tracks galore. Wild flowers and green grass and gorse gave color to an otherwise stark picture that would have made a Wyeth painting look splashy.

It was getting late in August; we had to turn back soon. We didn't have the time to make it to Cape Chidley and Hudson Strait, even though they were only a hundred miles away. Frobisher was also out of the question. We settled on Saglek as our turnaround point, smack in the middle of the Torngats. The course was west of north, the wind east of north.

In mid-afternoon Cape Uivuk, a two-thousand-foot cliff at the south entrance of Saglek Bay, appeared in view. The radar antenna of the DEW Line base jutted into the sky atop the cliff, the only reminder that the world wasn't quite at peace.

Just as we rounded Cape Uivuk with another Kikkertaksoak Island in sight ahead, the water suddenly was covered with a slick of oil. Not heavy stuff, but enough to see your reflection. Then, sickeningly, the sight of dead birds; puffins, eider, guillemots. What the hell? Had a plane crashed?

We dropped sails and powered around the cape to the bight, where there was a small supply base and some storage tanks. A red Canadian tanker was anchored with her stern to the base, and hoses were extended to the shore. Oil covered the water in all directions. We saw activity; a few small boats were going back and forth from ship to shore. I got on the VHF radio, but the ship's radioman didn't seem too enlightened. We inflated the rubber dinghy and sent Stocky and Jim Maclay ashore. When they returned, the story was that the hose connection had broken and that seven hundred thousand gallons of diesel had spilled into Saglek Bay. The boys were not greeted with open arms, and they said the circumstances looked strange to them.

We motored around to St. John's Harbour, where we found the campsite of the geologists in full view at the head of the harbor. No oil had flowed up the bay, and St. John's Harbour was a gem, with huge cliffs on both sides and a valley at the head. There were many eagles on the cliffs, and we saw a whole herd of caribou roaming up the tundra. We were not alone in this protected harbor. There were two icebergs, at least two whales, and a few seals that popped up around the ice.

No contact was made with the people ashore until the next morning, but then we discovered each other. They were indeed the addressees for Professor Morse's mail packet, and for our delivery service we were given a whole side of caribou meat. The story of the oil spill unfolded. It seems, the geologists said, that the men at the base were drunk on Saturday night and let the hose from the tanker loose. The tanker people had no idea they were pumping into the bay until the next morning. They had just rehooked the hoses when we arrived on Sunday afternoon.

All of us were shocked at the enormity of this spill and its potential hazard to wildlife, but according to the scientists the people at the base were keeping mum so nobody would get in trouble. To allow this oil to flow out into the south-going Labrador Current seemed like a tragic disaster to me. I'm not a tattletale, but this thing transcended the buddy-boy stuff.

My single-side-band radio was not working properly and the AM and VHF radios didn't have the range, so I asked the geologists why they weren't reporting the disaster on their radio to Nain. They feared incurring the animosity of the people at the base. It was then suggested that I use their equipment to call Tony Morse. I got hold of Morse in Nain and reported the spill. I then asked him to call the RCMP and CBC for good measure. He did as requested. Once the media has a story, the government has to act, and act they did.

That very evening on our way back to Mugford (with oil nearly all the way) we heard continuous newscasts about the spill at Saglek. Every day for two weeks it was headline stuff in Canada, rivaled only by activities in Nixon's Washington bunker. The Canadians are especially serious custodians of nature and their northlands. In forty-eight hours teams of experts were flown in to contain and sop up the spill, then estimated at five hundred thousand gallons. Fortunately it was diesel oil, which is far lighter than crude and therefore more easily evaporated.

Later, turning south, we had good luck all the way to Corner Brook, Newfoundland, where Stocky was to meet three college friends who would help him get the boat back to Connecticut. Mugford Tickle was bathed in sunshine and we were able to make three overnight passages without hitting any ice, except two glancing blows from bergy bits that shook us a little. Back at Nain, we again saw Tony Morse and reviewed what had happened. Then we had the great pleasure of an evening visit with "Aunt Katie" Hettasch, the Moravian teacher, who told us tales of the past and present. This was her last of forty-five years of teaching the Eskimos of Labrador, and she was preparing to retire and move to Bethlehem, Pennsylvania, where the Moravian Church has its North American headquarters. Just as Aunt Katie was finishing her fascinating story, the wind began to whistle from the northeast. We were forced to leave the dock and seek shelter in Kauk Cove, about three miles away. It was a nasty trip, for we had to power into a wind that reached force 10, and it was cold. Once around the corner in the cove, all was happy and relatively quiet. We slept like logs.

On the way south, one night we made it to Petty Harbour in the fog and anchored in the outer harbor around midnight. Had the visibility been fair, we'd have gone into the inner harbor, but the entrance was too narrow for navigating in such poor visibility — a stroke of luck for us that illustrates the hazards of sailing these northern waters. The next morning we were wakened by a sudden jolt which sounded like hitting bottom. Nothing of the sort; it was an incoming berg nudging us as it drifted in. Lucky we hadn't gone to the inner harbor, for we would have been plugged in by the berg. As matters happened, the berg grounded in the entrance to the inner harbor. It might have been a real fiasco, if we had had good visibility the night before!

Finally by 16 August we reached Corner Brook, and while we were there our engine cooling water intake line quietly ingested wood chips that were all over the harbor from the paper mill. By the time the boys got *Reindeer* to Halifax, the engine had conked out from lack of cooling water circulation, and they had to sail the rest of the way to Connecticut with no auxiliary. This cost one new engine, but considering the trip as a whole and the 5,800 miles covered since leaving Newport, the cost didn't seem excessive — or so went my rationale. It had been an interesting expedition that among other things confirmed the lure of the Labrador and succeeded in whetting further my appetite for the Arctic.

3

Thinking North Again

No SOONER was *Reindeer* back in commission after a new diesel engine was installed at Saybrook, Connecticut, than I was thinking of the Arctic again, considering a possible future trip to Iceland, Norway, Spitsbergen, and home via Denmark Strait. Back-to-back long-distance cruises were out of the question for me, logistically, financially, maritally, and in just about every way. The next year, the summer of '75, had to be fairly conventional. There would be the usual races in the Chesapeake, the Annapolis-Newport Race in June, and maybe the New York Yacht Club cruise, if I were a glutton for punishment.

At any rate the summer of '75 was not unusual for *Reindeer*. We raced her in the Annapolis-to-Newport Race and then joined the New York Yacht Club Cruise. In both instances I found myself out of the hunt. Not even a sniff of the silver. Boats went by me so fast I got the feeling the only thing I had going was a good paint job. Everybody said how pretty our topsides looked! Big deal. The only thing I wanted them to see was our stern, not our sides, and not be able to read the letters on it.

Later in August we went down east to Maine and in the Northeast Harbor Cruise we finally found some wind and won. That helped the ego and also put my thinking straight. No more thought of selling the boat. One wouldn't want to go to the Arctic in a brand new boat, much less an IOR monstrosity! I figured if we made it to the High Arctic and got back all right, then I'd strip *Reindeer* down a bit, put in a taller rig and just see if it were possible to win a race or two. If not, well, hell, at least we would have given it a try. Perhaps the racing game by then would have passed me by, judging from the direction it was taking.

By fall of 1975, a year after the Labrador cruise, my plans for the following summer had jelled, and I was able to get out letters at Christmas to a list of friends of several age groups who were likely candidates for crew. I had decided to cruise to Spitsbergen, the northernmost inhabited land in the world. It had a fascinating history, not to mention a strategic value in the East-West relations of modern times. A branch of the Gulf Stream reaches its west coast and in the summer opens up the fjords in most of the archipelago. Reading accounts of assaults on the North Pole over the years convinced me that Spitsbergen was accessible, and now I wanted to go there. I had heard about this intriguing land from an old friend of mine from Vancouver, whose grandfather had been a mining partner of John Munro Longyear, the man who discovered coal in Spitsbergen in the early 1900s. To bring this full circle, John Munro Longyear was an antecedent of Carol Munro Sheldon, Paul Sheldon's wife and shipmate and mistress of *Seacrest*. Funny how the lure of the Arctic gets into the blood!

I had always had a hankering to return across the Atlantic from Europe via the northern route. Once the farthest objective was picked, then the route was the next consideration. That depended to some degree on what we wanted to see and the available connections for possible crew changes. During this period of planning I tossed about in my mind the idea of a possible visit to Murmansk or some other Russian town. To grease the machinery for that objective I wrote to a fellow sailor, Senator Ted Kennedy, who had heard about the trip from a mutual friend. His reply was certainly generous. He wrote me that he had contacted our ambassador in Moscow and had requested that I be given permission to visit coastal villages in the Soviet Union. He was enthusiastic about the project, but, of course, could not guarantee the Russians would be so minded.

Selecting a crew was a continuing process on which I had been working since the summer of 1975. The first prospects were all people who had sailed and raced on *Reindeer,* knew the boat, and in turn were well known by me. It's almost impossible to get a nonretired person to go on such an extended trip. It doesn't figure to improve either corporate or marital relations. Therefore, I planned that the trip be segmented to allow for several crew changes, as well as the restocking of provisions. From the candidates among my acquaintances, sixteen accepted the invitation: eight adults, including women, and eight college-age types, including my three sons.

Having had such an excellent experience with the University of Delaware's College of Marine Studies (CMS) and knowing that its scientists' participation in my proposed cruise would give us the mantle of respectability, I called again on my friends Dean Gaither and Professor Daiber. They immediately jumped at the opportunity that such a trip might afford CMS. When I had first approached them about the Labrador expedition, they had responded cautiously, but this time their enthusiasm was instant and unbounded. Of course they had to get approval of the president of the university, but they assured me this should not be a problem. My emphasis on the dangers, which we could not afford to understate, and the necessity for thorough preparation seemed to increase their eagerness.

The university had so many applicants for the trip among their instructors and graduate students we had to screen them! We boiled their number down to six, plus two who simply hopped a ride to Newport on the first leg. I insisted that each of the CMS crew members spend at least one weekend on the boat to get oriented. These weekends gave Orlin Donaldson and me a chance to give a thorough indoctrination to the CMS people, to get to know them and evaluate their level of skill in seamanship. It amazed me that several young women wanted to go. This gave me a little pause, but only because I thought they didn't know what they would be getting into; rough seas and heavy work. I refused to accept any passengers for the Denmark Strait portion, male or female. In this respect, Frank Daiber, with his previous participation in the Labrador trip, was most helpful in picking those applicants he knew had some sea experience. As a result they all turned out to be splendid as shipmates and sailors. I was most fortunate to have them. Their involvement gave the whole expedition a legitimacy, especially to those to whom a private yachting trip might have seemed like a stunt. For instance, I knew the Russians wouldn't understand our purpose if no scientists were aboard. They would be suspicious anyway, but doubly so without CMS.

It seemed sensible to go to Norway to get firsthand advice and possibly a Norwegian shipmate, as well as the necessary charts, radio aids, navigational aids, and official approvals. I had written to Helge Amundsen in Hammerfest, to whom I had an introduction from Walter Levering, a New York Yacht Club friend of mine who had his boat in Hammerfest and was planning to circumnavigate the world over the top of Siberia and Canada. Amundsen's reply to me was prompt and informative. In regard to the weather, he warned me it would be chilly. He would try to find me a Norwegian shipmate if he couldn't make the trip himself. Also, I had been talking with people at *National Geographic* who were planning a trip to Spitsbergen in the summer of 1976 for a major story on that remote part of the Arctic. A letter from Gordon Young, one of their editors, confirmed a dinner meeting for the two of us in Oslo. Thus I had appointments in Oslo and Hammerfest. I then arranged to stop in London to check in with U.S. Navy people at NATO headquarters. The objective of the latter visit was to grease the wheels in the event that someone in Norway might later throw up an obstacle, purely on suspicion.

The flight went off smoothly, and soon Gordon Young and I were having Sunday supper at my Oslo hotel. We compared notes. The information flowed mostly from Young to me. He told me of difficulties with the Soviets, but he believed they would allow him to visit the Russian mining town of Barentsburg, probably in July, He explained the reluctance of the Norwegians to foster any sort of tourism at Spitsbergen. They had enough trouble dealing with the Russians, and their policy for their arctic islands was that they would be off limits to tourists. I was curious as to why the Russians were a problem, so Young explained that they continually pushed the Norwegians for more than the treaty allowed. They would use any pretext to obtain a stronger foothold, and Norway feared it was for military purposes. After all, the Germans had grabbed Spitsbergen in World War II and used it primarily as a weather station and an outpost on the flank of the Murmansk run. Young intimated there was much more to the Russian-Norwegian confrontation than met the eye. While listening to Young, obviously an old pro, I imagined myself in the middle of a drama in one of Ian Fleming's stories. When Gordon departed for his hotel, for the first time I felt alone in an uncertain environment.

Admiral Bagley and Captain Von Schrader, of NATO naval headquarters in London, had put me in touch with our naval attaché in Oslo. When I talked with him at the embassy, he assured me he would advise Norwegian Defense of our plans. We all understood the advisability of clearing any cruise in the Barents Sea, since that was a hot spot of cold war confrontation between NATO and the Soviet Union.

Later that day, I met at the Norwegian Polar Institute Dr. Lundquist, with whom I had already corresponded. The institute had official control over scientific activity in Norwegian polar regions, both north and south. Lundquist himself had been to Spitsbergen more than twenty-five times and knew all kinds of details, including where the polar bears might be found and how not to trust a mother bear who was with her cub.

Next morning I flew north to Tromsø via SAS. The flight was in the dark, but over the horizon there was a slight twilight that gave the white glistening peaks with a dark background a grandeur seldom seen in my part of the world. In midmorning, villages were clearly outlined by the streetlights. At Tromsø, a city of twenty-five thousand, I had to wait nearly an hour for a flight on a twin Otter to Hammerfest. I'll never forget landing at the world's northernmost city. It looked exactly like the movie *Ice Station Zebra*. Even though all the bays and fjords on the Norwegian coast were open, because of a branch of the Gulf Stream, the mountains, hills, roads, and towns were in deep snow. When we taxied up to the small airport building I saw a helicopter tied down, and I wondered what business in Hammerfest could support such a luxury, especially in January.

Reservations at the Grand Hotel in January were no problem and, once checked in, I walked over to the photographic supply store, Photo Co. Its owner was Helge Amundsen, Walter Levering's friend, the man I had come all the way to the top of Europe to see. He was either going to sail with me from Hammerfest to Spitsbergen or find me another Norwegian who could. He was also going to get me expert advice on the trip.

Helge addressed the crew question first. He knew a young man in

Tromsø, Knut Sørensen, who loved to sail when he wasn't running a bank in town. It was arranged for me to meet Sørenson at Tromsø on my stopover on the way back to Oslo. We then discussed Walter Levering's attempt to make a circumnavigation around the polar route. Walter's Norwegian wife was a friend of Helge's, and Walter's well-known attempt to achieve this feat had the assistance and support of Norwegians, not the least of whom was Helge. His 1975 attempt had ended in failure in the Barents Sea because of fierce weather and the loss of crew support. Soviet disapproval had been an issue, but extremely adverse weather in the very sea I now wanted to cross made the Russian problem academic — at least in 1975.

Levering's scheme to sail across the top of Siberia wasn't farfetched, but I had seen too much ice in eastern Canada to share his confidence about the part from Alaska to Labrador, let alone about the notion that he could do both Siberia and Canada in one season. His premise, however, was based on the fact he had only about four feet of draft and could work along the edge of land after the ice had receded. As for Siberia, this would require Soviet approval, and that was by no means assured. The Canadian stretch had been done in a sailboat, but the risk of being smashed by wind-driven ice was always present. No sailor in history had put the two together, Northeast Passage and Northwest Passage, in one season. That's about like climbing Everest and K2, back to back, as Helge agreed.

During my visit with Helge, an incident occurred that underscored the tremendous importance that the Norwegians and NATO as a whole attach to the northern waters, where the interface with the Soviet Union is no casual matter.

Helge had scheduled a meeting with a Norwegian whaling captain for supper at the Grand Hotel. Tuesday was Bingo night, and when Helge, the whaler, and I started poring over charts of the Svalbard Archipelago, we must have seemed a bit incongruous in the dining room. Just then I noticed two men looking at us from their table, as if to say "What in hell are those boys doing here?"

After my two dinner partners departed for the night, I went to the desk in the lobby to buy some postcards. While there I was approached by the two men that I had noticed in the dining room. Both looked to be in their mid-thirties. One was blond and pleasant-looking; the other was swarthy, had only one ear and several scars, close-cropped hair, two slits for eyes, a positively menacing sort.

The blond one casually asked me, "What brings you to the far north, if I may ask?"

I kept one eye on Scarface. "Oh, I'm just up here seeing some friends about your arctic islands." His suspicion was making *me* suspicious. I was damned if I were going to hand everything out on a silver platter, so I decided to give him a little of his own medicine.

"Are you fellows up here on business?"

"Oh, more or less," replied Mr. Nice Guy.

That convinced me these guys were on my tail. I'm no expert on James Bond, but one of my adversaries looked tougher than Odd Job. Who in hell was he? I thought. Soviet? Norwegian? American CIA? And the nice guy: Norwegian Intelligence? Who sicced these hounds on me? Suddenly it occurred to me I had never got back to our naval attaché's office in Oslo. Perhaps he hadn't had time to check with London. To him I was just a phone call, so maybe to head any trouble off at the pass he had simply handed it to CIA.

After I went to bed, trying unsuccessfully to get some sleep, I suddenly remembered the helicopter. That's how they got there! No other way. I was on the only plane and they hadn't been aboard.

At breakfast, there they were again. This was no joke. I needed to drop some aniseed somewhere to get these hounds off my scent. I packed my bags carefully, put the cuff links in one corner and toilet kit in the other. Admiralty charts and a new *Playboy* covered the rest. Helge drove me to the radio station, where I got some further communication information, which must have looked even less touristy to my two observers. Finally off to the airport, and as I checked in my two bags, there they were, smiling cunningly.

On the flight Nice Guy was in the seat behind me. I turned around and asked him a loaded question. "Hey," I said, "where in the States does your colleague come from?"

"Why do you think he's from the States?" he retorted sharply.

"I think I've seen him before," I said, lying through my teeth.

"No, he's from Mexico," he said, making some acknowledgment about the right continent.

Odd Job sat implacably four seats back. He never broke silence, except to grunt to Nice Guy in American idiom. When we landed at Tromsø I went into the waiting room to meet Knut Sørensen, Helge's choice for my shipmate. We only had time for a handshake and a few quick comments. It must have looked awfully conspiratorial. Nice Guy and Odd Job now had something to report to their superior, and I felt sorry for Knut. In any event, Mr. Nice Guy got off at Tromsø, and Odd Job stayed on to Oslo.

At Oslo I managed to change my reservation to an earlier plane for Copenhagen. To do this, it was necessary to switch the luggage, and the SAS man took my stubs and gave me new baggage checks. Everything was in order, he said. So off I flew to Copenhagen. Odd Job was not on board. I drew the conclusion that if these agents were on the ball they would have a look at my bags, and the only time for such a check was between flights at Oslo. Ergo, the bags would not be on my flight; they would come in on the flight on which they were originally scheduled, for the simple reason that there wasn't enough time for the inspection if the bags were put on the earlier flight. Meanwhile I concentrated on recalling just where my belongings were stowed in the bags.

Upon arrival in Copenhagen, sure enough no bags. My presumption was well founded, as the bags came in on the next flight, the original flight that I had booked. At the Hotel Angleterre I carefully inspected the contents and found my cuff links in the opposite corner of the bag from where I had stowed them. Also the Admiralty publications seemed stowed a bit differently. Even the folding of my sports jacket was unusual, but *Playboy* was somehow undisturbed. Agents of some country were on my trail. Of that there was no doubt, but at last I had finally escaped their surveillance. The only remaining questions were whose agents were they, and why was I a suspicious character?

Much later I pieced together information from the U.S. naval attaché in Oslo and another naval friend. Nice Guy and Odd Job were agents of Norway, put on me as purely a precautionary measure because Norwegian Defense did not have time to establish my purpose in going to northern Norway in January. Undoubtedly it was standard operating procedure for the Norwegian Polar Institute to inform the Defense Department of any visits to arctic areas by foreigners. This was precisely the sort of situation I had tried to avoid through our attaché's office, but perhaps I hadn't given them enough time. It was a spine-tingling experience that in retrospect added excitement to an otherwise normal trip.

My trip to Norway was productive apart from the sideshow. I brought back valuable information on the prospects of sailing to Svalbard, the risks and recommended procedures. I had charts and radio communication information. I now knew the procedure to get formal permission, and, most important of all, I had a prospective Norwegian shipmate.

Back at home, I addressed a follow-up memo to my crew. I passed along the information my contacts had shared with me, and also I stressed the delicate Soviet relations in the region. In particular, I urged the CMS crew to maintain a scientific mantle at all times, to avoid any suspicion of our being tourists or — even worse — spies. It was now time to get down to the short strokes, the details that would make the trip go off as planned.

Our biggest adversary on this arctic expedition would be ice. For up-to-date information, Orlin journeyed to Maryland, to the National Oceanographic and Atmospheric Administration, known as NOAA. This trip was a ten-strike so far as ice information and preparation was concerned. Their bulletins were loaded with facts, including an advisory on ice off East Greenland, which Orlin got hold of even before it went out to the fleet! After reading this advisory I realized the importance of a thorough study of ice, even though the Labrador trip itself had been a very good basic seminar on the subject.

Since our first port of call was in southwest Iceland and after that our course was through warmer water to the top of Norway, ice did not appear to be a threat for that portion of the trip. In any event, I studied the report Orlin brought back from NOAA. It was loaded with pertinent stuff, both on currents and ice, for the entire area of the North Atlantic.

The British Admiralty publication *Arctic Pilot* had a mine of information on ice, including very handy sketches of the expected ice distribution in the exact areas we wished to traverse. The *Pilot* states matter-of-factly: "Sea Ice presents serious hazard to navigation over much of the area covered by this volume throughout the year. The whole East Coast of Greenland is icebound for the greater part of the average year."

Since 1966, sea ice data has been collected by polar-orbiting meteorological satellites, and as long as storms don't obscure accuracy, information based on such data may be reliable. We were going to make every effort to get such data and keep it updated. The conclusion we drew from the Admiralty information was that the most we should expect of ice on the west coast of Spitsbergen was scattered loose pack and a few bergs. The north coast of Spitsbergen might be relatively free of the polar pack in late July but might just as easily be blocked by Siberian ice floes from the east.

On the east coast of Spitsbergen, in Hinlopen Strait, and around Northeast Land (Nordaustlandet), ice was expected to be generally bad. Only local knowledge, plus a lot of luck, would satisfy the requirements of safe passage in those areas.

In east Greenland even in August, the most ice-free month, a narrow belt of ice usually encloses the whole coast to Cape Farewell. If such ice were of the four-tenths coverage type, that appeared manageable. If seven-tenths coverage, forget it, for this would be dangerous. In any case, the big imponderable was the effect of wind. We learned that the prevalence of west winds would tend to scatter the pack off east Greenland, whereas a wind shift to the east, especially of high intensity, which was common around the southern portion (in the Icelandic low), would push it on the coast and make it impenetrable.

The charts I had of Greenland were like nothing I had ever seen. Many fjords and channels had absolutely no soundings, obviously indicating they had not been surveyed. I couldn't imagine sailing where no one had been or at least where no soundings had been recorded! Also, the chart I had of southernmost Greenland was colored and almost three-dimensional. It showed the glaciers and mountains, and in places the glaciers extended to the water's edge. I had no idea what this implied for a sailboat in the vicinity. It didn't seem safe if a piece of the glacier were to slide off as an iceberg does. Also, no indication of drift ice in the interior passages was shown on the chart. The Admiralty *Coast Pilot* showed pack ice prevalent in Denmark Strait all summer, and I had no idea of what this might portend. From our experience in Labrador, I knew that we had to be very careful with this type of ice.

When in Copenhagen, I had talked with Captain Toft, a famed Danish whaling skipper whom Tom Watson had consulted before

Palawan's great voyage beyond Thule. Even Major Tilman of the Royal Cruising Club consulted Toft, so I knew his word was *le dernier cri.* I wrote to him early in February, expressing some of my anxieties about the relatively unknown waters of Greenland and Denmark Strait.

My chief concern, I told him, was the ice, especially that of the east Greenland pack. I asked him about the possibility of getting into the village of Angmagssalik and also the passage through Prince Christian's Sound. I also requested all he could tell me about coping with the pack ice under different conditions. The unsurveyed interior passages worried me, so I asked him about that as well.

I hadn't told him we were a forty-three-foot sailboat with a fiberglass hull no greater than five-eighths of an inch thick. This omission was intentional; I was used to people looking at me with a jaundiced eye. Toft therefore assumed I had a heavy trawler and that I could push through loose pack ice as an icebreaker might. His colorful letter was based on this assumption — which amused the crew — but was nonetheless full of helpful information on what we might expect in the way of ice conditions, scenery, accommodations ashore, radio communications, and navigational aids. He warned us not to go north of any pack ice on the way to Iceland, and referred to the possibility of the ice "screwing" — a term I took to mean that condition in which the ice was pushed onto the coast by the wind.

In my research, I learned of a very interesting feature of sea ice called *polynya,* which is an area of open water amidst the pack ice. This occurs along the east Greenland coast sometimes as early as May, owing to northwest winds. It was these polynyas that must have permitted the Scoresbys, William Senior and Junior, to penetrate the east coast back in 1820. They discovered the largest fjord in the world, Scoresby Sound. William Scoresby, Jr., wrote an account of the voyage and mentioned the refraction phenomenon that we first saw in Labrador, called ice blink. Pack ice can look like a solid wall and icebergs can look inverted. When on board his *Baffin of Liverpool,* a small whaling vessel, William Scoresby, Jr., saw his father's vessel, *Fame of Hull,* at least thirty miles away. Commenting on this in 1822, Scoresby wrote:

On my return to the ship, about 11 o'clock, the night was beautifully fine, and the air quite mild. The atmosphere, in consequence of the warmth, being in a highly refractive state, a great many peculiar appearances were presented by the land and the icebergs. The most extraordinary effect of this state of the atmosphere, however, was the distinct inverted image of a ship in the sky, over the middle of the large bay or inlet before mentioned [Scoresby Sound] — the ship itself being entirely beyond the horizon. Appearances of this kind I have before noticed, but the peculiarities of this were the perfection of the image, and the great distance of the vessel that it represented. It was so extremely well defined, that when examined with a telescope by Dolland, I could distinguish every sail, the general rig of the ship, and its particular character; insomuch that I confidently pronounced it to be my father's ship, the *Fame,* which it afterwards proved to be; on comparing notes with my father, I found that our relative position at the time gave our distance from one another very nearly thirty miles.

I had read Nansen's *Farthest North, Three Years of Arctic Service* by Greely, and *Arctic Researches and Life Among the Esquimaux* by Charles Francis Hall, and the Arctic adventures of Elisha Kent Kane, the Navy doctor from Philadelphia. Their collective experiences ranged from the fantastic to the grisly. They thought nothing of being beset in the ice, but of course their vessels were heavy and reinforced for the expected pressures. Experience on the Labrador had given me an indelible picture of what ice can look like, maybe even in all its forms, but I shuddered to think what our remedy would be if we were somehow to become beset in the ice.

While thinking of this I began to envisage a scenario in which the ice staves us in and we abandon ship. We are too far from land to paddle there in the life raft, so we find an iceberg to climb upon and our life raft becomes a tent. The life raft does have a canopy and therefore would make a pretty good shelter. Then, dreaming on, I assess our position. We have no medicine for frostbite, but we do have emergency rations, a mirror for signaling, and a transponder to send out radio distress sounds that we hope might be picked up by airplanes. I foresee a long ride on the berg. Maybe I remember to bring the shotgun, but how do we retrieve the birds that are shot in water that is below freezing? Will this iceberg join the warm current of the Gulf Stream and melt, or turn around Cape Farewell at the southern tip of Greenland and join the north-going West Greenland Current? I can't make up my mind which is better!

The whole notion of a long drift on an iceberg was not an impossible idea. In fact, in the winter of 1872, Captain George Tyson, a whaling skipper from New London, was cast adrift on an iceberg with a small party that was part of a polar expedition led by Charles Francis Hall. They drifted south some fifteen hundred miles from October, 1871, to April, 1872, and were rescued near the Strait of Belle Isle, off Labrador, by one of the Bartletts of the famous seafaring family of Brigus, Newfoundland. Reading about Hall's expedition and Tyson's drift had left some fierce impressions on my mind.

Having just studied ice probabilities and what to expect, I received through the mail a warning from Knut Sørensen that predicted only a 5 percent possibility of getting around Spitsbergen, because of ice. I was aware of the extreme caution of the Norwegians, who, oddly, are not used to sailboats in the north, but as a result of his caution, I decided to consult counsel and was advised to get my crew to sign waivers of any claims in the event of an unanticipated disaster. I also wrote the governor of Spitsbergen, known as the *Sysselmann*, telling him our desires and the scientific nature of our visit. A little emphasis on the goals of the geologist from Delaware would give us respectability, I figured. In addition I wanted to allay any fears he might have of mounting a search and rescue operation, or even logistical support. The Sysselmann, whose name was Leif Eldring, replied with a formal letter extending his permission and good wishes.

When seemingly all the important information was assembled, the next step was to plot out the trip. This required knowledge of the facilities available and of course a careful estimate of the time it would take to make each passage. This would be the master plan, the schedule, and it would provide for eleven ports for crew change and provision for a total of twenty-seven hands in the crew in its entirety.

The expedition was divided into ten phases:

Phase 1: Delaware Capes to St. John's, Newfoundland (via Newport)
30 May to 7 June; open ocean passage

Phase 2: St. John's to Reykjavik, Iceland
14 June to 26 June; open ocean passage

Phase 3: Iceland to the Faeroes
28 June to 4 July; open ocean passage

Phase 4: Faeroes to Bodø, Norway
5 July to 10 July; open ocean passage

Phase 5: Bodø to Hammerfest, Norway
11 July to 20 July; coastal cruising

Phase 6: Hammerfest to Spitsbergen
25 July to 29 July; open ocean passage

Phase 7: Spitsbergen to Jan Mayen Island
2 August to 7 August; open ocean passage

Phase 8: Jan Mayen Island to North Iceland
9 August to 13 August; open ocean passage

Phase 9: North Iceland to St. Anthony, Newfoundland
15 August to 27 August; open ocean and coastal passage

Phase 10: St. Anthony to Georgetown, Maryland (via Baddeck and Halifax, Nova Scotia, and New York)
28 August to 15 September; open ocean passage

By February, 1976, I had gathered sufficient information to lay out the whole trip and schedule the crew changes. It didn't seem practical to take a sailing trip of over three months' duration with the same crew in its entirety, unless the crew were husband and wife. Even then, marital harmony could be strained to an undesirable limit. Nevertheless, for tactical reasons, I invited my wife to select any or all segments of the cruise. I suggested "all" first.

She looked me in the eye as though I were that Japanese admiral who exhorted his kamikaze pilots to join their honorable ancestors. After the admiral's instruction to dive down the enemy's smokestack, he then asked if there were any questions. One young officer is reputed to have said: "Yes, Admiral, are you out of your focking mind?" Anyway, Peggy selected the Norway coast for her fortnight aboard, and her choice was later rewarded with the best weather of the whole trip.

We were able to achieve an interesting variety in our crew selection, because of the separate segments of the cruise and the different people included on each.

Orlin and I would make the entire voyage, with the following crews:

Phase 1:	Lewis Smith	Phase 6:	Stockton Smith
	Hank Smith		Dicky Cromwell
	Dave Leu		Knut Sørensen
	Henry Lane	Phase 7:	Diana Russell
Phase 2:	Toby Garfield		James Demarest
	Paula Garfield		Stockton Smith
	Lewis Smith		Dicky Cromwell
	Hank Smith	Phase 8:	Same as Phase 7
	Henry Lane	Phase 9:	Salley Norwood
Phase 3:	Philip Parish		Stockton Smith
	Terry Lloyd		Dicky Cromwell
	Henry Lane		Courtenay Jenkins
	Professor Franklin Daiber		Michael Ponce
Phase 4:	Same as Phase 3	Phase 10:	*Salley Norwood
Phase 5:	Peggy Smith		Michael Ponce
	Philip Parish		Andy Harris
	Jeannette Parish		*Gary Madeira
	Terry Lloyd		Courtenay Jenkins

* Off at Nova Scotia

This variety was a bonus rather than a necessity, for despite what might seem to be the restrictions of close quarters, the daily routine aboard a cruising boat can enable several people to live harmoniously in a limited space for quite a long time. Making the boat go requires concentration and therefore a continuing watch system. This concentration is much more intense while racing, when at least four people must be active on the deck at all times. When cruising, except during storms, usually two people can handle the duties of the on-watch, permitting each member of the crew six hours off for every three hours on watch. While the on-watch continually adjusts the sails to changing conditions and of course logs the progress for the navigator, the off-watch is sleeping, or, perhaps, reading, and in any case relaxing. Meals are important times for the entire crew, and usually happily anticipated. Seldom is boredom a problem, except possibly during periods of flat calm. When cruising one can start the engine, so flat calms need not be as trying as they are during a race. They provide a chance to charge batteries.

Meanwhile the College of Marine Studies formalized plans for sending its personnel on different phases of the trip. Professor Daiber wrote up a proposal to the university administration, stressing the value of research in the eastern Arctic, since most polar research had concentrated on Antarctica and the western Arctic, where atomic testing and the Alaska pipeline have stimulated investigations.

Daiber outlined the objective of cesium sampling, the same type of study they had conducted on the 1974 trip. His presentation went into great detail on how they would get the samples and just what might be accomplished from the data obtained. They would bring a large number of plastic bottles, and the samples collected from towing a special apparatus every morning and evening would be measured to go into the data bank for CMS to correlate.

I chuckled a little over the precision of Daiber's plans. He made no provision for nausea that might hit the scientists in the North Atlantic, and I wondered if any of them had any idea of the conditions they might encounter as they approached the Icelandic lows, where storms fly across at regular intervals. I didn't want to discourage them, but I knew that daily samples would have a few holidays.

Professor Daiber made a separate proposal on bird life. I knew he was an avid observer and might even consider himself an ornithologist, but his high-sounding proposal translated to one thing: he was going to observe and count birds. I didn't tell him we had some pretty good hands on seabirds ourselves.

The last part of the proposal covered objectives in the field of marine geology. Professor Chris Kraft just drooled over the possibility of doing a photographic study of Spitsbergen. I looked forward to learning some geology from Jim Demarest of his department, who was to study the raised shorelines and relative sea levels of the coasts of Spitsbergen and Jan Mayen.

While we were moving forward with our major planning, the State Department was still trying to get us cleared for the Soviet Union. I had despaired of ever hearing from the Russians, having called their embassy several times and having written to them asking for permission to visit the Soviet Union at Murmansk. I'll say one thing for them; they can ignore you with utter consistency. Even though two Soviet scientists, A. I. Alkhimenko of the Leningrad Polytechnic Institute and K. A. Bilaskvily of Tbilisi State University, had studied at the University of Delaware CMS and Dean Gaither wrote to the director of arctic science at the Research Institute of Leningrad, we still met a wall of silence. The letter from Senator Kennedy evoked no response. I was therefore forced to conclude that an excursion into the Soviet Union would be at best a waste of navigation time and at worst a risk of arrest and detention. I would stick with Spitsbergen. We could visit the Russian town of Barentsburg.

As for preparing *Reindeer* herself, there was much to be done. Her accommodations were modern, albeit miniaturized. The compact galley area, located on the starboard side, aft, features an aluminum and steel stove on gimbals, so the pots wouldn't spill. There are three burners on top and two in the oven. We converted the fuel from alcohol to kerosene, which has four times the Btu. A couple of ten-gallon jugs of kerosene were all we needed for spare fuel, and if this were insufficient, kerosene was available most anywhere and cheap compared to alcohol. Someone told me that using alcohol was like pouring Beefeater gin in the tank, and according to my calculation we would have needed forty-five gallons for the whole trip! That of course was prohibitive in expense and, more important, space.

Stowage space was extremely important for a trip this long and to such isolated places. Fortunately, going north meant that ice in the icebox would last longer. Our box holds about two hundred pounds and is well insulated. Next to the icebox is the sink, which has two deep but small basins. We can pump fresh water from our tanks or salt water from the sea, which suffices for washing dishes on a long passage.

Opposite the galley on the port side is the navigator's area. The navigator has a desk that contains charts and instruments, like parallel rules, triangles, and the ordinary paraphernalia for navigation. The sophisticated stuff, like loran, radar, VHF, AM, and single-side-band radios are all mounted on the bulkheads above the desk, or recessed into cabinets on the port side. This area is also quite compact and has room for only one man, about like the galley. Forward of this area is the main cabin, which seats six people at a gimballed mahogany table.

The main cabin sleeps four, two on each side. Each of the total of six berths has a lee cloth or lee board to prevent one from falling out when the boat rolls. Just forward of the table is the mast, which comes down through the deck and rests on a structural beam that runs fore and aft,

Iceberg off Cape Mugford (Diana Russell)

Overleaf: Waterfall at Facheux, Newfoundland (Stockton N. Smith)

Burgeo, Newfoundland (Orlin Donaldson)

Hebron, Labrador, evacuated 1953 (Diana Russell)

Heimaey in the
Westmann Islands,
with Helgafell in the
background (Orlin
Donaldson)

Torshavn, Faeroes.
The building
features a sod roof.
Reindeer in the fore-
ground (H. G. Lloyd
III)

Overleaf:
Woody Point,
Bonne Bay,
Newfoundland
(Orlin Donaldson)

*Lyngenfjord, Norway. Photo taken from
the dinghy late in the evening (Orlin Donaldson)*

*Terry Lloyd, Peggy Smith, the Parishes
in dramatic silhouette against the
midnight sun, Norway (Orlin Donaldson)*

called the keelson. Under the floorboards are water tanks and below them the bilge. The main cabin is warmly finished in teak and koto, a lighter-colored wood, all varnished and clean-looking. There are a bookshelf, stereo, cabinets, and spare chart racks — all the comforts of home in one room that combines bedroom, dining room, and den. There are no port-holes; light comes through a skylight overhead that opens. Two ship's-type ventilators bring fresh air below and are baffled to prevent water from joining the air.

Forward of the main cabin on the port side is the head, which in *Reindeer*'s case is really compact. A man of six feet can't fully stand up, but he can take a shower if there's enough fresh water, and if the engine has been running he can even take a hot shower, albeit a "quickie" by land standards. On the starboard side opposite the head are two quite adequate hanging lockers. Then there's another transverse bulkhead, forward of which is a forepeak where sails, anchors, anchor lines, and miscellaneous items are stowed. There are two bunks in that forward area, but they were removed to provide more stowage space. My bunk and that of the first mate are aft on the quarter, with portholes that open into the cockpit well. I like it back there, because I can hear what's going on and I can get to the navigator's seat in a jiffy. All in all, it's a fully utilized space, and every effort is made to provide both necessities and comfort.

We carried enough tools to transform our home to a machine shop or an electrical shop, and on a long trip it's almost inconceivable that a cruising boat doesn't sometimes convert to such parameters. Often during racing, something goes wrong electrically or mechanically and a good portion of the crew are diverted to mend the item that's broken down. In the 1966 Transatlantic Race from Bermuda to Denmark, I remember on the Yacht *Challenge* we broke our spinnaker poles three times. That means one was broken twice. The forces of compression on those poles, under forty to fifty knots of wind, were too much. The deck was truly a machine shop as we fashioned wooden plugs to connect the broken aluminum poles, using bolts and steel strapping. So much metal was flying around that the skipper should have issued hard hats to the crew!

We worked at preparing *Reindeer* while she was at the yard in the spring. Orlin Donaldson, who had just retired as chief of photography for Bethlehem Steel, made ingenious improvements for the trip. His attention to detail was extraordinary. Orlin worked assiduously in the galley area, putting in better shelves, cutting boards, changing the stove from alcohol to kerosene, and taking care of many other special items. We consulted daily and worked together every weekend, making structural changes and preparing radio and electronics equipment, special equipment for a long trip to the Arctic, safety equipment, food and fuel storage, and tools and spares.

Phil Parish, whom I had known and been associated with at Georgetown Yacht Basin, was a close friend, and his supervision over the changes on the boat was much more than business. He loved *Reindeer*; she was his baby in many respects, and he eyeballed her daily from the stem head to the stern pulpit, including every clevis and cotter in between. Phil was adamant that she was not to leave the yard until he had reinforced her transverse bulkheads with aluminum plates or teak and fiberglass. The fact that Phil was going to be one of the crew augmented his ardor for safety. I urged him to pay special attention to our steering gear and the alignment of the sheaves. We had broken our steering cable four times since delivery in Finland in 1969. Nothing is worse than to have no control of the rudder. Minneford's Yard at City Island had finally fixed this defect, but I just wanted Phil to check it once more.

I concentrated on the radio and electronics. We got Colin MacDougall from Falmouth, Massachusetts, to install our single-side-band radios, and what a job he did! Single-side-band (SSB) is for long-distance high-seas calls, and its range is phenomenal. We had four separate frequency bands — four, eight, thirteen, and seventeen megaHertz. The choice of frequency is critical and is related to the time of day and the distance to the receiving station. For example, one might transmit unsuccessfully to New York because the signal could bounce off the ionosphere and skip New York; yet Miami might be loud and clear from the same location at sea. A letter from the Coast Guard spelled out some of the frequencies available for such important aid as ice information and illustrated the technical knowledge required for a trip of this magnitude.

Good communications were essential, and that also meant backup equipment in case of failure. Thus we had two separate SSB radios, one AM radio with sixteen channels (made by Sailor of Denmark), and a VHF set. The backstay, with insulators, served as the aerial for the SSB and AM radio and loran. The VHF had its own antenna at the masthead, because its signal is line-of-sight, so it needs maximum height for range of transmission. As backup in the event of dismasting, we carried a whip antenna that could be installed swiftly on the stern. To adjust for the change in antenna length it was necessary to have a special automatic coupler for tuning to the new length. The radar had its own rotating antenna, which sat atop a pedestal in the stern. To operate all this electronic equipment, we had to have an elaborate switching capability. I was fearful that no one short of Einstein would ever master all these hookups, but finally my son Stocky and I passed the course.

Meanwhile, I was having some difficulties with language barriers. Knut Sørensen helped in translating the Norske Radiostasjoner booklet that I had bought in Oslo. It had sending and receiving frequencies for Bodø, Tromsø, Hammerfest, Svalbard, and Jan Mayen.

Our special equipment included two rubber bladders for carrying extra diesel fuel on deck, a heavy-duty net for picking up chunks of ice for the icebox, a radiator to warm the cabin with hot water from the heat exchanger, two rubber inflatable dinghies (one a spare), a Seagull outboard engine for the dinghy, weather cloths to protect the cockpit, and many other items that Orlin thought of in his thoroughness.

Orlin's ideas for stowage were outstanding. He found space I didn't know existed. For instance, he devised a rack under the upper bunks that could hold nearly all our canned food. He had little baffles built in so each can could stow snugly, and he even put sponge rubber in these racks to prevent the cans from rolling and making annoying noise. We spent days discussing the appropriate place to stow nearly every item. Bulk items like potatoes, brown sugar, or flour could be stowed in a relatively inaccessible space behind the stove that was hard to reach and impossible to see, whereas Nepal pepper and oregano had to go in a special spice rack that one could see. I remember stowing twelve quart bottles of Hellman's mayonnaise around the water pump under the sink. We calculated the mayo consumption carefully, because it is available only in the U.S. After three months we had consumed 10.7 quarts, so the estimate was close.

Phil put a Lucite cover over the main skylight. This was far better than the canvas dodger, and one could stand on it. We also blew up the life raft on Phil's lawn to check it out and the emergency kit inside it. I had never been in a life raft, so it seemed wise to get the feel of it, and

I must say it seemed very cozy and well protected by its canopy. For the life raft we had a big bag of emergency items, including a transponder that would send distress signals that aircraft could detect. In the forepeak there were two wet suits and one rubber survival suit: only one because they were expensive. Oddly enough, the survival suit was in my size!

Food selection and stowage was one of Orlin's chief concerns. He made maximum use of mixes, powdered soup, Carnation milk, and Bisquick, as well as dried mushrooms, dried apples, and onions. He used the oven to an extent it had never known, baking bread and cake and roasting meat and potatoes. By converting the stove to kerosene, we introduced a few problems with the burners and the fuel tank, which unfortunately did not emerge until well along in the trip. Orlin, it turned out, had a far greater tolerance for kerosene fumes than anyone else.

When possible, we planned to purchase fresh fruit, vegetables, meats, and sundries ashore, but on long passages or in remote areas, our canned goods would be the mainstay. It is surprising how good a canned meal can be. For liquids at sea, beer is a luxury because it takes up a lot of space, but it can be rationed in such a way as to award meritorious young mates. The same goes for soft drinks in cans. We permit wine on special occasions, such as Independence Day, Bastille Day, birthdays, and any other day when the supply allows. On *Reindeer,* liquor is not consumed while at sea, because we are all pilots, not passengers. In the north, hot drinks were more popular than cold drinks, and we carried plenty of coffee, tea, cocoa, and dried soup mix.

In the medical department, a thorough consultation with doctors was a must. We carried a broad supply of medicines, including antibiotics, antidotes for burns, and even sutures. The usual pills to regulate one's plumbing were handy, and on that score we had to be careful not to overcorrect in any one direction.

Safety equipment was given the highest priority. Probably most important in this category were safety harnesses, which are worn over foul-weather gear. At sea, in the Arctic particularly, the most important thing is to stay in the boat. Life preservers are fine for keeping afloat, but how long can one live in water temperatures ranging from the forties to the upper twenties? Years ago we used to wear safety belts, but I recall, from racing in England in 1961, that an English crewman on another boat fell over the side and was dragged through the water fanny-first until he drowned. That gave rise to the harness type of belt, which would drag a man headfirst if he went over. The main point is to be hooked in to the standing rigging so that a rogue wave or a sudden lurch or slip (both of which I had experienced several times, especially on the foredeck or in the pulpit) would not put one overboard. The watch captains were charged with the responsibility for enforcing the rules on belts.

We installed wire rope along the deck in the waterways to hook our safety belts onto when working forward so that we could move about without having to unhook and rehook all the time.

Perhaps the most sophisticated precautionary steps that we took involved the X-rays of mast and rig fittings. After the 1959 Halifax Race, I had a bronze toggle at the base of the backstay explode and very nearly lost the mast. That shook me so that before the Bermuda Race of 1960, I had all my turnbuckles, toggles, and clevises X-rayed. Four of them showed defects in the casting and had to be replaced. In that 1960 race, it blew a full gale or more, and one of those new toggles let go! Fortunately it was on a lower shroud. Had it been the upper shroud, the mast would have gone. Now we had all stainless steel fittings, but even these weren't foolproof, and there were no ship chandleries in Denmark Strait.

One of the last major changes that we made was to remove all the inside lead ballast, which totaled 1,800 pounds. If we were to take a roll-over or, worse, pitchpole (a somersault), I didn't want lead raining down on our heads from beneath the floorboards. This lead was recast into a shoe, which was then fitted to the leading edge of the existing lead keel. The new shoe weighed 1,350 pounds, but since it was much lower down, the boat's righting moment was increased substantially. This gave us more stability; in other words, she was stiffer.

We had more tools than I knew how to use and more spare equipment than ever before. One addition was a small Honda portable air-cooled gasoline generator that was to prove invaluable. So much electrical stuff depends on the two twelve-volt house batteries and the one engine starter battery that any failure or run-down of them would put us in the proverbial soup. Again, some previous experience had taught me to be mindful of what can go wrong. In the 1963 Transatlantic Race to Plymouth, our engine wouldn't start after four days past Nantucket. Thus we couldn't put a charge into the house batteries with the engine alternator. The skipper had a portable generator, but it too was on the blink. The race was slow and took twenty-one days, so we made do without juice, even for running lights. The compass lights were the only battery consumption permitted. When an English electrician came aboard in Plymouth after the race, he found the trouble in five minutes. Our earth (ground), he said, was disconnected! So the little red Honda found a place in the forepeak.

By late May we were ready to leave the yard. Orlin and I recognized there would be things we had not thought of, but we felt assured we would catch up with any loose ends by the time we arrived in Newfoundland. Everything seemed to be in working order. At last we pushed off from Georgetown and headed up the bay for the Chesapeake and Delaware Canal, where, after a brief stop for the crew's wives and mothers to see us off, we would pass into the Delaware and out to sea. Ten thousand miles of ocean lay ahead. It was an exhilarating feeling to be on the wind and wave; all cares were left ashore as we departed.

4

To Newfie and St. Brendan's Land

OUR UPCOMING EXPEDITION across the Atlantic and on to the Arctic called for a little celebration. If not Holy Communion, then perhaps a last supper ashore at the Canal House in Chesapeake City. The Chesapeake and Delaware Canal gets an enormous amount of coastal and international traffic, and the maître d' makes a big thing of the name of every ship, her tonnage, her home port, and her destination. At night they even dim the lights in the restaurant to watch the ships go by. Our little vessel remained tied to the dock while all the exotic foreign merchantmen went by and were announced, as we enjoyed the food and wine that were served.

Finally, after hugs and kisses, we cast off for the trip to St. John's via a short stop at Newport to pick up my sons Lewis and Hank. Besides Orlin Donaldson and me, the crew for this leg included Tom Campbell and Dave Leu from the University of Delaware, and two of their Delaware friends who were to be replaced at Newport by my sons, one of whom was graduating from a nearby school. With the mainsail set, we powered down the Delaware River until early morning. Then we set the number one genoa and turned the corner at Cape May heading straight to Newport, reaching with a light westerly breeze. There was a slight swell to the sea, not much but enough to make the Delaware boys sick. Along toward evening on Wednesday, 26 May, the wind backed to sou'west and we set the 1.2-ounce spinnaker. As Tom worked in the galley preparing fancy hamburgers with peppers and onions, Orlin and I stretched our legs and swapped sea stories in the cockpit. He told me classic stories about the crew of *Malay*, and I told him equally implausible exploits of *Reindeer* and her friends. When the going is easy at sea, that's the ideal condition for telling yarns.

We continued sailing downwind until early on Thursday, when we had to turn on the engine to keep up speed. Then in the afternoon an eighteen-knot nor'wester came in. We made landfall at Montauk Point, Long Island, in late afternoon. After supper the wind died, and again we needed the engine the rest of the way into Newport.

Newport was gearing up for the 1976 Bermuda Race, the finish of the Transatlantic singlehanded race, and the arrival of the Tall Ships for the Bicentennial celebration. The merchants had already festooned their stores with flags and welcome signs. Nobody had the slightest interest in a little blue boat going in the opposite direction. I saw a friend at the head of a pier where we topped our tanks. He asked where we were headed.

"Norway," I said.

"Are you out of your mind?" he replied.

Maybe we were at that. By then Lewis and Hank had joined us and we set sail, rounded Brenton Reef before supper and headed for the Cape Cod Canal. On Sunday evening we weathered Cape Cod off Province-town and put to sea on an east northeast heading for Newfoundland. It was a great feeling, even though the air was light and the engine occa-sionally required. The bird life took on oceanic character. There were fulmars, greater shearwaters, sooty shearwaters, and once we saw a Manx shearwater. Wilson's petrels were common and blackcapped petrels occasional. We also saw red and northern phalaropes, but only near the shore.

We passed about seventy-five miles southeast of Halifax and quite close to Sable Island and then sailed through the middle of a Russian fishing fleet. One of the trawlers in this fleet had Cuban markings. Her name was *Golfo de Tonkín* and home port was "La Habana." Perhaps the Russians were using Cuba as a base.

All week the weather was cooperative, with the winds northerly and dry. On Thursday, as we closed the Newfoundland coast near Cape

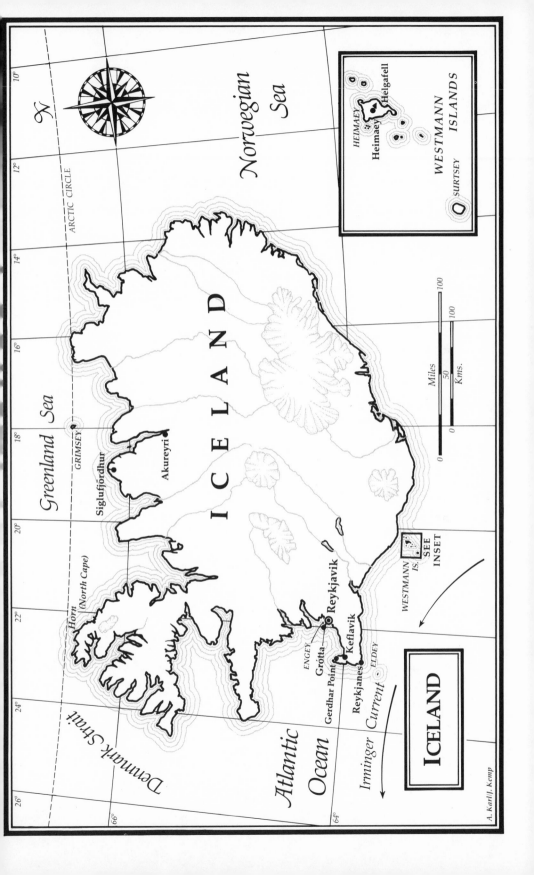

N

Norwegian Sea

ARCTIC CIRCLE

Greenland Sea

Horn (North Cape)

GRIMSEY

Siglufjördhur

Akureyri

I C E L A N D

Denmark Strait

Atlantic Ocean

Irminger Current

ENGEY

Grótta

Gerdhar Point

Reykjavik

Keflavik

Reykjanes

ELDEY

WESTMANN IS. SEE INSET

WESTMANN

Miles

Kms.

HEIMAEY

Heimaey

Helgafell

WESTMANN ISLANDS

SURTSEY

ICELAND

A. Karl/J. Kemp

Race, a Canadian armed forces helicopter paid us a visit and seemed satisfied. I was reminded quite naturally of the last time a Canadian chopper had concerned herself about us, but there couldn't be another smuggling act! The weather forecast mentioned strong westerlies, and when we rounded Cape Race the wind started to build in force until it was blowing over fifty knots. By shortening sail we kept the rail out of water and our feet dry. The boat showed her stiffness from the keel addition and behaved very kindly. It was such a short fetch from land that sea conditions were remarkably smooth, just the combination to fly. And fly we did; nine and ten knots on the "steam" gauge.

Bird life was outstanding. The gannets were our top choice — the way they soared and dived, their wingspan of six feet, and their distinctive white, black, and yellow coloring. The gannet is without question my favorite sea bird. Pictures of the new supersonic jet, the Concorde, look like carbon copies of a gannet in flight. Occasionally we heard the sonic boom of the Concordes; no wonder New York objected to those noisy newcomers.

The single-side-band radios checked out well. I talked clearly with New York and through the New York high-seas operator to home and elsewhere. I wanted future shipmates to know we were alive and well and to gain the confidence that good communications impart. Our radar and loran were also fully operative, except that close to shore the loran became ineffective. Sun sights with the sextant were useful to remove cobwebs from my celestial navigation, although I was fully aware that farther up north there would be no twilight, and therefore no star sights, because the sun would not set all night.

One thing that pleased me was the state of our equipment, although Orlin and I continued to make lists of little things needed. Even the fuel transfer from the rubber bladder on deck into the forward tank took place without spillage or mishap.

On Saturday, 5 June, *Reindeer* quietly slid into St. John's and tied up to an old fishing schooner at the head of the harbor. On the way, we passed the Soviet Union's research vessel *Moldavia,* which was lying at dockside. Our two new shipmates, Toby and Paula Garfield, both oceanographers from CMS, had already made the acquaintance of the Russians, who showed a lot of interest in the cesium samples which the

Garfields were going to collect as part of their study of the ocean's absorption of nuclear fallout from atmospheric tests. Cesium is a trace element in nuclear fusion, and by comparing the amount of it present on the ocean's surface and relating that to past known quantities, scientists could derive some idea of the ocean's tolerance for nuclear fallout.

While my sons and I flew home for my daughter's wedding, Donaldson, Henry Lane, a teacher at Hill School, and the Garfields took care of further provisioning and a myriad of small details, including procurement of an Icelandic flag, which we had been unable to buy back in the States. It is always proper courtesy to fly the flag of the host country at the starboard yard. The stores in St. John's didn't carry foreign flags, so young Crispian Barlow generously made us a flag that was a good copy of the Icelandic colors. My friends Sir Christopher and Lady Barlow attended to our needs and made the crew most welcome ashore.

When Lewis, Hank, and I returned to St. John's, we were met by Lady Barlow and Orlin, and after stowing our gear on *Reindeer* we went straight to the Soviet ship *Moldavia,* where the captain and his chief oceanographer, plus interpreter and commissar, entertained us for drinks and a light supper. Somehow Orlin had ingratiated himself with the Russians. They gave us a carefully guided tour and after that a pleasant reception in their wardroom. I couldn't help but notice that nearly every piece of equipment on the bridge was made in East Germany. Two things were apparent: the Russians' interest in the cesium sampling, and their admiration for our sailing trip in general. They seemed to respect us as sailors. Just for conversation and to test their reaction, I asked them what they thought of entertaining capitalists aboard a Soviet ship. Though we could not be sure how the interpreter translated that to the ranking officer, the latter firmly replied, "We talk sailing, not politics." That promptly put me in my place.

Later, when I entertained three of the Russians on board *Reindeer* for morning coffee, one of their younger men asked me what my boat cost. He was apparently amazed when Henry Lane told him the boat was owned by me personally, not by the government. I didn't want to exacerbate an already apparent disparity in life-styles, so I merely told him, "Too much."

They were also curious about the coming presidential election. I was tempted to tell them that if the American people didn't like their President all they had to do was vote him out of office. But again the problem of going through an interpreter made such a remark useless for the purpose of impressing them with the value of freedom. I remember Jamie Wyeth's telling me about his experience in Moscow with an interpreter who kept translating his conversation in such a manner that *his* farm became *the State's* farm.

Later, while Orlin and I were busy tidying up in the cabin and I was lining up my charts, two more Russians in civilian clothes paid us a visit. They said they had had the duty during our visit to their ship but were interested in our program of sampling cesium and would be glad to give the Garfields any data they had collected. The one who did all the talking spoke fairly good English. Said his name was Vasily Shurbitov. He mumbled his colleague's name, but I didn't get it. The colleague was apparently the scientist, as Shurbitov translated in Russian our answers on scientific matters.

Later, while Toby showed the mute one his collecting apparatus, communicating by hand, Shurbitov and I discussed our planned itinerary. He asked if I intended to visit the Soviet Union, and I told him that our ambassador in Moscow, at the request of Senator Kennedy, had asked permission for us to enter the Soviet Union, but we had received no reply. For that reason and also because of the shortage of time, I told him we would go straight to Spitsbergen from the North Cape. I purposely did not tell him I intended to visit the Russian town of Barentsburg, because I assumed that that might trigger a lot of red tape and perhaps even a refusal. I figured when and if we ever got there it would be better to act dumb, which wouldn't be difficult.

Mr. Shurbitov changed the subject and asked me if I had ever heard of Walter Levering.

"Of course," I said. "How did you know about him?"

"Many know about heem. A leetle crazee, no?" the Russian said with a smile.

"Oh, I don't know," I told him. "This year I understand he's got permission from Ambassador Dobrynin to visit Russia."

Shurbitov gave me a funny look as though this caught him by surprise. "I wish heem luck," he said, recovering his poise.

Shurbitov asked me what interested us in our tour of his vessel. Since the last thing I had on my mind was the Soviet research vessel, he found me dull. On the other hand, Orlin and Toby were much more effusive and seemed to hit it off well with him. Orlin told him how marvelous the Russian bread was (which it was); I don't think Shurbitov had any idea how much bread Orlin had already conned from them. While they were conversing I kept a weather eye on the other Russky, the silent one. Something about him bothered me. He just didn't look the part, and he wasn't comfortable when I was obviously surveying him. In my Machiavellian mind these guys weren't scientists or sailors, just spies. Damn it, I thought to myself, Shurbitov seemed too urbane for a Russian naval officer. He must be in the KGB, I concluded.

I wondered if I should report their visit to the Office of Naval Intelligence in Washington. And perhaps I should throw in *Golfo de Tonkín* for good measure. The bastards were up to no good. But then reason returned to my addled mind. Our guys would probably just listen and then thank me, all the while thinking I'd been to some spy movie and was trying to get into their act.

So I decided to leave spy games to the pros. Playing dumb was not dumb; it was smart. For all I cared, the Soviets could keep on talking about shrimp and cod and boundary layers and all that. Who were they kidding? I knew damn well what they wanted was what we were transmitting at Cutler, one of our low-frequency communications stations in down-east Maine. That Shurbitov was an engaging guy, but something about him was fishy.

On Tuesday, 15 June, we finally got underway for *Reindeer*'s first trans-Atlantic crossing, my third. Our destination on this leg was Reykjavik, Iceland. To put on a little show, we sailed out of the harbor flying a blue and gold parachute spinnaker. The Barlows were up on the ramparts of Battery Hill waving the Union Jack. To return the salute we dipped the Stars and Stripes; then we were off and away from the North American continent.

Putting to sea always lifts the spirit. It feels like the removal of a burden, like being airborne above the clouds. To communicate my carefree mood, I broke out in song, actually one of old Sherman Hoyt's ditties:

Oh, the starboard watch
Made a hell of a botch
Of the things they had to do.
They fouled the mainsail,
Buggered the staysail,
And snarled the halyards too.
Oft times at night,
With a star in sight,
They'd loudly claim a sail-l-l,
But when it rose on high
They'd heave a sigh
And pee o'er the weather rail.

CHORUS

Then blow ye winds high-ho,
And a-racing we will go.
We'll stay no more on Newport's shore,
So let the music play-i-ay.
We're off in the fog and rain
To cross the raging main.
We're off to Plymouth,
May God be with uth,
Three thousand miles away.

Then Orlin in much better voice topped me with his rendition of the Bermuda racer's ballad:

We'll say farewell to Newport's shore
And put her out to sea.
And when we sight St. David's light
How happy we'll be.

Once out of sight of land, the wind backed to sou'east and down came the chute. The wind and sea gradually began to build, and the temperature of both air and water plummeted, the water to the low forties and the air to about 36°F. It felt very cold, and it stayed cold for a week.

For four or five days I never removed my heavy woolen trousers, even when getting into the down-filled sleeping bag. I remember taking draconian measures just to prevent the slightest piercing draft of air from coming into the bag and down my neck when I was trying to sleep. While it was both wet and cold on deck, we kept warm reefing the main and changing headsails to meet constantly changing wind conditions. The main cabin was comfortably warm by virtue of a charcoal fire in the compact little fireplace. Occasionally, when we ran the engine for battery charge, the radiator along the cabin sole also put out some heat. With air temperature below 40°F., and the water not much above that, we kept the hatches closed except when cooking.

During this ten-day passage covering sixteen hundred miles, we were hit by four full gales. We must have been on the back side (the northwest side) of a low-pressure system, because the first three gales packed winds from the northwest. We reached with a working jib and double reefed main. At times we used the number four genoa, until the whole clew pulled out with a report like that of a cannon shot.

Being in midocean in a storm is an exhilarating experience. The fact that I had known total paralysis made me appreciate even more the thrill of slicing through heavy seas, feeling in command of the situation. One must never underrate the force of nature's wind and sea. It can be awesome. The shrill whine of the wind in the rigging and flying spindrift, wave tops blowing horizontally across the water, are ocean phenomena one enjoys only after a certain amount of experience. Then, too, knowing the boat, and what she can take, goes a long way toward calm acceptance of such conditions. Sometimes the roar of a storm is so great that it's impossible to hear a man shouting five feet away.

For circumstances such as these, we had installed canvas (Dacron) weather cloths around the cockpit to help keep waves out. These cloths were securely laced to the lifelines and the stainless steel stanchions, but the force of the water was so great that one little wave bent two of our steel stanchions inboard about 40 degrees! Such is the force of ocean waves. The boat usually rides on top of big swells, but occasionally wave and boat get out of synch. When that happens and a big wave crashes down on you, about all you can do is huddle in the cockpit and hold your breath until air reappears. The foul weather gear keeps you dry, although at times, especially when you're working forward or on the lee deck,

Breeze building on the way to Iceland (Lewis Smith)

water penetrates even the best-prepared defense. That's no bother on the way to Bermuda, where the water is relatively warm, but in the North Atlantic it's chilling and downright uncomfortable.

In weather of this sort, the watch on deck usually keeps active adjusting the sails. Even the helmsman gets good exercise. Down below it's dry and comfortable, but in a storm the noise outside and the shuddering of the whole hull can be intimidating to those on the off-watch. Sometimes you find yourself praying that all holds together. The worst noise comes when the hull drops off a big wave and smacks the surface many feet below, like a falling elevator hitting the basement. By and large, if you're not pushing the boat as in a race, the incidence of slammers of that type is not very high and nothing to fear. When it happens, however, I have to admit it scares hell out of me.

The worst of the four gales that hit us before we got into the warming Irminger Current, an offshoot of the Gulf Stream near Iceland, was hard on the nose, force 10 to 11. That's close to hurricane force. I decided not to risk gear failure and hove-to by backing the storm jib and countering that by lashing the helm in the opposite direction. Thus, when the jib took over, the bow would fall off, but since the hull would then move ahead, the rudder would steer the bow back into the wind. *Reindeer* thus stood up on her feet, and all of us went below for a full seven hours of good sleep. I didn't even worry about being run down by a ship, if indeed there were any other fools out there. After all, we had a radar reflector and running lights. There were no icebergs where we were, and our maximum speed was only about two knots. Maybe I should have posted a lookout, but I didn't.

Later on the radio I heard reports of casualties in the Transatlantic Singlehanded Race from Plymouth to Newport. Some lives were lost; several boats were towed to shore. I was reminded of Carlton Mitchell's old axiom: you can make almost any wind dangerous by carrying too much canvas. Conversely, I thought to myself, you can make almost any wind benign by shortening sail. Nothing is shorter than bare poles, and that would have been our next step. It didn't come to that, but seventy knots is a hatful of wind all the same.

Since I felt secure about our trip at least as far as the North Cape of Norway, I spent a lot of time reading and talking about early voyages through these same waters: for example, the voyage of Brendan, the Irish monk who sailed to Iceland via the Faeroes in the early part of the sixth century with a group of monks. His boat was made of oxhide on wooden frames, and his journey covered seven hundred fifty miles of the North Atlantic. As far as anyone knows, he was the first white man to discover Iceland and was followed by many Irish ascetics fleeing from difficult conditions at home.

The Viking migrations, including the takeover of Iceland, began three hundred years later, when the Norse population virtually exploded to places all over the known world. The very name *Viking* means "men of the bay," or "watermen," an apt name since their route was always by water. We know from the sagas that these seagoing plunderers were warriors and cold-blooded killers of strangers. The total disappearance of the Irish monks suggests that they were slaughtered by the Norsemen, who centuries later were known to have killed off the Skraelings (Eskimos and Indians) in Newfoundland. On the positive side, the Vikings overcame the toughest obstacles that nature hurled at them. They were, first and foremost, sailors, and my crew was interested in relating our experience to the history and exploits of these unusual people.

The early Viking settlements in Greenland were actually Icelandic.

Viking longboat, Oslo Museum
(Franklin Daiber)

Erik the Red and his followers had first settled in the west of Iceland after leaving their native Norway under clouded circumstances. He had to keep on the move to avoid the forces of justice.

In the books I had read, the Greenland nomenclature, such as the so-called Eastern and Western Settlements, puzzled me, because in actuality the two settlements were north and south and both on the west coast, as opposed to the real east coast facing Denmark Strait. I was also amazed by the assertion that Leif Erikson's epic voyage first took him to Baffin Land, which was northwest of his point of departure. On further reflection, however, this traditional theory is readily understandable. First, the West Greenland Current had to push him north and, second, the prevailing wind was likely from the west or southwest. That makes a landfall at Baffin Island possible, albeit unlikely.

W. A. Munn's very well-documented condensation of the sagas and deductive interpretation thereof explained some of these mysteries. In fact, every subsequent discovery, such as the archeological digs at L'Anse aux Meadows, has supported Professor Munn's conclusions to a great extent. According to Munn the Eastern and Western Settlements were so named because the early cartographers believed Greenland to be a peninsula running northwest to southeast. The earliest settlements were those of Herjolf Barnarsson and Erik the Red, who founded what might be called the Eastern Settlements around 986. The Western Settlements were farther up the west coast in the area that is now Godthaab, the capital. Since magnetic variation at Cape Farewell, the southern tip of Greenland, is about thirty-six degrees and at Godthaab about forty-four degrees, it's understandable how the later voyagers who had compasses thought the coast ran much more to the west than it actually did. But magnetic compasses didn't come into use until the mid-1300s, so the geographical error had another origin. In none of the early sagas is there any description of what I call East Greenland, the coast facing Denmark Strait and the Greenland Sea. Presumably, the pack ice deterred the Vikings from any probe in that direction, as indeed it did others for centuries, and still does.

Professor Munn further straightened out the geography. He put Leif Erikson's "Helluland" at Hamilton Inlet in Labrador and "Markland" a little to the south at the Porcupine Strand, which we visited in 1974. He put "Vinland," or, as he called it, "Wineland," at Pistolet Bay around the corner from L'Anse aux Meadows, where he suggested Erikson first landed. In 1961, a Norwegian archeologist, Helge Ingstad, authenticated a true Viking settlement at L'Anse aux Meadows, and it is now thought that this was the wintering place of Thorfinn Karlsefni in 1005, and possibly the landfall of Leif Erikson around A.D. 1000. So far, no one has either proved or disproved Professor Munn's conclusion that Leif's settlement was in the Pistolet Bay area. That Vinland was the northern tip of Newfoundland is now indisputable, and all the stories about Cape Cod and Newport can be put to rest.

Our great circle course northeast to Reykjavik took us within two hundred miles of Cape Farewell on our port hand. I found myself focusing on the problems of coming home and wondering and indeed marveling at the seamanship of the Vikings in their longboats, which crossed this strait around 985 to 986. Erik the Red, who had a penchant for trouble and was forced to leave Iceland, managed to explore the southwest coast of Greenland perhaps as early as 982. Then he returned to rally his friends to join him in settling in this "exotic" land to the west. One such friend, Herjolf Barnarsson, managed to found his colony even before Erik landed from this same expedition. His village, Herjolfnes,

is a cable or two across the water from the present day Greenlander village of Frederiksdal. I thought this was the logical settlement for us to
visit on the return trip, as long as we could make it through Prince
Christian's Sound and the other fjords which make up the inside passage
inboard of Cape Farewell.

Sometime after 986, Bjarni Herjolfsson, son of Herjolf, made a trip
to Greenland, in the course of which he was blown far off course to the
south and west. However, it is inconceivable that he was as far west as
Cape Cod, as many apocryphal stories have surmised. Munn thought
that Bjarni's sightings were probably along the east coast of Newfoundland and possibly Belle Isle. Since Bjarni's trip predated Leif's, he might
therefore be considered the first white man to have seen the New World.
And it was Bjarni's father's settlement that we hoped to visit on our return trip from Spitsbergen — if we could negotiate Denmark Strait!

The Western Settlements around Godthaab were founded a little later
than the Eastern Settlements but became extinct earlier. For that matter,
the whole Viking culture disappeared by the end of the fifteenth century. The Western Settlements expired about 1350; nobody knows precisely why. There had been as many as ninety farms in that district.
Historians and archeologists have speculated on a number of causes of
their demise, any combination of which could have been the culprit. To
begin with, from my own observation of coastal people in isolated out-
posts, I would conclude that thinning of the blood from intermarriage
would be an early cause of weakness. It was a known fact that the early
Vikings did not mix with the Skraelings, so intermarriage could have
debilitated them. Second, during those years mankind suffered from re-
curring epidemics, the worst of which was the Black Plague. If the germ
of this disease reached Greenland, it easily could have wiped out all the
families of the Western Settlement. Another cause of the decline, according to the Viking historian Finn Gad, was the reduction in the number
of walrus and narwhals along the coast, which could have caused a
diminution of commerce in tusks with Europe or trade with seafarers.
The ivory from the tusks of these mammals was much sought after in
those early days before African elephant ivory became available.

The Eastern Settlements are thought to have existed until around
1480, and then they too disappeared. The clues on their demise are
perhaps better documented. Examination of bones dug from graves

showed a strong evidence of malnutrition. Also, there were signs of a sudden end. This could have been the result of attack by the Skraelings but more probably an assault from the sea by the Basques, who were known to have fished these waters as early as the fourteenth century. There has been mention of the presence of the Basques in Newfoundland around 1372, one hundred and twenty years before Columbus. The English explorers and fishermen got cranked up later in the fifteenth century, but it's doubtful that any of them preceded Sir Martin Frobisher's "rediscovery" of Greenland in 1576 to 1578. Another, and I think most convincing, clue to the date of the last survivors of the Eastern Settlements was the Burgundian style of caps found in graves. These were in vogue on the European continent in the latter 1400s. Archeologists have found it hard to explain what happened to the people who buried the last survivors in these graves. This leads to the theory of attack from the sea and possible burial of the victims at sea.

In any event it seems safe to conclude that the Viking civilization in Greenland had a duration of about five hundred years. Subsequent attempts by the Danes to go to the relief of these people were failures, especially those that tried to cross Denmark Strait. The *stor is* (great ice pack) greeted the newcomers with impartial disdain. For example, in 1607, the Danes sent out an expedition, which is described by Finn Gad as follows:

> The ships tried in vain to break through the ice belt. According to *Den gronlandske Chronica,* published in 1608 by Claus Christophersson Lyschander, royal historiographer and pastor at Herfolge in Zealand (the only source material we have concerning the expedition), the ships reached as far north as 64°. Towards the end of June and during the first days of July they made a final attempt to break through the ice. This was a hazardous enterprise, and the sailors may have realized the risks they were taking. At least they learnt a good deal about the nature of the ice, and they only seem to have escaped its grip by a stroke of good luck. At long last they had to give up, and they reached Denmark on July 25.

Then in 1652 King Frederik III of Denmark gave one Henrik Muller a charter to trade with Greenland. One of his ships under a Captain

Dannel managed to reach the west coast of Greenland and acquired (from the Eskimos) tusks and skins, which he brought back to Copenhagen. His second voyage is described by Gad as follows:

> The meagre results of the voyage did not stop Henrik Muller from sending Dannel on a second Greenland expedition the following year. This time the ships left Copenhagen on April 16 and, setting a northerly course, they reached Jan Mayen on May 4; they then steered south-west and sighted Iceland on May 11. Five days later they were in Reykjavik, and on June 6 again sailed westwards. They sighted land at 63°40′, but were prevented from going ashore by a coastal ice belt 50 to 60 km. wide. Steering a west-south-westerly course they were now caught in the ice, now free of it, and in this way they followed the ice front as far south as 58°10′. On July 2 they sighted Cape Farewell in ice-free waters. In 62° (i.e. at the present Frederikshåb) the first few Eskimos came on board while the vessels were still some 25 km. out to sea; it was found that they were returning from hunting gulls still farther out! The most remarkable feature of the second Dannel voyage is the frequent mention of fishing, giving the impression that this voyage was dedicated to the second kind of fishing mentioned in the charter.

Reading these accounts in the middle of the Atlantic while only a couple of hundred miles south of Denmark Strait put my mind back in the boat and on the problems at hand. Our hands were full just getting to Iceland, so further reflection on the past was clearly a luxury, as our logbook reveals:

18 June
Since late yesterday we have been in a dry norther. Winds have increased to a steady forty knots, and today the sea has built up and is quite lumpy. Much of the day we were getting puffs to fifty-five knots. Lewis continued on Marezine and so far hasn't been sick. However, no such luck with Paula Garfield, who seems to be a permanent fixture in the starboard upper berth.

Everything is holding together. Reduced to number four jib and double reef in main. Still averaging eight knots on the steam gauge. Toby takes his cesium samples. Waves are breaking over the whole boat. I pray this lets up soon.

19 June

Wind continues at whole gale force, but it's across the deck and we go like a roller coaster. Bird life not as prolific now. Bloody ugly fulmars still follow us, but no more petrels. Still have greater shearwaters though. Water got to 36°F. Air 41°F. No whales. No porpoises. Water clear blue and no kelp.

Supper cooked by Orlin. Beef bourguignon, Uncle Ben's Rice with chopped dried mushrooms, and salad. Really stuck to the ribs.

20 June

More of same weather, only worse. Doused working jib; put up storm jib. The anemometer was now pinned at sixty knots, its maximum reading. Puffs were around seventy-five knots and the rigging had a steady whine and the sea really built. I call it twenty foot seas, meaning forty feet from trough to tops. Some of the wave tops are at masthead level, or fifty-seven feet. The crew are all uptight, not saying much. Orlin and I keep up a banter to boost their spirits. Paula is miserable, poor girl. Lewis and Hank are putting up a good front but I can tell they're scared. Toby is terrific, and of course it's Orlin's meat. These waves are just plain huge. Orlin finds that water has leaked into his bunk and ruined his camera, which really distresses him.

Supper was chicken à la king with added boneless chicken. A great rough weather meal. I was chef with Orlin adviser. Henry Lane and Toby Garfield were real chow hounds. Lewis and Hank were borderline cases. Paula remains in her sack.

21 June

At 0100 wind shifted to northeast and again started to howl. Now we're on the wind; it's on the nose. Seas getting really big. Doused main. Sheeted storm jib to weather and lashed helm to windward. Boat hangs in to windward. Spindrift hits our faces like hail, and it hurts. All go below and sleep. Blowing at least 70 knots steady. Hove-to seven hours.

22 June

Slogging into big and confused seas, which occasionally break over the whole boat. All hatches are secured shut. Had to fall off below our course. Pumped bilge. Engine on to charge battery. Supper is delicious beef stroganoff.

23 *June*

Winds abated but still on nose. Sun came out. Saw arctic skua for first time. Also immature kittiwake. Had roast beef dinner with wine. Wind eases to twenty-five. Broke out reef. Sent note in wine bottle. I wonder if someone will get the note in Scotland and write to us, as happened in 1974, when Stocky sent a note from Labrador in a wine bottle, and later got an answer from a schoolgirl who found the bottle on the rocks of northern Scotland.

24 *June*

Wind picks up. Number three genoa is too much; go to number four. Reef main. Terns, pomarine jaegers, all kinds of birds showing up. It rains hard at times, but water is much warmer. Ditto air. Water color changes. Looks like Gulf Stream! Wind again force ten, maybe eleven. Gauge pinned at maximum reading of sixty. Again we furl the main. The number four genoa clew pulls out with a loud report. Wind hurricane force. Go to storm jib.

25 *June*

Storm abates. Orlin and I go on deck to set sail. We make 080 to 090 magnetic. In the afternoon the engine shuts down for no apparent reason. Orlin and I work two hours on engine and drain the filter. Got her started again. Found trouble in fuel line filter and drained it. Wind again piped up, but temperature warmer.

26 *June*

Reached along at eight knots. Winds around thirty knots. Not bad. Doing fine. Sighted land at 1600! It was Eldey, an islet with the largest gannet colony in the world. Chart shows a few sunkers around. Kept a close watch. Proceeded up coast from Reykjanes to Gerdhar, past Keflavik's towers. Orlin cooked us spaghetti and meatballs, and we polished off the last of the salad.

Rounded Gerdhar and headed in toward Reykjavik, twenty miles to the east. Wind in the west, thirty knots. Ran in until Grotta Light appeared unlighted. Rounded Grotta. Dropped storm jib. Broke out full main and started engine.

Soon engine quit. We had to bleed it. Got it started again. As we got to the harbor, it stopped once more. Bled it again and it started. Orlin and I drained the separator. I called the harbormaster on VHF and was instructed to lay alongside an Icelandic fish transport ship. We were inspected, given papers. Then the very kind customs officer gave me a ride to the Loftleider Hotel, where I got us all registered, and then called home.

Iceland is a Nordic country, free and independent. However, the people we saw didn't seem entirely happy, although poverty was nowhere visible. There was a sameness to the Icelanders, but that's a characteristic of all the Scandinavians, who are not used to invasions by foreigners. Alcohol is apparent as a problem of the youth, not that Iceland has any monopoly on that. Probably the worst national problem is inflation, caused by an imbalance of trade. She exports only fish, and most everything the people wear, eat, and ride is imported. The government runs a deficit and the consequent inflation depreciates the value of their currency. Cab drivers prefer to be paid in foreign currency, even if it's illegal. The Icelandic people are the best read in the world and have more bookstores per capita than anywhere. The riddle is why with such intelligence they haven't developed an export trade, as have the Germans, who are also short of raw material.

We had been at sea for ten and a half days, most of them rough, and it was now time to relax and revitalize, then clean up the boat, restock the larder, sew up torn sails, and change part of the crew. It was also time for a quiet whisper of thanks to God, who seems much closer when you are out at sea. My sons departed for home after an all-night sampling of nightlife at the discotheques. Replacing them and the Garfields were Terry Lloyd, Phil Parish, and our old friend Professor Franklin Daiber. Henry Lane and Orlin Donaldson remained aboard.

Our shore headquarters, the Loftleider, was a very modern operation with fair cuisine, sauna bath, and a rather cosmopolitan atmosphere. After a full quota of sleep well into Sunday morning, Orlin, Henry, and I returned to the boat and hung everything out to dry; sails, bedding, life jackets, and everything affected by moisture and salt water. We worked all afternoon, scrubbing and cleaning and even doing a little carpentering. To dry sails, we had to move from our berth alongside the fishing vessel to the lee of one of the town docks and let the sails fly out in the wind. There, a crowd of polite but curious spectators gathered to look us over. It was a sunny afternoon, and the people were Sunday strollers. One of the spectators seemed to take unusual interest, and out of the corner of my eye I sized him up. In fact, he was one impressive-looking fellow of about fifty-eight, tall and military-looking. When our eyes met, he smiled and asked me in perfect English where the boat was built. He was clearly knowledgeable and had already noted the modern stainless steel shrouds of ribbon cross-section and the slab reefing arrangement for the mainsail. We introduced ourselves. His name was Peter Shuve, a flight captain with SAS, the Scandinavian airline. It turned out he was a yachtsman who kept a boat in Oslofjord. He also had flown with the RAF in the war, a man of poise and obvious seniority. He knew all about Nautor, the Finnish builder of the Swans, of which *Reindeer* was an early copy. After a thorough tour of the vessel, we arranged to dine that evening at the Loftleider, where he also was staying.

Frank Daiber came over from his hotel, and we all ate together with Captain Shuve. It turned out that SAS flew twice weekly from Copenhagen to Greenland. Peter said the passengers were government people together with a certain number of corporate representatives, mostly involved in mineral prospecting. We discussed radio frequencies, and Peter agreed to monitor our single-side-band eight-megaHertz frequency. Meanwhile he would keep a log of the ice conditions in Denmark Strait on his way across to the airport at Narsarssuak. Then, when we called him, he would pass on his latest observations. This sounded just fine, and we all congratulated each other for being so lucky.

On Monday, Terry Lloyd and Phil Parish arrived and helped us move *Reindeer* across the harbor to take on fuel, water, ice, and engine oil. While engaged in this operation I had an expensive mishap. As I was paying the fuel bill with American Express cheques and Icelandic currency, suddenly two American fifties blew out of my hands, which were a bit numb from the cold and wet weather. The two crisp bills, with General Grant's picture on them, landed on the surface of the water and took off like dinghies downwind. While the two Federal Reserve notes coasted across the water we all stared dumbfounded; no one volunteered for a swim. Lloyd finally stabbed at them with a boat hook. Finally the crew cast off lines to try to fish the money out by hand, but just as they appeared to be in good position, both bills nosed under and disappeared. Not an auspicious way to start our leg to Norway — a one-hundred-buck boot in the tail. I wondered how many dockside observers thought this was some new ritual practiced by American yachtsmen trying to buy off Davy Jones before putting out to sea.

5

Off to the Faeroes

THE NEXT LEG of the journey was to complete the crossing of the North Atlantic to Norway. We would detour slightly for a look-see at the Faeroes, Viking stepping-stones in the outward thrust to Iceland and Greenland. The Faeroes lie nearly due east of the southern coast of Iceland, only four hundred miles downwind under usual weather conditions.

On the evening before leaving Iceland we ate our last meal ashore at the snappiest restaurant in town. All of us were amazed at the prices, which were comparable to New York's. It was as expensive as La Grenouille or Caravelle, and since I don't frequent such high-tone temples of the gourmet, it came as a shock. The whole crew decided we couldn't afford not to go to sea.

On Tuesday, 29 June, we sailed out of Reykjavik harbor, leaving Engey to starboard and Akureyri to port. We beat westward toward Keflavik, tacked out to weather Gerdhar Point. Winds piped up to force six, and we fetched along with a reefed main and number three genoa. Rounding Gerdhar, we tacked south to pass between Rykjanes and the gannet-populated islet, Eldey. I never tire of watching these birds peel out of the air and dive into the ocean as deep as fifty feet below the surface, where they then attack an unsuspecting school of fish from below. Before Eldey was colonized by the gannet, it was the last nesting place of the now-extinct great auk. This nonflying northern counterpart of

Antarctica's penguin was finally driven to extinction in the 1840s by the world's greatest predator — man.

Once around Reykjanes, the southwestern tip of Iceland, we eased sheets and rolled eastward toward the Westmann Islands, which are volcanic outcroppings approximately fifteen miles south of mainland Iceland. Surtsey, the latest addition to these islands, poked up through the ocean in 1963 — a fiery and smoky spectacle if ever there was one, judging from pictures I had seen. As we passed Surtsey, only a few hundred yards to starboard we could see one lone guard standing watch on this totally black islet. His function was to keep people away so that scientists could study the evolution of life without human interference. We saw black guillemots, razorbills, and puffins, but the only birds that had started to nest on Surtsey were fulmars, whose eggs and chicks are often attacked and consumed by the great black-backed gull.

From Surtsey we sailed quietly northeastward to Heimaey, the capital and only town of the Westmanns. These islands are smack in the middle of a branch of the Gulf Stream known as the Irminger Current, which moderates the air temperature all year. The average temperature in summer is 57°F. Rainfall measures close to fifty inches a year. Heimaey is seven thousand years old, like Surtsey a relative newcomer to the world. It is dominated by an active volcano called Helgafell, which last erupted on 23 January 1973. The entire population of 5,200 was evacuated to the mainland without a single loss of life. Teams of men with fire hoses poured twenty-nine thousand tons of water per hour on the flowing lava, which then formed a ninety-foot wall extending out into the harbor and prevented the rest of the flow from covering more of the town beyond. This lava wall is still solidly intact, including an extension to form a natural breakwater that further protects what was already a good harbor for the fishing fleet. After a full year to clean up the mess of cinders, pumice, and ash, the entire population returned, and Heimaey is once again a thriving and busy fish town with a processing plant that packages fish for export, chiefly to the United States.

The north side of the harbor of Heimaey is dominated by a nine-hundred-foot concave cliff, mostly brown in color, topped by bright green grass, where sheep graze on incredibly steep slopes. The cliff is teeming with nesting birds: murres, puffins, kittiwakes, razorbills, and even dove-kies. The murres, standing up in the crevices with their white vests, look

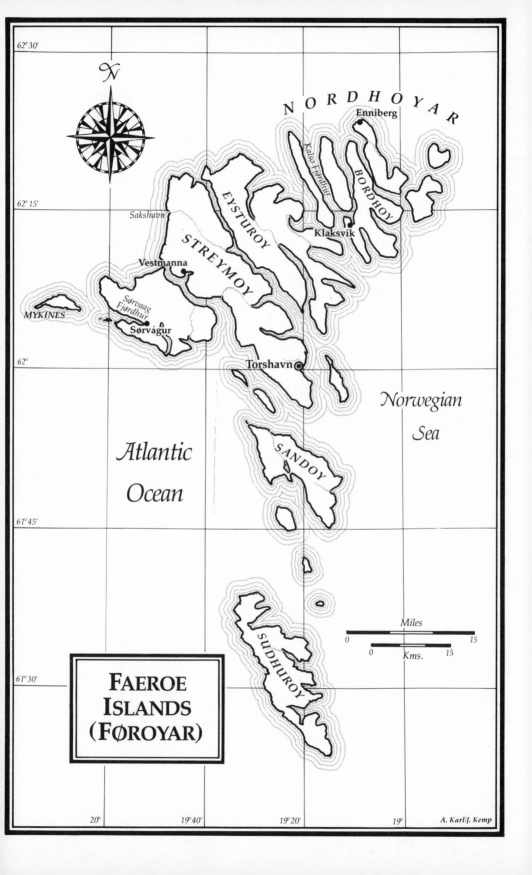

FAEROE ISLANDS (FØROYAR)

N O R D H O Y A R

Enniberg

Kalsø Fjørdhur

BORDHOY

EYSTUROY

Sakshavn

STREYMOY

Klaksvík

Vestmanna

Sørvaag Fjørdhur

MYKINES

Sørvágur

Torshavn

Norwegian

Sea

Atlantic

Ocean

SANDOY

SUDHUROY

Miles
0   15

0   Kms.   15

62°30'

62°15'

62°

61°45'

61°30'

20°   19°40'   19°20'   19°   A. Karl/J. Kemp

The leading edge of the lava at Heimaey, Westmann Islands (Orlin Donaldson)

like miniature penguins. Hovering, always within menacing distance, are the jaegers and skuas. A parasitic jaeger attack on a highly maneuverable kittiwake is fascinating to watch. The predator attacks when the kittiwake has a fish in his bill. The kittiwake will cut and turn and avoid the jaeger by superior maneuverability, but he will drop the fish, which the jaeger will then spear in midair or pick up on the water. It is an amazing show. Sometimes the pursued bird will upchuck a piece of fish; other times he will simply drop it from his mouth.

For some reason, the three species of jaegers and the great skua command the skies from the south coast of Iceland all the way to the Faeroes, while the fulmars, who were our constant companions everywhere else, disappeared in these waters. Nor were there any shearwaters or petrels. Indeed, I never saw these two ocean birds anywhere above the Arctic Circle.

After dropping our sails we powered into Heimaey and tied to a trawler at one of the docks. Orlin, Phil, and I went on a tour of the fish factory, which was busy packing and freezing fish for the Long John Silver chain in America. Most of the workers in the plant were women,

Tied up to a fishing trawler at Heimaey (Orlin Donaldson)

the wives and daughters of fishermen, all neatly dressed in white uniforms. In the winter they work up to sixteen hours a day; in the summer, only eight — for two dollars an hour.

The village looked almost Mediterranean. The houses had whitewashed stucco walls and rust red or green galvanized roofs. Heimaey was exactly what it always had been: a village of people whose lives are wholly dependent on the fishery.

On the way out of the harbor early in the afternoon, we motored toward the caves at the base of the huge cliff on the north side. While we were looking at the plethora of birds in their perches in the rocky cliffs, an immense seal suddenly broke through the water's surface. He appeared to weigh at least four hundred pounds and was no more than ten feet away when he surfaced. At first I thought he was a walrus without tusks. He and I stared at each other in disbelief. His eyes kept blinking, and in this respect he bore a remarkable resemblance to Terry Lloyd. He was what the Norwegians call a *storkobbe*, much bigger than the type of seal one sees around Maine and Nova Scotia.

We proceeded out of the harbor and set sail downwind to the Faeroes. The trawlermen in Heimaey had given us some pollack and cod, so Orlin made a fabulous fish chowder for supper. Something told me this leg of the trip was going to be a piece of cake; the barometer was steady and the wind moderate and following.

That night and the next day we saw several Icelandic trawlers, accompanied as always by slews of gulls. Thank God the cod war was over; I did not want to be mistaken for a Britisher or German after the recent unpleasantness over fishing rights in these waters. British MP's had talked tough about their constituents' rights to fish near Iceland, as they had done for centuries, but Iceland was not going to let Britain's Parliament dictate its fishing limits. Icelandic limits were first put at three miles, then twelve miles, later fifty miles, and now two hundred miles! Icelandic gunboats enforce these limits, much to the displeasure of the British and Germans.

What's more, Iceland had the trump card in this dispute, a little item called the NATO base at Keflavik. One doesn't have to be a geopolitical professor to recognize the importance of Iceland to the security and defense of the Western World. Should Iceland fall under the dominance of the Soviets, the whole containment strategy, particularly that which pertains to our northern flank, would come apart at the seams, so while I didn't wish higher fish prices on my English friends, in this matter my sympathies were with the Icelanders. To permit others to intrude on their one resource just doesn't seem fair.

Aside from the cod war, which reminds me of the oyster wars between Virginians and Marylanders, there is, of course, a much bigger cold war being waged in the chilly waters to the north and east of Iceland where we were heading. Indeed, this war of the silent service (the submarines) is, if anything, more intense and arcane than ever before, an exercise employing the highest technology. Also I had been amazed to read in an article in a London paper when I was there in January that American atomic submarines were planting mines on the ocean floor of the Barents Sea and that these mines or torpedoes could be actuated remotely to home in on Soviet submarines. That this and a lot more was right in the public press was startling. I knew from my Navy friends, more by what they didn't say than what they did say, that we had a substantial undersea presence in these northern waters. I knew we would not see our nuclear submarines, but I had been assured they would see us.

With that background we scanned the horizon daily for periscopes and for surface ships, especially hoping to see the Russian Navy on maneuvers. We knew they were around there somewhere. The Soviet Navy has been steadily increasing its muscle and probing the West on its northern flank. Certainly the Russians' experience with ice conditions is at least as great as the West's. With their fourteen-thousand-ton Delta class nuclear submarines armed with atomic missiles of five thousand miles' range, the Soviets presumably could duck under the polar pack, emerge in the Canadian Arctic, and aim their missiles anywhere from Key West to San Diego. It made me a little uneasy. I was used to Uncle Sam and John Bull ruling the waves.

While my mind was abuzz with Russian armaments, Orlin started praising the Soviets, especially those we had met in St. John's. He kept saying what a great guy Shurbitov was, insisting that he was genuinely interested in our trip and truly wished us success. Orlin's Quaker good-will toward a guy I suspected was a spy began to irritate me. Shurbitov was up to no good; I knew that. After all, if the Norwegians could get paranoid over my little January trip to Hammerfest, think what the Russians could do! I began to regret I had not fed them some cock-and-bull story about a military mission just to make them waste some money.

I told Orlin I thought Shurbitov was not a member of the ship's company on *Moldavia*.

"Why do you think that, Newbold?"

"Did you notice his clothes? They didn't look Russian to me. That guy was in the KGB. He probably learned English at McGill, or even Harvard," I said.

"Aw, come on, he was just a well-educated and courteous Russian naval officer or scientist," asserted Orlin.

I couldn't understand Orlin's refusal to recognize the subtle difference between Shurbitov and the others. I tried to tell Orlin that just because he *said* he was from *Moldavia* that didn't mean that he was. He knew damn well we weren't going back to *Moldavia* to check on him! Furthermore, with Ted Kennedy's letter and my contacts with the Russian embassy, wasn't it logical they might have a little curiosity about us? And how about his knowledge of Walter Levering? The whole thing fitted. Again I was under surveillance, only this time by the other side. Yet curiously, I got the distinct impression he wasn't so worried about me. He was really checking on his own people. We soon quit talking politics, to everyone's relief.

Orlin was the acknowledged chef supreme; no one came even close to him in that department. However, in his occasional impatience with errant burners on the kerosene stove he would throw in alcohol as a primer to get the damn burner started. Despite the availability of a Bernzomatic torch, he felt he needed to supplement the starting process with wood alcohol. Uncombusted kerosene fumes are bad enough, but adding alcohol to the alchemy produced fumes so noxious that all the flies in the entire cabin died. On one occasion everyone but Orlin hit the deck for air. Orlin's leathery lungs could tolerate anything. Daiber staggered to the rail with nausea, but the worst hit was Lloyd, who had the misfortune of being asleep in an upper berth in the main cabin. When Terry finally made it topside, he was pale green and had water in his eyes. He wasn't happy. "God damn it, Orlin," he said, "you can buy us gas masks when we get to Norway."

We kept rolling eastward under easy conditions, which allowed us to read books, study charts, and even play liars' dice after evening chow. One day as the sun rose, Orlin saw the green flash, which is a refractive phenomenon sometimes seen at the upper disc of the sun at sunrise or sunset. As the name implies, it appears as a sudden blink of green as the ball of the sun dips below the horizon. You have to be quick to catch it, according to Orlin.

That day the sea was like glass. It was windless, and we had to run the mill all day. At 1500 land was sighted dead ahead; it was the island of Mykines, westernmost of the Faeroes. Closing the islands, we passed near a Danish frigate, which we later learned was transporting a sick fisherman to the hospital in Torshavn, the capital. Mykines is a famous bird haven, and as we passed close to its northern shore, we could see puffins, razorbills, and guillemots literally blackening the skies.

Leaving Mykines to starboard, we took a lucky course as we headed into Sørvaag Fjord, which has some of the finest scenery in the Faeroes along its outer coast. Especially interesting were the rocks that ancient winds and waves have carved into archways and pinnacles that look like Roman ruins. When we dropped anchor off the tiny village of Bo, we marked the end of *Reindeer's* first and my third Atlantic crossing.

The next morning we sailed up to Sørvagur, a town at the head of the fjord, to make our entry official. While the townfolk gathered at the dock to eyeball the American boat, we had an interesting chat with the customs official, who told us we just crossed paths with the Irish oxhide boat *Brendan,* bound from Ireland to Iceland. She was the creation of a young Irish group which wanted to celebrate the true discoverer of Iceland, the monk St. Brendan. She had just passed through and caused a stir and wide publicity. It was in some respects like the *Kon-Tiki* trip of Thor Heyerdahl, in that it was undertaken to prove that it had been done. I didn't wonder that the local population was all excited about *Brendan*. It was a fascinating undertaking by a gutsy guy called Tim Severin. However, in no place in my research have I found the slightest hint to support the postulate that the Irish monks went from Iceland to America. I guess the Irish can throw their hat in the ring, along with the Italians and the Vikings, but I think their evidence is dubious. On the other hand, I have nothing but admiration for the Irishmen who in two summers sailed their boat of animal skin across the

Arrival in the Faeroes. Phil Parrish in the foreground (Orlin Donaldson)

North Atlantic. All I say is that they were the first Irishmen, not the second, to do it.

The Customs officer at Sørvagur suggested that on Sunday we visit a festival at Vestmanna on Streymoy. This is a Danish tradition on the fourth of July that actually started as a celebration of American independence. Denmark is the only country other than the U.S. to celebrate that famous day. This was Saturday the third, so to use the time, the customs people recommended we take a short trip north to Sakshavn, a fine anchorage and a good spot for salmon fishing and bird watching.

When we got there we found anchoring impossible. It was blowing a half a gale and the water was too shallow to get in the inner harbor, where it was protected and where presumably one found the salmon. The birds were prolific as advertised, and we added the king eider and the oyster catcher, which happened to be familiar to me from Chesapeake Bay. When we looked in the Faeroes tourist guide, we found it was the national bird and that his arrival in spring was an event not unlike the arrival of the Punxsutawney groundhog in Pennsylvania. I could tell by Lloyd's expression that I had scored one on Daiber!

Of all my memories of these emerald islands, the one most outstanding is that of the bird population. Never have I seen so many seabirds and shorebirds. Even in this era of conservation, Faeroese hunters still shoot over one hundred thousand guillemots and I don't know how many puffins a year. Fowlers get another fifty to one hundred thousand more. Such birds as the arctic skua, the great skua, king eider, red phalarope, ringed plover, and whimbrel are commonplace. Even the whooper swan is a migratory visitor.

After a brief look at Sakshavn, a very pretty bay with no people or houses, we sailed around to Vestmanna, where we tied to the pier and prepared for our two hundredth birthday. The significance of our hail-port on the transom — Philadelphia — was apparently not lost on the population, who knew that was where the Liberty Bell rang on the first fourth of July. We heard it mentioned frequently on the radio.

The Faeroese are a happy and independent people, true Vikings by descent. Just as with the Icelanders, their ancestors arrived over a thousand years ago from Norway and the Shetlands and Outer Hebrides. As children in school, the Faeroese are taught the sagas, which contain all the romantic history of the early leaders, their struggles for independence and their conflicts over the imposition of Christianity by the kings of Norway, most notably Olav II. Many Faeroese ships are still named after the gallant warriors of the tenth and eleventh centuries, such as Trondur, Sigmundur, and Leimur.

Sunday the fourth was a perfect day. We dressed ship, using all our signal flags. Unfortunately we didn't have a Faeroese flag, and it would have been improper to fly the Danish one. The Faeroese are unique and proudly independent, so much so that the high commissioner from Copenhagen has to keep a low profile. The designer of the Faeroese flag was none other than Winston Churchill, who recognized the necessity for Britain to continue receiving fish from the Faeroes during the war. Since flying the Danish flag would have invited attack by the Germans, Churchill gave them their own flag, using the usual cross of the Scandinavian countries.

Lloyd, in his inimitable way with higher-ups, had somehow made contact with the mayor, and he and Daiber had invited the mayor and his brother for cocktails after the races on board the boat. We presented him with a Bennington flag (with "'76" inside thirteen stars) as a sou-

The author with the mayor of Vestmanna, Faeroes, Fourth of July (Orlin Donaldson)

venir. The mayor's brother had been to the States as a seaman and both of them understood a little English. They invited us for Sunday lunch, but we declined, feeling that would have been an imposition.

Shortly after lunch the boat races began, and the mayor watched from our cockpit. Crews, including girls, came from all over the Faeroes to compete. Crowds lined the docks and other vantage points, and cars were bumper-to-bumper on the roads that overlook the harbor. The total population of the Faeroes is only forty thousand people, and at least half of them were at Vestmanna cheering their favorite crews.

As soon as the boat races were concluded, we got underway for Torshavn. Like a damn show-off I decided to leave the dock under sail alone, and, in the course of my so doing, some signals between me and the foredeck were misunderstood. As a result the bow pulpit of *Reindeer* smacked into the ferry boat tied nearby, leaving the ferry boat intact but *Reindeer* with a mangled pulpit, which would have to be repaired in Torshavn.

The sail to Torshavn introduced us to the fierce wind-driven currents of the Faeroes. Although the tide does not have a high rise and fall, the

Women's crew race, Fourth of July, Vestmanna (Orlin Donaldson)

currents, mostly driven by wind, are fierce. We made it to Torshavn around suppertime on Sunday the fourth and proceeded to dock near the center of town.

Torshavn, compared to the rest of the Faeroes, is a cosmopolitan place. While the population is only twelve thousand, the activity there suggests a city twice that size. We saw several foreign vessels in the harbor and a continuous hustle of people both in town and on the waterfront. One of the incongruities that met the eye was a sod roof on a prominent downtown building. This is an old Viking practice, usually seen only in country houses, where it provides insulation. We had errands to take care of, but the bent pulpit would have to wait 'til the next day, when the machine shop would be open.

Having completed our chores, written postcards, and finished supper, it was time for the sack, but Terry Lloyd and I somehow decided to hit the streets of Torshavn. We soon found unusual foot traffic entering a dimly lighted doorway with the name *Cockatoo* painted above it. This name had a familiar ring to me: oh, yes, it was the name of a famous hangout in Copenhagen, where gorgeous blondes asked and presumably received as much as a hundred dollars for their services. In any event, I suggested to Lloyd that we might slip in for a lager or two. Lloyd showed no hesitation; in fact his heart immediately seemed to thump at a faster pace. The joint was humming like a Third Avenue disco, while scantily clad, well-proportioned waitresses kept a steady flow of drinks running from bar to tables. We gravitated toward the bar and sat on stools. Our respective seats were separated by a stool occupied by a young Norwegian sailor who was of the crew of a cruise ship in the harbor. Lloyd seemed to be getting bearings from this lad while at the same time training his guns on a pert blonde waitress, whose cleavage could hardly be improved. His approach was uncomplicated; I never saw his eyes rise above the level of her front. While I couldn't hear what he was saying, clearly Lloyd was achieving some tactical success, judging by the steady closing of the distance between them.

Just then my attention riveted on a slender brunette two seats to my left, at least momentarily unescorted. Ah, I thought to myself, this is much better than the waitress. A bit older, true, but unencumbered by a job, at least that night. Also, I was sure that Lloyd hadn't thought ahead. His twenty-four-year-old strawberry blonde was probably some-body's daughter, meaning of course they couldn't go to her house. They'd have to climb up the hill where the sheep were pastured. No question, the slender brunette was the much better bet. And anyway, she was better looking, probably about thirty-eight. By great fortune our eyes met and I thought I detected a slight smile. This gesture gave me the nerve to move onto the stool next to her. Since I don't smoke, I couldn't open with the suave "Would you care for a cigarette?" approach. The girl had style, and I didn't want to boot it by anything crude or clumsy. After all, I wasn't a gob on liberty; I owned the boat! Of course I couldn't pull that one either. This wasn't Amarillo. Something told me to open with a compliment, which, by the way, was not that hard to conjure. I made some comment about how snappy her bag looked. Of course it was Gucci, which gave me a hint she wasn't local. It turned out she was English and on summer holiday. She was a passenger on the same cruise ship from which the sailor apparently came. What a good looker, I thought. Brunette, high cheekbones, radiant complexion, hues of peach and apple. She was an outdoor type. Refined-looking but sexy.

Bang! Just then Orlin dropped a pot on the galley sole, and I was startled out of my dream! Reveille had never been so unpleasant, and I was really annoyed. Not only did he interrupt what I was doing, but he prevented me from getting her address and telephone number! Lloyd was snoring away in the main cabin, and I decided not to tell him the part he played in my nocturnal fantasy. Better have a healthy Lloyd than a horny Lloyd. Thinking back on my dream, what made it most implausible was that the Faeroes are dry! Not a gin mill in all eighteen islands, not even a public bar in Torshavn for the trawlermen. Good-looking women, on the other hand, abound, and use of alcohol in private houses is permissible. It comes from Denmark and is strictly rationed. Only paid-up taxpayers can qualify to buy spirits. This fact seems to encourage drunkenness among the young, who regard the possession of alcohol as some badge of importance, much as they do in Iceland.

Monday was a bright and busy day. Phil and Orlin got the pulpit fixed at a machine shop, and Henry Lane and I shopped for fresh food. I called home to make sure everyone knew we were on schedule. When Phil and Orlin returned with the reshaped stainless steel pulpit, they brought with them the owner of the shipyard, Poul Mohr, who does all kinds of repair work, mostly on fishing trawlers. He insisted on giving us this repair job free of charge. I couldn't imagine an American shipyard treating a visiting Faeroese with such generosity, but I could be wrong. The Danish high commissioner also stopped by to say hello and couldn't have been more cordial.

By early afternoon we embarked for Klaksvík, the northeasternmost town of importance in the islands, which is situated on Bordoy. The sail north from Torshavn along the east coast of Eysturoy was like a sleighride down Buzzards Bay, reaching with a smoky sou'wester. The difference was the stronger currents and the mountain scenery, where sheep grazed on the damndest slopes one could imagine. We only stopped at Klaksvík long enough to take on ice at the fish plant, and again the Faeroese generosity emerged, as we received gifts of halibut and salmon from the men at the plant. The grocery store even opened especially for us at 2100.

By 2230 we were again underway north, going downwind in Kalso Fjord, soon passing the great promontory of Enniberg on our starboard hand. Enniberg is the northern extremity of the Faeroes, a sheer cliff rising 2761 feet out of the water, the highest in the world according to the Faeroese. I don't think that includes Greenland, but this we would find out in August, unless we were nipped by Siberian ice or locked up by the Soviets.

Thus we departed from one of the really delightful countries on the globe. We will always remember the Faeroes. The whole population seems connected with the sea, sheep, and birds. They are fishermen or fowlers, hunters or herdsmen, and their chiseled faces reflect the wear and tear of nature, much as does the sculpture of their rocks and rills. What a pity it would be if this were our last visit to these Viking islands! That was my thought while the great cliff of Enniberg slowly dropped below the horizon and *Reindeer* reached northeastward, course 060 True, through a deceptively tranquil sea.

6

Norway

For three days and nights *Reindeer* moved across the Arctic Circle toward northern Norway, amid fully lighted nights. The Arctic Circle is that latitude at which there is one full day of light, presumably 21 June, and one full day of dark, 21 December. The Norwegian Sea — that part of the ocean north of the North Sea and east of the Greenland Sea — is distinctly different from the Atlantic. None of the swells you get in the Atlantic and, much to my surprise, little observable life. We sighted no whales at all and very few fish, except for an occasional basking shark. Birds were few and far between until we neared the coast. Moreover, for the first few days the seas were quite calm and the wind no greater than a soldier's breeze.

I kept scanning the horizon for periscopes and warships. No dice. No excitement. No intrigue. The only vessel we sighted was a British freighter out of Hull bound for Archangel to take on a cargo of timber, information I got on VHF from her captain. Of course I wondered how the Soviets would treat him. Murmansk, not far from Archangel, was by now the world's largest naval base, home of the Soviet Navy in that part of the world and closed to foreigners.

Suddenly, as we powered along at seven knots in a smooth sea, the engine ground down and stopped. We had tangled the propeller in a floating derelict, a polypropylene fishnet, which had wrapped around the prop in a viselike knot. Polypropylene is so light in specific gravity that

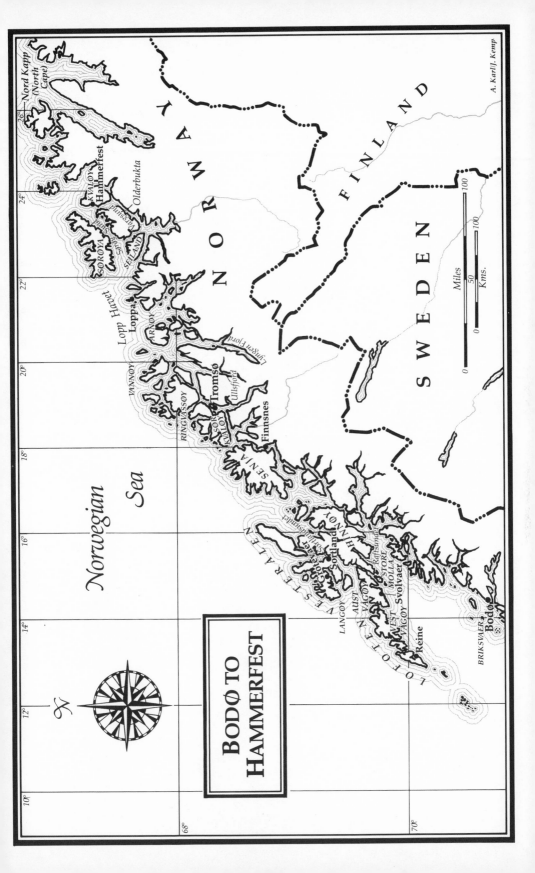

BODØ TO
HAMMERFEST

Norwegian
Sea

NORWAY

FINLAND

SWEDEN

A. Karl/J. Kemp

Nord Kapp
(North
Cape)

Hammerfest
KVALØY
Olderbukta
SØRØYA Finnsoy
SEILAND
Loppa
Lopp Havet
VANNØY
ARNØY
RINGVASSØY
Tromsø
SØRØ
KVALØY
Ullsfjord
Lyngen Fjord
Finnsnes

SENJA

VESTERÅLEN
LANGØY
HINNØY
Sortland
Rolla
Skjoldehamn
AUST
VÅGØY
STORE
MOLLA
Raftsundet
VEST
VÅGØY
Svolvaer
LOFOTEN
Reine
BRIKSVAER
Bodø

Miles
0   50   100
0   50   100
Kms.

it floats and can therefore be a hazard to a surface vessel. Had a fishing trawler run over this stray net at night she would have been disabled. Such are the problems of some products of modern technology. Professor Frank Daiber was at the helm, and he hadn't seen the net, which was an absolute menace to navigation.

In any case, we were disabled, and the only way to fix it was by sending someone overboard — a risk we had to take. Phil Parish put on a wet suit and with all hands in support, slipped overboard to cut the net off the prop. Every forty-five seconds at the most he would surface for air. I was really afraid he'd be conked on the head by the bobbing hull of *Reindeer*. Finally, after a tremendous expenditure of energy, Phil cut the net off the propeller with a hacksaw. He did a super job; all go again. We were very lucky not only to get the prop cleared, but also to get Parish back unscathed.

As we resumed our steady passage northeast toward the coast of Norway, both the air and water temperature actually rose. On Wednesday the water temperature reached 54°F., its highest since the Gulf of Maine, thanks to the Gulf Stream that keeps Norway's west coast ice-free the year around. In the afternoon, we saw two jet contrails in an east-to-west direction at very high altitude. Otherwise the total environment belonged to our forty-three-foot sloop, which was now sailing on the wind in a light norther. For dinner we ate curried lamb fortified by Swedish meatballs and pineapple slices, all washed down by a hardy Burgundy.

On Thursday the wind shifted to north by east and started to howl, in fact scream. We wasted no time in double-reefing the main and shortening to the number four genoa, which was really a working jib. The wind continued unabated for the better part of two days, and since we were beating into it, the boat never heeled less than twenty-five degrees and pounded like mad into the seas.

Such conditions made visits to the head damn near a federal project. Unless one has sat on a nautical toilet during a beat to windward in a choppy seaway, it's hard to imagine the geometry, if not trajectory, that eliminations take. It takes a full court press to do the job. Someone once likened ocean racing to taking a shower with a full suit of clothes on, while at the same time beating your own head with a hammer. (I might add to that, "While using the other hand to tear up hundred-dollar bills.") In any event, the difficulty of executing normal ablutions under these circumstances cannot be exaggerated. Indeed, gravity is not always in one's favor. On top of this, none of us had flies in our foul-weather gear, so just preparing for a visit to the head was a debilitating exercise, pulling off all outerwear.

While pounding along under reduced canvas, we began to notice a leak that required pumping the bilge at least once a watch. As in so many other mechanical and electrical problems that arise at sea, this annoying leak for a long time remained a mystery bound in an enigma, as Churchill would say. When such mysteries develop aboard ship, "experts" come out of the woodwork, or in our case, the fiberglass. The chiefs usually outnumber the Indians. In electrical matters I find it better to remain an Indian, but in plumbing I feel I've earned my Ph.D. Phil Parish, of course, is a genuine expert in all the disciplines where things go wrong, but on my own ship's plumbing I felt I had a leg up, so to speak. Orlin wisely kept out of this one, as he had singlehandedly nearly asphyxiated the entire crew with his attack on the recalcitrant stove and its kerosene leak.

"Phil, you don't s'pose there's a leak in the raw water intake, do you?" I naturally spoke deferentially to the man who had endangered his life to unsnarl the prop.

"Hell, Newbold, there's not that much water in the engine pan. That couldn't be it," he said.

"I checked the head and I checked the knot indicator throughhull fitting, and they look okay."

"What about the stuffing box?"

"It's okay," I replied, "and all that water can't come from the icebox."

Just then Orlin tacked the boat. I continued to look for the leak. Then I noticed it had stopped.

"Hey, Phil," I shouted, "I've got it. The bilge pump ball check valve must not be seating. It doesn't leak on this tack while the overboard drain is out of water."

I was right. In ten minutes Phil had the check valve fixed, thus ending a leak that had defied us for nine straight watches. Then I remembered we were getting a little low on fuel. So we transferred our spare diesel oil to the forward fuel tank and secured the empty bladder inside a polyethylene bag in the forepeak, thus keeping diesel oil from dripping below decks.

It continued to blow, and the sea remained choppy, so to improve creature comfort I altered course to pass inside some islands south of Bodø. Under reduced visibility such a course might have been hazardous, but the sky was clear and the inside route delightful. The sea was much reduced by the string of islets, and the navigational marks were reasonably intelligible. The Hydrographic Office *Sailing Directions* and British Admiralty *Pilot* were both very accurate and helpful in terms of pointing out the landmarks and the preferable passages.

Saturday morning dawned with a bright sun and much reduced wind, although the sea still retained a lot of lump. To our starboard was glorious Norway, in my mind the most scenic nation in the world, with nearly four million of the world's nicest people.

This was my fifth trip to Norway. I went first in the Navy in 1946, second as part of the crew on *Challenge* in the Transatlantic Race of 1966, third when I was breaking in *Reindeer* in 1969, traveling as far north as the Sogne Fjord; then in January 1976, by air. These northern waters, like those of Labrador, appear warmer the farther north one gets on a course that leads away from the open sea and into protected areas.

As I gazed at this magnificent coast with its mountains and snow fields in the distance, its greenery near the coastline and tiny farms that, together with a rich fishery, support a resourceful population, I marveled at the lushness of Norway and the pride of its people.

Norway has length, not breadth. This is especially true of the coast from Trondheim northeast to Kirknes. The total outer coast is 1,643 miles long, but including all the fjords and bays it would expand to 12,500 miles. Above Trondheim the width, or distance from the coast to the eastern border, is nowhere more than fifty to a hundred miles except in part of Finnmark, the land of the Lapps. It is mountain country with only a strip of soil near the sea. From Bodø north, the coast is protected by a string of islands of granite, which face the open ocean. Inside these islands are some of the world's prettiest passages, which in summertime are busy with cruise ships and fishing boats, but very few sailboats.

It is readily apparent that a large portion of Norway's population is oriented to the sea, as it has been for centuries. Its neighbor Sweden, with twice as many people, has been far better endowed with raw materials and agricultural land, but the arrival of oil in the North Sea may have altered the balance. Some people say that in per capita income Norway will soon lead the world. Unlike Britain, which shares the oil wealth of the North Sea, Norway will not suffer any energy shortage once the North Sea fields are depleted, owing to her inexhaustible water power, which readily translates to electricity. Thus, unless strident socialism negates their vigor, the Norwegians may once again rule the roost like their Viking ancestors, only this time economically.

At 1700 on Saturday, 10 July, we sailed into the busy little harbor at Bodø to rendezvous with my wife, Peggy, and Phil's wife, Jeannette, who would take Henry Lane's and Frank Daiber's places. *Reindeer* was right on schedule. The harbor master, who doubled as Customs and Immigration officer, examined my papers and issued an official permit to cruise in Norwegian waters. He allowed us to tie up to his cutter, which was in the small-boat part of the harbor and afforded us easy access to the grocery store and the ship chandlery.

The wives had arrived the night before, right on schedule. They came down to the dock to greet us, board the boat, and give us big hugs. They didn't realize that part of our elation came from being there on time so we didn't have to pay an excessive hotel bill, but naturally we played that down. It was nifty to see them, and they brought us up to date on all the gossip, the state of the dollar, the Olympics, and the cost of hairdos in Norway. After luxurious baths in our wives' rooms we all had supper at the ultramodern SAS Hotel, where there was an orchestra and dancing, and Phil and I slept ashore for the first time since Iceland.

It was a good sound sleep. Nice not to have to go on watch for a change. I had almost forgotten what clean cotton sheets felt like. Since the next fortnight encompassed leisurely cruising along inside passages where dangers were minimal and the temperature would be hospitable, there was no cause for anxiety or possibility of a nightmare. Back in the States the Democrats and Republicans were going through their respective quadrennial conventions to nominate presidential candidates. At this distance politics at home somehow held little interest. In fact, I was more interested at that time in Norwegian politics and government. I would keep my ear to the ground.

The next afternoon, while we were down working on the boat, a newspaper reporter from the *Nordlands Framtid*, a local paper, came aboard for an interview. His name was Odd Seljesaeter. Odd spoke very good English and also knew something about sailing, but of course we couldn't be sure what the article was going to say. When I did see it later, all I could recognize was the picture of all of us on the front page. The first lines read: "Den elegante amerikanske havseileren med lett norskklingende navnet 'Reindeer,'" which translated means "the elegant American sailboat with the Norwegian-sounding name *Reindeer*." I didn't think we looked too elegant, but I was glad we sounded Norwegian. One thing I did learn from Odd was the whereabouts of Walter Levering. I had seen and heard his name on television and in the papers, but none of us could figure out what they were saying about him. That he was front-page copy was obvious.

Odd told me Levering was safe in Hammerfest, which was a relief to hear. Unfortunately his image in Norwegian minds was something akin to a cross between Don Quixote and Evel Knievel. All of Scandinavia was sure he would either be swallowed by the ice or arrested by the Russians and shipped to Siberia. When Odd's article was published in the *Nordlands Framtid*, Walter and Elsa Levering of course read it. They were in Tromsø at the time. The article, translated in part (and referring to us), read as follows:

They said, "We hear that Walter Levering is missing up north. He is a friend of ours and a very good seaman but he is getting older and perhaps has not been careful enough." Captain Newbold Smith on Reindeer had been long at sea and was not up to date about the news in Norway, but he and his wife were relieved to hear that Levering gave up his attempt to sail through the Northeast Passage and is safe in the harbor of Hammerfest. Perhaps they will meet on their way. Captain Smith is on his way north to Finnmark and Hammerfest.

I don't know what Walter and Elsa thought when they read that stuff, but I did not tell Odd that Walter was senile or that he wasn't careful. Odd was obviously adding two and two and coming up with eight. I had no idea what the article said until Mrs. Geoffrey Smith in Philadelphia kindly translated it for me almost a year later.

On Monday, 12 July, we split up into teams. Lloyd and Donaldson bought and stowed the food aboard; Phil and I bought the fuel, water, and ice and purchased miscellaneous gear at the ship chandlery; Peggy and Jeannette gathered the laundry, a mixture redolent of my perspiration, Orlin's sweat, Phil's diesel oil, Lloyd's kerosene, and one or two other unpleasant properties, and turned over the whole noxious bundle to the unlucky chambermaids on duty at the hotel. It must have watered their eyes.

The next several days were expected to be pleasant cruising with stops every night at scenic spots. This is what the girls had flown to Norway to do, not roughing it with all-night passages. It was also to be a restful sojourn that would restore our vigor and recharge our batteries for the toughest parts of the trip that lay ahead.

Finally by midafternoon we got underway for the Lofoten Islands via a one-night stop at the island of Briksvaer, which resembles many of the islands off Maine, such as Isle au Haut and even Matinicus. We ghosted along in light air through the passages of Briksvaer and took note of several new birds, most notable a sea eagle, which in rarity was in a class by itself. It was also the first time I had seen a hooded crow, although ornithologists wouldn't be impressed, as they are common in northern Europe. On the western side of the island we found a well-protected uninhabited cove and anchored there for the evening. Orlin broiled the halibut we had purchased in Bodø and, with Terry Lloyd as his sous-chef, prepared one of the more memorable meals of the trip.

The next day we beat to windward on a course of north nor'west past Reine, a little fishing village on the island of Moskenes, into a completely protected harbor surrounded by mountains as high as three thousand feet, with a few unoccupied cottages visible in the hills above. Most of these fishing villages in the Lofotens are seasonal, inasmuch as the cod take is limited by regulations, and once the limits have been attained the fisherfolk return to their mainland homes. A town like Svolvaer, capital of the Lofotens, is permanent; it even has a small airstrip. In many of the fjords one sees penstocks, which are special sluices for hydroelectric generators that take advantage of the abundant water in the mountain lakes. As on the mainland the snow fields never entirely disappear, but in mid-July the temperature is comparable to that of Maine in the summer. At 68° north, the sun did not go below the horizon at night, and at 0530 when we up-anchored, the sun was already strong enough to burn the skin.

The next day was placid, and we powered till midmorning, when the wind came up, permitting us to reach northeastward past Svolvaer and inside the island of Store Molla to Raftsundet, a very picturesque sound, where we found a nifty gunk hole on the port hand, called Ulvo. Here we anchored in six fathoms, and to keep *Reindeer* from swinging onto the rocks had to tie a stern line to a bush on the opposite shore. Shortly after anchoring we saw a rarity for these waters — another sailboat, also cruising. She wore Swedish colors, which didn't surprise me, because the Swedes have not only affluence but also more extensive interest in sailing than any other Scandinavians or northern Europeans.

The next day, again cloudless and warm, we pushed northward through Raftsundet to Sortlandsundet. This sound was amazing. On the port hand were beaches and behind the beach were hayfields and rolling hills like those of Camden, Maine, or even more so, the Bras d'Or Lakes of Nova Scotia. The seaward side of these islands is rocky, but the inboard side is pastoral. On the opposite side of the sound were the more typical rocky hills and in the distance snow-capped mountains, perfectly exquisite scenery. In the sun our thermometer read 94°F.; in the shade it was 74°F. at two o'clock in the afternoon. We saw low islands with white beaches like those of the Bahamas, all of this at almost 69° north. Women wore bikinis, but our most powerful binoculars mounted on Orlin's gyro stabilizer produced no one in the nude.

In the town of Sortland we took on fresh water and bought popsicles and the paper — the *Nordlands Framtid*, with our pictures on the front page along with the story we couldn't translate. It said something about elegant Americans, which started an argument about who gave them that impression. I maintained it was I because of my jacket and tie. Peggy announced that I was the most inelegant American she knew. I had no sense of color, my clothes didn't fit, and I made no effort, she said. Cleverly she made sure these remarks applied only to me, so the rest of the guys began to think they were elegant. It was a losing proposition for me, so I managed to change the subject.

Late in the afternoon we found a splendid anchorage in the tiny island group called Grotavaer, where the view included both white sand beaches nearby and snowfields in the mountains. Supper was roast pork, mushrooms, and eggplant. The beverage wasn't half bad; Vosne-Romanée 1964. That bottle had covered some distance! From France to Maryland to Canada, Iceland, and finally Norway. After supper I hit the sack, but the others climbed to a little promontory and photographed the midnight sun, which was visible over the Arctic Ocean to the north. At midnight the sun was a full diameter above the horizon.

The only mechanical problem was the stove. The burners had never worked right; now the kerosene tank sprang a leak. Phil and Orlin finally hauled the whole tank up on deck and resoldered the top, where they had found a pinhole leak. This put us back in business as far as the stove was concerned, and that was important.

Friday was another tropical day, and we anchored for lunch, rowed ashore, went swimming and flower-picking. When we disturbed a huge kittiwake rookery, the males made such a big fuss that we had to retreat. Sailing along in the afternoon we watched the action of the herring gulls, kittiwakes, and the fearsome parasitic jaeger attacking until his prey regurgitated. Phil threw a string of hooks in the water where a raft of gulls had been sitting and hauled in six blue cod for dinner with the greatest of ease.

That night we anchored across the sound from the town of Finsnes, a prosperous-looking place that commands the narrows between Senja and the mainland and in the morning continued on through the inside passages to Tromsø, which is the largest city in northern Norway and capital of the district of Troms. Tromsø sits astride a sound by the same name and is a thoroughly modern city. In fact, all of northern Norway is relatively new and modern, thanks to the Germans who destroyed all the original towns in World War II. In Tromsø we met Knut Sørensen, the young banker who would join us later in Hammerfest.

To my amazement the first people to meet us at the dock in Tromsø were Walter Levering and his wife, Elsa. This called for a celebration, so we all enjoyed together a dinner of reindeer steak at a very nice restaurant. Walter filled me in on his fantastic attempt to cross the top of the earth. He made it all the way through the Kara Strait, south of Novaya Zemlya. The Russians refused to let him land, despite the letter he produced from Ambassador Dobrynin. Then, after he made it past the Kara Strait, his Norwegian mate got cold feet, so Walter had no choice. He had to turn back. This was the second year in a row that

Walter and Elsa Levering with Phil Parish at Tromsø (Orlin Donaldson)

Walter had been thwarted in his effort to get through the Northeast Passage. I don't know what would have happened had he enlisted some Russians or perhaps even some Americans. Clearly, however, the Norwegians were not too keen on Levering's goal. They were justifiably scared of what the Soviets might do to them, and they had been indoctrinated that high Arctic excursions were only undertaken in fortified trawlers. So Levering had a strike against him which he had not initially realized. On top of whatever the Russians' suspicions were, they clearly regarded Walter's plan as a wasteful lark. In my opinion it could be done; after all, Nordenshiold of Finland did it and described his trip vividly. As in our own trip, however, it would take some planning that perhaps Walter didn't care to bother about. Walter and I made arrangements to meet in Hammerfest, where he would sell me his canned goods and a sack of potatoes, at a bargain price, I hoped.

It was such good fortune to meet the Leverings and to have Knut with us that I celebrated a little excessively. Peggy issued me several warnings, so to show her how sober I was I went straight (well not quite straight) to the one-armed bandit and on my first play hit three bars for the entire jackpot. I couldn't even count all the kroner that fell out, but it was more than enough to pay for the entire dinner. I tried to argue that the fates would never have favored me had I been abstemious. The truth is I wouldn't have played the slot machine if I had been entirely sober.

The next evening, after departing from Tromsø, we dropped the hook well up in Ullsfjord, after running under spinnaker between mountains, snowfields, and glaciers, a continuous treat of really awesome scenery. We moved farther north after supper and finally anchored in beautiful Nordlyngen. At 0200 I felt the warm rays of the sun on the back of my neck just before turning in for some needed sleep.

The next day we sailed to Loppa in Finnmark. We were hoping to see some Lapp families, as Helge Amundsen had told me they would be interesting. The Lapps are a distinct race unto themselves, like the Eskimos. No one is absolutely sure of their place of origin, but from their physical appearance it must be Mongolia or thereabouts. They are tiny in stature, rarely more than five feet in height. There are some 33,000 Laplanders, of whom 21,000 are in Norway, 8,000 in Sweden, and 2,000 each in Finland and Russia. The Finnmark district accounts for the greatest concentration, and most of them live in the uplands, where they tend their reindeer herds. Some, however, have adapted to the sea and live on small farms near the water's edge. We saw one of these farms on the island of Seiland, not far from Hammerfest. We anchored in a bight and knocked on the door of a frame house that had smoke coming out of the chimney and a dogsled with wooden runners and some ancient tools nearby.

When no one answered, Orlin and Phil looked in the window and saw the family hiding. After some hand signals Orlin managed to get the father to open the front door, where a nonconversation took place. Orlin thinks he got them to understand we lived on the blue boat at anchor. For his part, the Lapp father made it clear the sailors weren't invited in the house, and Phil noticed the look of fear and bewilderment on the wife's and children's faces.

Later Knut explained that while some Laplanders, usually men, have mixed enough with outsiders that they enjoy their own uniqueness and are happy to display themselves in colorful Lapp dress, the great majority prefer to be left alone. Knut's description made it clear that the Lapps have a position in Norway (and presumably the other countries as well) comparable to that of the American Indian on a reservation. They are a protected species who are allowed unlimited hunting and fishing rights together with welfare payments, all of which exceed the rights of the regular citizen. In this respect, there is some resentment felt toward them, but for the most part the attitude of the thinking person is that the state owes these people special dispensation. After all, they have been there since before Christ, and if they weren't protected, their culture and civilization would be wiped out in no time.

It is a fascinating experience to see at first hand a culture that could have existed centuries ago. It was as though we had rolled into Washington's headquarters at Valley Forge in a modern tank with a couple of 105-millimeter howitzers. His poor rabble in arms would have run for cover, thinking we were from outer space.

It was my birthday, and Orlin bought a fresh salmon from a fisherman, since we had not caught any. I gave everyone a break by taking a shower, and the girls baked a cake. We found a good anchorage at Olderbukta on Seiland. All the afternoon Phil Parish had been catching *sei* fish, which were put on ice for breakfast. Supper was quite a treat, and my fifty-first year was ushered in with some flourish and great anticipation of Hammerfest and what lay ahead. We were getting close now to another crew change, and with it the beginning of the most exciting part of our trip — Spitsbergen, Jan Mayen, and Denmark Strait. My son Stockton was presumably in Hammerfest waiting for us with his friend Dicky Cromwell. Stocky had flown from the States to London and then to Norway after his summer cruise as an ROTC midshipman. Cromwell, whose parents were living in South Africa temporarily, had flown from his home in Baltimore to Capetown for a visit, then on to London, where he joined up with Stocky — going from nearly as far south as one can go to almost as far north.

In late morning we set sail in overcast weather up Vargsund to Straumen, which is the sound between Seiland and Kvaløy. Hammerfest harbor is situated on the northwest coast of Kvaløy. We reached the entrance at about 1700, and as we turned into the harbor, there was the Grand Hotel on our starboard hand, the same Grand Hotel where I had stayed in January. What a difference! No snow around the harbor. Instead, a bustling port, albeit a tourist place. I looked up at the hotel, saw someone waving but wasn't at all sure who it was. We had the ensign at the taffrail, the Cruising Club burgee at the truck (masthead), and the beautiful Norwegian flag at the starboard yard — three flags we were very proud of. Again we were right on schedule.

Hammerfest, the city at the top of the world! In winter it is Ice Station Zebra; in summer it is the jewel of the North, a veritable melting pot of nationalities. We saw a French cruise ship in the harbor, two Norwegian cruise ships, a Greek ship, and the biggest of them all, the *Maxim Gorky,* pride of the Soviet passenger liners, out of Odessa, Russia. There must have been twelve thousand people in a town of eight thousand, but everything was business as usual. We furled our mainsail, stowed the headsail, and tied up to a couple of sealers at a dock not far from the hotel. Stocky and Dicky had seen us as we entered the harbor and came running down to the docks in time to take our lines as we secured to the outboard of the two sealers. As a present to the boat, Cromwell brought two bottles of South African red wine.

After cleaning up the boat and putting all the laundry on deck to take to the hotel, I decided I needed a little hot water for a shave. Rather than heat a pot on the stove, I elected to use the engine to heat the water. However, for some reason the engine wouldn't start. Immediately our best technical brains were put to work on the problem, and, after trial and error, found a faulty ampmeter in the engine circuit. Phil and Stocky found a new meter in town and installed it, but the engine wouldn't start up immediately because the batteries were drained. We then dug out the Honda portable generator that Dan Strohmeier had suggested, and it paid for itself right there. In short order we had the engine started and the alternator putting out its steady charge to the batteries. Had this happened up in the Arctic Ocean or in Denmark Strait, we would have been in a real pickle. Of all the mysteries that long-distance sailors encounter, electrical problems are the most unfathomable. It is a discipline for which I have the least aptitude, despite four years of electrical engineering at Annapolis. On instrument circuitry I am weak, on engine circuits I am a probable loser, but on radio and electronic circuits I am completely hopeless.

We took our laundry to the Grand Hotel, and after all hands bathed and put on shore garb, we gathered in the dining salon to celebrate our progress north and toast those who had just arrived and, regretfully, those

Passing Maxim Gorky, *the Russian luxury liner
on a visit to Spitsbergen* (Stockton N. Smith)

who were about to depart: namely the Parishes, Peggy, and Terry. Knut
Sørensen had joined us, and our crew to Spitsbergen would be only five
until Diana Russell and Jim Demarest met us at Longyearbyen. Walt
Levering, who was arranging for winter storage for his boat, also joined
us for dinner.

The new camera that Orlin had wired a friend in New York to send
him did not arrive, and after Orlin told Walter the story about all his
cameras and equipment getting soaked in salt water during one of the
gales going to Iceland, Walter generously gave his camera to Orlin for
the rest of the trip. Now that we were heading to Spitsbergen, Orlin had
to be equipped for picture taking.

On Friday the twenty-second of July we busied ourselves with errands,
purchase of food and the miscellaneous items one always needs before
going to sea, and at 1700 we cast off for the north. We set the mainsail
and number two genoa and glided past *Maxim Gorky,* which dwarfed
all else in the harbor. In a light easterly, we put out to sea through
Sørøy Sund, took a bearing or two on Nordkapp, and set a course for
Bear Island in the Barents Sea, half way to Spitsbergen. I recall my
disbelief at finding Nordkapp (North Cape) on the exact same longitude

as Istanbul, Turkey. That's how far east we had sailed, and now we were heading a little west of north. Every mile we sailed now was one more mile farther north than any of us had ever been before.

We hadn't gone twenty miles when a Norwegian Orion reconnaissance plane buzzed us twice at damn near mast height, then disappeared in the clouds. That told me we were being watched, which was fine with me. Our only armament was a combination shotgun and rifle, which lay in a plastic case above my bunk in the port quarter, and that was to defend against a miscreant polar bear, not a Russian bear. Bear Island was the only bear on my mind, for one good reason — it had a consol station. We were now beyond the range of loran and there were no RDF stations. It never got dark, so star sights were out. Of course, we had radar, but its range was short, so dead reckoning was the order of the day, especially when we later found Bear Island's consol station was on the fritz. I just hoped there would be no Siberian ice floating westward. Knut assured me that the Polar Institute said it would be clear, but their weather prognostication turned out highly inaccurate. Not long after the aircraft visit we plunged into fog. Nothing you don't get in New England, but here it necessitated extra vigilance, owing to potential ice floes together with our inexperience in the polar regions. Also, of course, there was no audio aid of any sort. Bear Island had no foghorn. Compass accuracy therefore became paramount, and in far northern latitudes, magnetic anomalies are commonplace. One had to have faith.

At 0400 on 25 July, *Reindeer* emerged from the fog and found Bear Island only one point off our port bow. Stocky Smith had done well as our navigator, and I was pleased with the compass, which so far seemed undisturbed by the expected vagaries of North Polar magnetism. Bear Island was bleaker than I expected. At that time of year there would be no polar bears, because the ice had mostly disappeared and with it the *storkobbes,* those great seals that are the staple of a bear's diet. I thought about sailing east to Kong Karls Land, the easternmost islands of Svalbard, but the ice in that area was said to be very bad, so we pressed on, leaving the island to port.

As we passed by Bear Island we made an effort to do so as close to its eastern shore as was possible yet safe. The greater part of the island was flat plain, one hundred to two hundred feet above sea level. There were two terraced hills on the island. The one in the south corner was called Mount Misery and it rose to about twelve hundred feet. Along the northeast coast were a few dark sandy beaches with walrus bones strewn about. There were several huts in this portion of the island and they looked to be for hunters and trappers. We observed no human life, nor was there a trace of grass, bushes, or trees. Only tiny polar willow grows on the island, which is totally drab and gray. Bird life was, however, abundant all along the coast.

Visibility remained about one-half mile, but at least we had a following wind for a while. I wasn't much concerned about colliding with ships, just bergs and bergy bits, and our radar told us we were in the clear. Nevertheless I rehearsed time and again our emergency procedures, assigning the right man according to his special strength. On that basis Orlin had the stove, Stocky the electronics, Knut did the transmitting, and I pumped out the head, or if necessary took it apart. It was reassuring to know that with our new crystals in the single-side-band radio we could ring up the Polar Institute in Oslo via Rogaland Radio and get ice information by satellite. This wasn't Tilman's style, but I found it reassuring to know we could talk with the mainland.

We were heading for Sørkapp, the south cape of Spitsbergen. In reduced visibility I managed to get a consol cross between the Soviet station at Rybachiy and the Norwegian station at Andøya. I had become adept at counting the "beans" (the dots and dashes) on Nantucket consolan, and European consol stations worked the same way. On the basis of this fix, we changed course ten degrees to the west. Finally, on Tuesday morning after several unsuccessful attempts to pick up land on our radar, Knut sighted mountains to port. We had completely missed our intended landfall. In fact we weren't even close. It was like missing Larchmont Harbor, having left from New York City. Must have been magnetic vagaries. We had to tack and beat for some twenty miles in order to weather South Cape (Sørkapp). But what scenery! Unbelievable! Breathtaking! There it was, just like the pictures, like nothing I had ever seen at first hand. Great snow-covered mountains, glaciers, and snowfields sweeping down to the sea! This was Spitsbergen, truly a polar island. Here for the first time were polar gulls. Fulmars became blue fulmars. Never mind the magnetic anomaly that put us so far to the east

Russian trapper's hut surrounded by whalebones, Hornsund, Spitsbergen
(Orlin Donaldson)

of our rhumb line. The sun was now out and the glistening snow, the vastness, the silence — reminders of all that we had read of this land, redolent of history, measured in millions of years, not centuries.

We worked around the cape and entered fabled Hornsund. It might easily have been a fairy tale, and for the moment we were all little boys again, God's children, looking at what only He could have wrought. Then we began to think of the men of endurance who had preceded us, the whalers and maybe a few trappers. We picked a bight on our starboard hand in which to drop the hook. It had a Norwegian name meaning Goose Bay and turned out to have been one of the favorite anchorages of the whalers during the heydays of the 1800s and earlier.

We were just off a gravel beach, part of a moraine left by the early glaciers. We saw a hut intact near the beach and great quantities of whale bone, including the full carcass and jawbone of a sperm whale, according to Orlin, who knew his whales from New Bedford days. Near the hut was a grave marked by a weathered wooden cross, which we deduced was Russian from the mortise of a missing second cross — the

Hornsund, Spitsbergen. Jim Demarest,
Knut Sørensen, Stockton Smith (Orlin Donaldson)

Isfjord from the air (*Diana Russell*)

Overleaf: Reindeer *and glacier at Hornsund* (*Orlin Donaldson*)

Woodfjorden from the moraine (Orlin Donaldson)

Reindeer *anchored in Woodfjorden. Metamorphic formations in the background
(Stockton N. Smith)*

Prins Karls Forland, Svalbard, after
a light snow (Stockton N. Smith)

Overleaf: Schmeerenbergfjorden. Wind on the rise (Stockton N. Smith)

Eastern Orthodox cross. It was amazing how the cold preserves things, including the wooden shack itself.

That night after a fine dinner, no one needed an invitation to sleep. One Norwegian, three Pennsylvanians, and one Marylander were in Never-Never-Land. The fact that we had arrived in the Polar Arctic and were safe and sound in the protection of this faraway bay made for deep sleep and a chance for our own batteries to recharge.

I remember that evening vividly. How happy I was that my vessel had arrived in what the old explorers called the High Arctic! How extraordinary it felt just to be there! From Hornsund, the next stretch of our journey would take us to the very gateway to the North Pole — the west coast of Spitsbergen and the Arctic Ocean.

7

The Polar Gateway

THE NAME SPITSBERGEN is Dutch. It means land of pointed peaks. This name was aptly picked by the Dutch explorer William Barents, who was purportedly the first seafarer of the modern era to discover this archipelago. He was the precursor of a long line of Dutch seamen who over two centuries dominated the whale fishery of east Greenland and Spitsbergen. Between 1620 and 1635 more than three hundred Dutch ships and eighteen thousand men were on the coast, and Amsterdam Island in Spitsbergen became the flourishing center (in summer) for this important trade.

The impetus for the discovery of Spitsbergen was the search for a polar shortcut to the Orient, the so-called Northeast Passage. The idea of a passage to the Orient was probably first suggested by Robert Thorne, a British merchant, in the year 1527. He wrote a paper to King Henry VIII recommending that such exploration be undertaken, in part to catch up with the trade already started by the Portuguese and Spaniards to both East and West. He maintained that a trip to the Spice Islands via the North Pole would be shorter and that maximum advantage could be taken of the twenty-four hours of daylight. It was in such a quest that Sir Hugh Willoughby, a mid-sixteenth-century English captain, sought a route north to Cathay as early as 1553. His fleet, having taken off with pious instructions about morning and evening prayers and warnings from Sebastian Cabot about mermaids, left for the North Cape via the Lofo-

12°   18°   24°

N

Arctic Ocean

MOFFEN I.   80°

NORDAUSTLANDET

AMSTERDAM I.
FUGLØYA
NORTH NORWAY I.
NORWAY I.   **Gråhuken**
DENMARK
Schmeerenbergfjorden
Woodfjorden
Magdalenefjorden
KONG   *Bockfjorden*   ANDRÉE
ALBERT I   KONG   LAND
LAND   HAAKON
VII
LAND

Kongsfjorden   *Hinlopen Strait*

Ny Ålesund
Engelskbukta   **SPITSBERGEN**

PRINS KARLS FORLAND

Forlandsundet   BARENTS I.

Kapp Thorsen

Isfjorden   *Adventfjorden*
Longyearbyen
Kapp Linné   **Barentsburg**   78°
Grønfjorden   **EDGE I.**

Barents Sea

Hornsund

▲ **Hornsundtind**

SØRKAPP

Miles
0   75

0   Kms.   75

**SPITSBERGEN
(SVALBARD)**

A. Karl/J. Kemp

tens. The tiny fleet got separated in a storm in the waters where we were headed and made for Lapland, where they all froze to death in the winter of 1554. Sir Hugh's log and the remains of his vessels were found by Russians a year later.

These early mariners were not oceanographers in the modern sense, but they were the true discoverers of the gateway to the Polar Arctic. Only Spitsbergen, northern Greenland, and the northern tip of Ellesmere Island are truly in the Polar Region. Two Soviet possessions, Franz Josef Land and Severnaya Zemlya (north of Siberia) are also within ten degrees of the Pole, but they are totally inaccessible because of ice and political realities. Since history is replete with voyages of discovery in these northern regions on the part of great seamen, it seemed wise to examine their collective experience for our own orientation.

Barents, the Hollander, made at least three voyages to this northern area before he perished, and he was given credit for the first discovery of Bear Island, as well as Spitsbergen. He perished in the ice around Novaya Zemlya in 1596. The Barents Sea was very appropriately named after him, as no one else had even approached him in terms of the exploration of these waters.

In 1603, one Stephen Bennett, under the auspices of Sir Francis Cherie, found Bear Island and named it after his patron. Thus, Bear Island is sometimes called Cherie Island by the British. After Bennett, Jonas Poole went to the arctic ice fields, but his expedition had more of a commercial coloration, bringing back walrus ivory in great quantity and more news on the prospective whale fishery. Fotherby was another explorer of that era, but of all of them the greatest was unquestionably Hudson. In 1607, the English navigator Henry Hudson explored east Greenland and Spitsbergen trying to find a northeast passage to the Orient. Ice turned him back when he got as far as the north coast of Spitsbergen, but his voyage spurred remarkable interest, not only in discovery of a short route to Cathay but also in an opportunity to exploit the potential fisheries of the North. In 1608 Hudson tried again unsuccessfully to make it east through the Kara Strait, north of Russia. In 1609 he was hired by the Dutch East India Company, once again to find the shortcut to the Orient. This ubiquitous seaman, captain of the ship *Half Moon,* found his way to the American coast, discovered the Delaware River, probed up what was subsequently named the Hudson River, and then went back to England and Holland to report his discoveries, which led to the early establishment by the Dutch, Swedes, and English of the middle colonies of America. In 1610, convinced there was a Northwest Passage, he made his fateful voyage in *Discovery,* in which he sailed into Hudson Bay and spent the winter. In June of 1611, mutineers put Hudson and his son in an open boat and left them to perish, while they then returned to England.

Hudson's voyages were extremely significant in that they gathered valuable information for succeeding generations. For example, he was completely stymied by the east Greenland pack ice, which never yielded the opening that he sought to the West. Considering the range he covered from 1607 to 1609, the total lack of knowledge of the waters and no charts, Hudson's voyages must be regarded as nothing less than epic. His observations and discoveries resulted in a vast expansion of commerce and colonization by the English and Dutch for the next two centuries.

In 1773, Captain Phipps, later Lord Mulgrave, sailed for Spitsbergen in HMS *Racehorse,* along with HMS *Carcass.* He was blocked by ice at latitude 81° N. It was on this expedition that young Midshipman Horatio Nelson, on his second sea voyage, had his famous encounter with a polar bear while on an ice floe. He was about fourteen years of age and might easily have lost his life right then, in which event there might not have been the Nile, Copenhagen, and Trafalgar, his three most epic battles, which are commemorated by the three white stripes on bluejackets' jumpers (in both the Royal Navy and the U.S. Navy). Phipps made it beyond 81° N. before turning back and abandoning his struggle for a passage to the Far East via the polar route.

In 1775, Captain Phipps wrote a book about his trip "to the Pole." It was primarily a report of his 1773 expedition with a foreword in the form of a letter to King George III, which said in part:

Sire:
As a sea officer addressing Your Majesty on a professional subject I might justly be accused of singular ingratitude, did I not avail myself of this opportunity of reminding the World that the voyage to explore how far Navigation was practicable towards the North Pole was undertaken at a Period peculiarly distinguished by Your Majesty's gracious Attention to Your Navy.

In a time of profound Peace, Your Majesty, by a liberal addition to the Half Pay of the Captains, relieved the Necessities of many, and grateful the Ambitions of all, at once demonstrating Your Majesty's Regard to their Welfare, and the Remembrance of their Services.

The main body of the book was Phipps's log, written on *Racehorse* during the voyage. This detailed log contained a mine of information about Spitsbergen, because the ice conditions in the Greenland Sea forced the two ships into the warmer waters of the West Spitsbergen coast. His observations of conditions in late July around Schmeerenburg Fjord, Denmark Island, and Amsterdam Island were particularly illuminating. He noted, for example, that noon temperature and midnight temperature were not far apart. One was fifty-eight degrees Fahrenheit and the other, fifty-one. Another temperature observation at noon on 16 July was forty-nine degrees in the shade and eighty-nine in the sun. On another occasion he noted that when a slight breeze came up the temperature dropped immediately ten degrees.

An important aspect of the *Racehorse* log was the repeated observation of wind conditions in July and August. I was amazed how often it was reported flat calm. Then when there was wind, often it was from the north, northwest, and northeast. It was seldom that they had a cloudless day, but, on the other hand, precipitation at that time of year was minimal. In fact, they had to take on fresh water from the glacier-fed streams. Phipps praised the quality of the water from that source.

On 15 July, Phipps's men could see solid pack ice north of Norway Island as far as the eye could see, but by 25 July it was clear of ice at Moffen Island. When they went ashore at Moffen they found a round atoll, two miles in diameter, with a frozen lake in the middle. They saw three polar bears and all kinds of ducks, geese, and birds. No mention was made of walrus. Phipps made an extremely perceptive comment about Moffen Island. He was amazed, he said, that no earlier mariners had ever reported this island, and judging by the meticulous way so many of them had reported other northern outcrops, maybe the island hadn't previously existed? Coming from a naval officer, not a geologist nor on the other hand a mystic, that's an extraordinary observation. He must have seen the terraces along part of the Spitsbergen shore, and he must have noted the evidence of coastline a hundred or more feet high in the fjords. In other words, he might have known that Spitsbergen and its outlying islands were rising. Otherwise, king and country would have branded him a kook.

Phipps mentioned that he found no rivers in Spitsbergen, nor any evidence of volcanic action. He mentioned the "blink of the ice" as an early indicator that the pack was not far away. On the northern shore of Spitsbergen he found driftwood, which he said was fir but of which he was at a loss to explain the origin. Since the objective of this officer was to get to the opposite side of the globe, over the Pole if possible, he pushed on to the north and east. He became embayed in ice north of Nordaustlandet (Northeast Land) and only a providential gale out of the east set him free. Since this took place in early August of 1773, I thought it was worth noting, for we might be there at approximately the same date in 1976. The most notable aspect of Phipps's log was his notation of the sudden changes in wind, weather, and ice. I doubt that that pattern had altered in the two hundred intervening years between his northern voyage and mine.

The last attempt of the Royal Navy in this particular area was that of Captain Parry in 1827, who apparently was one of the earliest sailors whose single aim was being first to get to the Pole. After the Napoleonic Wars, Britain had an excess of naval officers looking for something to do, so in 1812 a squadron of the Royal Navy was actually ordered to seek out the polar reaches. Many of the officers of this squadron became famous in their own right as explorers of the North. They included such names as Franklin, Parry, Ross, and Sabine. Captain Franklin, later Sir John Franklin, in HMS *Trent* and Captain Buchan in HMS *Dorothea* tried to reach the Pole by way of Spitsbergen but were turned back at 80° 40', which was well below Hudson's penetration in 1607, over two hundred years before. In Captain Parry's attempt, ice stopped the ships below 81°, but he then engineered a trek across the ice, dragging small boats by hand. Amazingly, they made it to 82° 45', but, finding no open water, they had to retreat to their ship at Spitsbergen.

It is a wonder how certain everyone was for centuries that the North Pole was in open water in the summer; that all one had to do was get over the ridge of ice that surrounded the polar sea. After Parry's courageous but unsuccessful attempt at the Pole, the experts of the day were so wedded to the open ocean theory that they believed Parry would have made it had he left earlier, say in June. By consulting my *Arctic Pilot,* published by the British Admiralty in 1974, an excellent guide, I could readily see that Parry couldn't possibly have come near the top of Spitsbergen in June because there would still have been seven-tenths coverage by ice as a mean limit. Of course there were good and bad years, as we found out ourselves, but I doubt that the weather was so drastically different a hundred and fifty years ago that Parry could have done better in June. The theory of an earlier start was probably right in one respect. Once on the ice itself, he probably would have had less southward drift that early in the season. But the price of that would have been a lot longer walk, to say nothing of the supply and logistics problems.

The primary aim of the North Polers of the nineteenth and twentieth centuries was fame and immortality, immortality at the price of mortality more often than not for their comrades. Probably the first of these North Pole seekers was the Navy doctor from Philadelphia, Elisha Kent Kane. As early as 1853, he put together an expedition for the ostensible purpose of finding out what happened to Sir John Franklin, whose earlier expedition had disappeared and was presumed lost. Franklin, with the full approval of Her Majesty Queen Victoria's government, was seeking a northwest passage to the Orient across the top of Canada for the worthy purpose of stimulating trade with the Far East. Kane, however, appears from the start to have harbored an ambition to strike out for the Pole. His vessel of 140 tons, the *Advance,* was specially constructed and outfitted for arctic exploration. In addition to the support of the Navy, which may have been the real purpose for the idea of the relief of Franklin, he had the financial backing of prominent citizens of the day. Many bays and capes were named after such sponsors, so obviously this was the technique used to raise the money. Indeed, it was a technique used by all the American North Polers. The Danish and Canadian governments have not seen fit to change these names, such as Cape George Ingersoll, Cape Morris Jesup, Rensselaer Bay, Grinnell Peninsula, and many others unilaterally conferred by explorers on land that wasn't even American. Many of these polar explorers did not get as far north by vessel as we would be when we got to Spitsbergen. The reason for this, of course, was that a branch of the Gulf Stream, the North Atlantic Drift Current, warms the waters of the Barents Sea and makes a sea approach to the Pole from Spitsbergen appear more feasible at first. Those explorers using

Spitsbergen as a base to attack the Pole failed only because of the tread-mill effect of the south-flowing polar ice. Those making the jump from the northwest of Greenland or Ellesmere Island, Canada, had better luck, although their accounts of physical sufferings and loss of life can hardly be described as "luck."

One Arctic cruise, in fact a Spitsbergen cruise, which took place in 1856 on a private yacht, no less, was perhaps the closest parallel to that which we were attempting. This was the cruise of the schooner yacht *Foam,* owned and skippered by the Earl of Dufferin. Lord Dufferin kept a meticulous log. Considering the fact that his was a yacht, not a man-of-war, not a whaler, and had no auxillary, no RDF, no loran, no consolan, no radar, not even much in the way of celestial tables, Lord Dufferin deserves the highest mark of any of the Arctic sailors. If the Blue Water Medal of the Cruising Club of America had existed in 1856, it should have been awarded to Lord Dufferin and immediately retired forever.

On the trip north from Hammerfest *Foam* ran into impenetrable pack ice not far from Bear Island. Since there was no apparent lead open to the south cape of Spitsbergen, Lord Dufferin tacked to the west toward the Greenland Sea. After a sawtooth course westward and northward, he finally found open water and a lead eastward to the west coast around Prins Karls Forland. He made it to English Bay, now called Engelskbukta, where he spent four days climbing on the glacier and shooting game. (It is interesting to note that the *Arctic Pilot,* an Admiralty publication, still quotes Lord Dufferin's description of Engelskbukta as an aid to present-day seafarers in that region.) When *Foam* quit Spitsbergen, she did so by retracing her route. Lord Dufferin wisely held westward to the east Greenland pack before turning south and thundering on down before half a gale in Trondheim.

Spitsbergen has been a subject of interest off and on for almost four hundred years. Right now, as mentioned, it is on again because of its mineral and military potential. Aside from that, it has been and will continue to be an earth scientist's dream. It is the seaward gateway to the High Arctic even though the gate is closed for nine months of the year. Orlin Donaldson and I had done a little homework; we didn't think we would be disappointed. And we weren't.

Much of my preparation for Spitsbergen was library research, and naturally I couldn't ask my crew to undertake that sort of work. In this connection, Orlin was an exception. Not only did he do research on his own at the Lehigh University library, but he also kept feeding me literature he had dug up. He was indefatigable in his investigation. One book, which my friend Dr. Paul Sheldon, the famous Labrador sailor, lent me was *Report of the Company,* an account of several northern passages by Dudley Talcott of Hartford. Talcott's father-in-law was a Tromsø sealer named Isak Isaksen, a real salt of a guy, with whom young Talcott bought the ninety-nine foot sealer *Nordkap II* back in 1932. Talcott tells the story of Morten Isaksen, the father of his father-in-law, who in 1872 at the age of twenty-five joined an expedition of five sealing vessels to the north coast of Spitsbergen. Sealers in those days were well aware of the dangers of ice and knew enough not to overstay their welcome and get caught by a late summer freeze. Young Morten's companions, however, were doing so well with seals and reindeer that they made the fatal mistake of staying too long and found themselves caught in a snowstorm and September freeze. Their boats made it to a protected cove called Graa Huk, but there got caught in the ice. After two months of sitting and waiting, part of the group decided to walk halfway down the west coast to the mouth of Isfjord, 175 miles away, where they knew there was a hut at Kapp Thorsen. This group, deciding it was a better gamble to keep moving than to sit and freeze to death, gathered all the food and supplies they could drag in small boats and took off across the ice, figuring that if they came to open water they could jump in the boats and row. They knew there were coal and emergency rations in the hut. Of course there was no winter settlement of any sort on Spitsbergen in those days, so they gambled that these rations would last the winter.

The second group, led by the skipper and cook of one of the vessels that lay in the snug cove — one that had not been crushed by ice as two others had — decided to stay for the winter. They had plenty of meat in the hold and their guess as to the probabilities of survival was as good as anyone's. However, as a result of that decision, they were never seen again.

A third group, which young Morten joined after first going off with the hikers and then turning back, decided to stay in their boat outside the cove and pray for a break in the early cold spell or, alternatively, tough it through the winter. This wouldn't be the first time Norwegian fishermen had involuntarily spent the winter beset in the Arctic ice —

or the last! About a week after this group had made their decision, along came a hurricane-force blow out of the northeast that broke up the ice and set them free. They then battled a combination of pack ice, head winds, leaking bilges, incipient starvation, and finally fearsome freezing of ice up topside and in the rigging. But on Christmas morning they sailed into the harbor of Tromsø, home and alive to tell the tale.

In the spring as soon as the ice would permit, a rescue crew was put together to sail north to Isfjord to retrieve the survivors of the march — if any among the seventeen had indeed survived. After working their way through chunks of ice of every size and dimension, the rescue vessel anchored at Kapp Thorsen in sight of the hut, from which no smoke was visible. Young Morten Isaksen was of course among the rescuers, and when he saw no smoke he assumed the men were out hunting.

Morten hopped ashore and scrambled up to the hut. When he opened the door the first thing he saw was scattered human teeth, evidence of scurvy! As his eyes became accustomed to the darkness inside the hut, gradually what appeared before his eyes were the frozen corpses of all seventeen men, some sitting in chairs, others lying in their bunks or leaning across the table. Such are the stories of man's struggle in the Polar Arctic, Spitsbergen, east Greenland, and Denmark Strait.

Fortunately, not all trips to Spitsbergen have ended in such a ghastly fashion. One of the most valuable and certainly the most recent experience was that of the incredible Britisher, Major H. W. Tilman of the Royal Cruising Club. I realize that an incredible Britisher might be redundancy itself. They are all a bit incredible. But when you have a British gentleman, mountaineer, sailor, and horseman, then you have redundant redundancies. I didn't know Tilman personally. But anyone who can quote Epicurus, speak German, French, and Greek, climb up mountains and ski down them, sail to Patagonia and back for a little diversion, and treat Spitsbergen and Hinlopen Strait with utter disdain deserves a great deal of respect.

Tilman cruised into Longyearbyen in '74 in a seventy-two-year-old pilot cutter with an old one-lunger engine that was somewhat questionable in forward gear and positively inoperative in reverse. His very appearance at the wharf after a couple of thousand miles from the Solent would frighten the average and elicit sorrow from the salty. All he asked from them was black or rye bread, on the theory that since black bread becomes less palatable with time, the bread would last longer on the return trip! Some of Bill Tilman's shipmates have been a bit sketchy; yet Tilman apparently saw no link to the chow he provided. If they made it (twice they did not), it was, so to speak, not by bread alone.

Tilman made it in spades all the way round Spitsbergen and down Hinlopen Strait between Vest Spitsbergen and Nordaustlandet — a very dangerous passage of heavy ice and horrendous current. His vessel *Baroque,* while under power and in a three-knot current, ran hard aground off Hinlopen Strait. During nearly a whole day's pounding from bergy bits that kissed his hull as they passed by, the crew tossed out all of their inside lead ballast, and finally, after losing first one anchor, then another, kedged off with the help of tide and sail. In typical Tilman fashion, he replaced the lost ballast with rocks gathered at the next anchorage and carried on. When fog set in, he calmly took off for home. His account never mentions the fact that he sailed farther north at 80° 04′ than any yachtsman in history. He probably didn't know it and couldn't have cared less. Parenthetically, it is sad to report that Bill Tilman disappeared at sea in the early months of 1979 on his way south along the coast of South America. He had been hoping to scale an Andean mountain on his eightieth birthday. Thus ended an active and adventurous life and one that will long be remembered in the annals of the Royal Cruising Club.

The High Arctic is part Canadian, part Russian, part Norwegian, and part Danish. People have been living in this region since perhaps as far back as seventy thousand years ago. The so-called Peking Man goes back possibly a quarter of a million years. Toward the end of the Paleolithic Age, the Old Stone Age, man is believed to have left traces in the eastern Arctic regions. Probably the earliest traces were of mongoloid stock, as archeological finds have definitely linked these eastern people to the wild game that is characteristic of the region, like musk-ox, seal, and polar bear.

The western Arctic seems to have been developed much later, primarily by prehistoric maritime Indians starting about 2500 B.C., and later by nomadic Eskimos. Thus archeologists are certain that man did not originate in the polar regions but migrated there in his search for food. Moreever, nature seems to have compensated these northern migrants for their cold environment by endowing them with physical features that specially suited them for coping with low temperatures. Their bodies are smaller, thus they have less surface area from which to lose heat. Their low-bridged noses, fleshy faces, and mongoloid eye-folds all contribute to cold-weather adaptability.

This is not to say that once man penetrated to the northern extremities he necessarily stayed there. Indeed, quite the opposite may be the case, and in all probability the chief determinant of his tenure and his boundaries was weather. This so-called Upper Paleolithic Man ranged across the Eurasian land mass, leaving rock paintings that show his preoccupation with hunting. He followed the retreating glaciers during periods of warming and either left or was wiped out during periods of cooling.

Again, as we know from the Viking experience in Greenland in recent times (in archeological terms), nature had many options for population control, including temperature change of both air and water as probably the most fundamental. Then there are divers other factors, like pestilence, alteration of patterns of fish and game, and, lastly, the nature of man in his relation to man. The latter is usually a competitive, not a cooperative, relationship, but it also is susceptible to idea transfer. For example, I believe our observations of the Canadian and Greenland Eskimos and their relationships with the culture of the white Canadians and Danes showed a microcosm of a human society in flux. In Labrador, when we saw the so-called "livyers," predominantly white people with some Indian and/or Eskimo blood, it seemed that they were an example of whites adapting to the exigencies and the dictates of the North. In the case of the Greenlander of mixed blood, from my small vantage point, I would have to say the pull was toward the Danes. Overall, there is no question but that the culture of the white man of the temperate zone has the potential to envelop, if not obliterate, that of those more indigenous to the Arctic, namely the Eskimo, the Indian, and the Lapp. I'm not prepared to say that this is good or bad, but that's the way it is.

It is not that we wish to destroy them or even change them, but we want what they sit on — minerals and other resources, maybe even ice. The Moravian and Anglican missionaries who taught the Eskimos it was wrong to kill newborn girls and to let the aged and infirm simply die were not intending to demolish their culture, but unwittingly they did a pretty good job of it. When the native depended on the limited game the hunters could obtain, his survival necessitated an animal code. Now that white man's culture, including his latest product of genius — welfare — whether administered by Russian, Finn, Norwegian, Dane, or Canadian, has been made available to and in most cases forced upon the native of the North, the latter's days to extinction may well be numbered.

My earlier trip to Labrador and much of the impetus for the polar probe originated in my fascination with the nature of the Labrador coast, its scenery, its flora and fauna, its ice, and its people. Its inaccessibility made more precious that which was there. Because of the weather and temperature between Labrador and Greenland, one is limited in his Arctic aspirations in that sector, although in 1974 Tom Watson, in his motor-sailor *Palawan,* defied the elements to reach 77° north, beyond Thule. To go much farther than that, one would have to walk! Therefore to get a look at the polar regions by sailboat, one really must select Spitsbergen as his target, for no other northern region has the moderating thermal influence of a finger of the Gulf Stream.

Spitsbergen has not always been where it is, or if it has, then our world once rotated about another axis. Otherwise, how did this most northerly inhabited place in the world get minerals like coal? Most geologists sub-scribe to the theory of continental drift, which holds that the surface of the earth has shifted around its iron core and that every five hundred million years or so the poles might even exchange places. Surely the process by which oil, gas, and coal are formed is not one that takes place in the climate of the Arctic. As early as the 1700s coal was known to exist in Spitsbergen, but it was not till early in the 1900s that an Ameri-can geologist and iron mine operator, John Munro Longyear, put together a company to mine it. In 1906, Longyear and his associate Frederick Ayer started the Arctic Coal Company at Adventfjorden off Isfjord, which is now the location of the present-day town of Longyearbyen, named for the American founder. (The Arctic Coal Company operated until just before World War I, when it was sold to a Swedish group.) Longyear-byen today is entirely a company town: it is the seat of the government of Svalbard, the archipelago of which Spitsbergen is the largest island, and the only one of commercial significance, populated by some 1,100 Nor-wegians and 2,200 Russians.

Svalbard lies betwen 74° north and 81° north latitude and 10° east and 35° east longitude. The total area of this island group is about one-fifth of mainland Norway. Most of the land in Svalbard is covered by glacier. That which is not has permafrost under the surface to a depth of 150 meters in the lowlands and 300 meters in the uplands.

Unlike Norway's, the waters around Spitsbergen are comparatively shallow, with skerries and occasional banks, making anchoring no problem. One unique aspect of these arctic islands is the fact they have been rising since the last ice age waned. This presents an unusual opportunity for a marine geologist, who can observe the shoreline of ten thousand years ago at perhaps one hundred feet above water. It also produces broad terraces that were once ocean bottom. This rise in the land derives from the slow alleviation of the weight of the ice, as the glaciers are still retreating, often leaving moraines before them, and these moraines are made of the ground-up rock from glaciation. (In America, two good examples of terminal moraines are Long Island and Cape Cod.)

Perhaps the most striking aspect of Svalbard is its infinite variety. In some fjords, like Woodfjorden in the north of Spitsbergen, there are solid gray granite and granitic gneisses on one side and sedimentary red sandstone on the other. Metamorphic strata, often heavily folded, are common, and there are even a few outcroppings of volcanic activity such as hot springs. Again, unlike Norway's, the snowfields and glaciers sweep down to the water's edge. Some of the mountains are staircased, while others, especially on the west coast, are rugged with jagged peaks.

The government of present day Svalbard is vested, as we've seen, in the Sysselmann, a governor appointed by the administration in Norway. Though Norway had historic claims to these northern islands it was really a no-man's-land until 1922, when the Treaty of Svalbard was signed. The treaty was ratified by the last of the signatories in 1925, formally recognizing Norway's sovereignty with certain restrictions stipulating that all signatories had rights to stake claims, much as a U.S. citizen has a right to mineral leases in any state of the Union. The Russians have been the only country to exercise this right actively, and their mine at Barentsburg is surrounded by their permanent community. Another stipulation, which now takes on important dimensions, is that no military installation of any kind is permitted in Svalbard. This is proving to be a sticky covenant to administer, but Norwegian authorities are living by the law and insisting that the Russians do likewise.

We had been apprised of all the laws, including even the rules on game. In Knut Sørensen we had a knowledgeable citizen who knew the ropes and had the necessary sensitivity. So, with the knowledge of the present rules and a fair understanding of its history I thought our crew were well prepared for Norway's gateway to the Pole — Spitsbergen.

8

Spitsbergen

AFTER A LONG SOUND SLEEP at anchor in Gåshamna Cove in Hornsund, we arose around 0800 and breakfasted on oatmeal and good hot cocoa, all the time feasting our eyes on the spectacular scenery which surrounded us. It was clear and crisp, a great day for photography. Hornsundtind, one of the highest mountains in Spitsbergen, was enshrouded in altocumulus, but occasionally its peak would protrude and assert its sovereignty over the entire sound. The sky was azure, with billowing cotton clouds scudding by from the northeast. The temperature was not inhospitable; we didn't need earmuffs or even gloves until we left the sound. Air temperature was in the low fifties Fahrenheit.

After breakfast Dicky Cromwell and Orlin rowed ashore to investigate the shack that stood up boldly on the moraine in front of the glacier in Gåshamna. When they returned, they were gushing with wonderment. In addition to the complete carcass of a sperm whale and the nearby grave marked by the Orthodox cross, they found Russian words painted on a rock nearby. Orlin felt that the hut could easily have been there since the eighteenth century, but I would settle for middle nineteenth. There is no question that the arctic cold does a remarkable job of preservation, and Orlin may well have been right. For example, when the crew of *Nordkap II* broke through to Cape Hold-with-Hope, Greenland, in 1931, they found on Pendulum Island complete stores left by the Baldwin Ziegler Polar Expedition of 1900! They broke open the tins marked "Armour & Co." and ate beef that was still perfectly preserved.

How Orlin could be so positive that the skeleton was that of a sperm whale was beyond me, but he had a whale book and I accepted his judgment. The spooky question was: how did the man die and who buried him? We concluded he was a trapper who froze to death and was buried the following summer when his body was found.

I told the crew the story of Ivar Rund, the Norwegian adventurer who spent the winter in Hornsund and wrote a book about it called *A Long Day's Night*. Rund and his husky dog lived off what he trapped and shot or what fish he occasionally could catch through the ice. We all agreed that no amount of royalties would be enough inducement to spend a winter in Hornsund, beautiful though it was even in the dark.

The summer, however, was a different story. Donaldson began to salivate over the photographic possibilities, so we weighed anchor and got underway to explore the sound and take in the scenery in this virgin vista, known only to God and a handful of mariners. The sound was full of bergy bits, at least along the northern shore, and there were some half dozen icebergs. At the forward edge of many of the glaciers, which ran down to the water, was an occasional blotch of blue ice. This was where a berg had recently calved, leaving a raw-looking spot behind. These were not big bergs by Greenland standards, but still large enough to put us away in a hurry if we happened to collide with one.

Orlin, with camera in hand, cut loose in the Avon dinghy, and by walkie-talkie instructed us what to do to suit his artistic desires. In a breeze of twenty knots we set a chute, sailed between a berg and the glacier, and in general put on a show, all the while dodging the bergy bits and trash ice. Knut, who was still getting used to us, thought we were crazy messing around in all that ice. He was greatly relieved when I gave orders to knock off the exercise and get underway for Isfjord.

Sørensen had checked around and knew a lot about Svalbard, in part because his cousin had been a radio operator at Isfjord Radio. Unlike the British, who would go anywhere on a dare, the Norwegians have an ingrained reticence when it comes to venturing into the polar ice. Too many of their countrymen have been lost in the North for them to regard ice as anything but an enemy. Not many of them would consider an arctic cruise in a sailing yacht as something to do for a vacation. They would much prefer to be in heavily constructed motor vessels. Knut was an exception because he had a background of sailing with Helge Amundsen in Hammerfest. The whole Norse nation were weaned on the exploits of Nansen and Amundsen, but these great explorers were not yachtsmen and their vessels were of very heavy construction. I could tell from the looks on the faces of most Norwegians who saw us that they thought we were slightly off our rockers.

Reaching at eight knots with spinnaker flying in Hornsund was "pour le sport" for us but totally asinine to Knut, and the look on his face showed that clearly. When the spinnaker came down and we got clear of the drift ice, Knut suddenly became a new man. He caught on quickly to our routine and our sense of humor. Meanwhile, his ability on the radio transmitter was of great assistance, as was his monitoring of Norwegian radio broadcasts. We were much more secure than we might have been without him.

Working north from Hornsund past another fjord, scenic Bellsund, we found the outer coast very different from the glacier-covered Sørkapp (South Cape) and the outer coast south of Hornsund. In this stretch of coastline, the rock looked like sedimentary sandstone, almost a Mediterranean look for part of the way. The sun remained bright all night, and we sighted a collier heading south, probably carrying coal to Russia. Our destination was Barentsburg, the Soviet town on a bay just inside the entrance of Isfjord, which is about halfway up the west coast and the only commercial waterway in all of Svalbard.

After a pleasant overnight sail, we turned into Isfjord and past Kapp Linné to Grønfjorden, arriving there at 0530, before the town of Barentsburg was awake. We tied up at a ramshackle wharf behind a Russian freighter that evidently was delivering lumber to the mining town.

On the way into Barentsburg we were amazed to see a huge sign on the hill overlooking the bay which read "Peace and Goodwill to Man" — in English. This message amazed me, especially when very few foreigners ever go there and, from what I had read, are not especially welcome. Why was this message in English? Perhaps they felt that all Westerners would understand English, and wanted anyone who happened by to construe them as people of purely peaceful pursuits. Funnily enough, I think that most of them are peaceful and, in fact, do hold

Westerners in awe. We saw no hostility in any Russians whom we met. Orlin, of course, took the opportunity to mention the civility of Shurbitov and what a decent person he had seemed to be. Even I, at this point, conceded that Shurbitov was a nice guy. Excellent manners and all that. Maybe it was I who had been brainwashed — by the American press?

The first people to greet us were dock workers just arriving for work. They were curious but we were unable to communicate. Soon, however, the cook or commissary officer from the freighter next to us came over and invited us to the crew's mess for breakfast. We jumped at the invitation. Maybe the Soviet courtesy flag that we were flying at our port yard had some effect at conveying friendly intentions. The Norwegian courtesy flag was quite properly flying on the starboard yardarm, which is the honor side. I doubt if anyone ashore knew or cared about these nautical niceties, but the simple display of the hammer and sickle flag might have seemed a friendly gesture, and that is why we flew it.

Breakfast in the crew's mess aboard the freighter was interesting, but Orlin had the only stomach that could tolerate pickled herring for breakfast. The rest of the meal consisted of white bread, butter, and boiled potatoes. The tables were attended by waitresses who were part of the ship's company. None of them would win a beauty contest, so I did not push the obvious question of how they handle a bisex crew.

While we were eating, an interpreter (probably also a commissar) came down to find out what we were doing there, and he seemed much relieved when I told him we were leaving immediately to head up the fjord to Longyearbyen. He politely wished us good luck and left.

Our host took us to meet the captain in his quarters, and he turned out to be a rather jolly sort who spoke English fairly well. He told us he had taken his ship to Chicago, which surprised me because the vessel seemed too small for transoceanic trade. Then again I remembered that there was a regulated trade between the two countries, albeit small in volume. The captain introduced me to his chief engineer, who spoke only a little English but was quite affable. He had several teeth made of solid gold, which, at current prices of the precious metal might net him a small fortune in Chicago.

I invited both officers aboard *Reindeer* for a mug of java and they responded with enthusiasm. We had a pleasant gam, and when I mentioned that my wife, who had visited Russia, much preferred Russian

Soviet workers at the dock in Barentsburg (Orlin Donaldson)

The author with the captain and executive officer of the Russian freighter at Barentsburg (Orlin Donaldson)

vodka to the U.S. stuff, the captain immediately ordered a bottle delivered from his vessel as a gift. We gave him one of our Bennington
flags. I also pulled out the printed speech of Brezhnev which the Russian
visitors in St. John's had left aboard as a "gift," along with little
medallions with Lenin's picture featured on them. The captain appeared
to scoff at this stuff as though he too knew it was pure propaganda. At
one point I asked him about the Russian square-riggers that had joined
Opsail '76 to celebrate our bicentennial. I told him that the papers said
that *Kruzenshtern,* one of the biggest of the Tall Ships, had pulled out
in some sort of dispute. He too had read about it in the Soviet press. The
captain of *Kruzenshtern* had a German name and I asked him about
that. His answer was an amazing snarl, "He's a Jude!"

I could not believe my ears. I felt like saying, "What's that got to do
with the price of eggs?" but I restrained myself. Race, creed, and
polemics seemed a bit out of place in nature's surroundings.

After our guests went back to their freighter, I climbed up on the
dock. I noticed some pretty big boxes being unloaded along with the
lumber. That intrigued me. I was sure these boxes contained small arms
or something more lethal. As I was staring at them, someone came up to
suggest I better embark on my boat. There was absolutely no doubt in
my mind that the Russians were putting at least small arms in stockpile
for the day they chose to take over all of Svalbard.

The wind was due east, force 5 or 6, so we had to beat to windward
in order to get to Longyearbyen, twenty-five miles away. It seemed late
by the sun when we pulled away from the dock at 0930 and headed out
of the harbor and into Isfjord. On the way out the only obvious military
or potentially military material that I could see was electronics. The
docks were nothing, and Barentsburg did not appear to have much mining activity. Housing was barracks-like, but that could be a function of
winter. There was a graveyard nearby but no church. Altogether it was
a puzzling place. Knut, who was aghast that I would go there without
permission of the Sysselmann, was even more dubious and suspicious
than the rest of us. He had spoken of the endless trouble between the
Russians and the Norwegian government, and he was certain the Reds
were violating all kinds of provisions of the treaty. As to requesting permission to visit Barentsburg, I knew it would be easier for the governor
to say no, and by stopping there on my way to Longyearbyen I wasn't

violating any laws, because I had already been cleared to cruise in Norwegian territory. As we left Barentsburg, Knut's spirits took a turn for the better.

Working upwind, *Reindeer* played the south shore of the big fjord. We passed some abandoned mines of the drift variety, and saw quite a lot of geological interest. Keeping close to the shore, we passed a grazing musk-ox, which is one of a species originally imported from Arctic Canada, where it was a northern relative of the buffalo. Around 1400 we reached Adventfjorden, an inlet to starboard, where the mining town of Longyearbyen dominates the landscape. Like so many other names in Spitsbergen, Adventfjorden is a corruption of an English name, Adventure Bay, which derived from the name of one of the ships in a British whaling fleet in 1656. Dropping our canvas, we slowly powered into the harbor, passing by the airport and much of the automated equipment connected with the mines.

As a temporary measure we tied to a motor patrol boat, which turned out to be the official craft which the Sysselmann used to visit distant parts of Svalbard. Knut conferred with various people on the dock, including some young officials of Store Norske, and the Sysselmann himself wasted little time in coming from his quarters up on the hill to join us for tea. The way Knut had talked, I fully expected the governor to be standoffish, if not pompous, in the manner of so many British colonial governors who take themselves so seriously. Not so; the Sysselmann was friendly and, while not effusive, was obviously satisfied that we could handle ourselves. He had just returned from a round-the-islands visit, and told us that ice conditions in Hinlopen Strait and farther to the east were not good. Also, he implied he knew of our every movement since our arrival, including the visit to Barentsburg. I detected a little sign of displeasure over that, so I mentioned that we had made a brief stop out of curiosity. I told him we did not see much mining going on, and his reaction to that might well have been "Are you telling me?"

Knut remained quiet and in the background as if to say, "Governor, I had no part in that Yankee caper." We soon got the conversation around to our itinerary and what we needed, as well as news of the world. The Sysselmann warmed up, and when we parted I felt we had passed the litmus test. No doubt, Isfjord Radio had informed him of our doings, and the radio boys knew about us as soon as we contacted Bear Island. Again, Knut was relieved when the Sysselmann left and no fireworks had occurred. Without any question, one could feel the Norwegian-Russian tension in the air, and the Sysselmann said nothing to relieve that tension. For the first time in a long while I had a longing for company — the company of the United States Navy! Americans don't very often have the feeling which I had — a bare tail to the wind. The only people who could assist us were Norwegians, and where we were going there wouldn't even be any of them around.

At this point Knut introduced us to an acquaintance of his, one Tøre Wassbakk of Tromsø. Tøre (pronounced Tura) owned a Colin Archer–designed motor ketch called *Caroline Mathilde*, which was just then on the opposite side of the dock from us. She was under charter to a West German financier, who with three Norwegian mining engineers was prospecting for uranium. They claimed to have discovered both coal and uranium already and were on their way north to find more. Tøre had a ship's captain called Alf, who had been in the merchant navy and spoke perfect English. Alf was a splendid fellow with a marvelous sense of humor. Tøre and Alf insisted on entertaining us in their warm and spacious cabin. A party got underway spontaneously, and there was so much laughter and merriment that we were soon joined by some young engineers from the coal company. This was a stroke of luck, because Knut was able to make arrangements to requisition food and supplies from the company commissary. Meanwhile, the party lasted until 0330, when our two new shipmates arrived from the airport — Jim Demarest and Diana Russell. They had just flown in on the one weekly flight from Tromsø. The sudden presence of a young woman gave a real fillip both to the party and to the brotherly feeling which *Caroline Mathilde* transmitted to *Reindeer*. Alf combed his hair, preening like a peacock, and Knut and Tøre gave him the needle.

Alf strummed a mean guitar and the place was alive with Norwegian songs, the "Battle Hymn of the Republic," and finally "Dixie," rendered by the two boys from the University of Virginia.

Somehow *Mathilde* had an ample supply of Scotch whisky in bond. That being a rare item, I offered Alf a trade: Diana for one case of

Scotch. Alf quickly raised the ante to two cases, at which point Diana, not wishing to be treated as barter, fumed at me. "Newbold, shall I get my duffle bag?"

This cracked up the Norwegians. Straightaway we planned a rendez-vous up north and to that end arranged radio frequencies to keep the two boats in touch. Knut, not allowing Alf to score the last goal before turning in, had one final remark: "Tøre, you boys are unfair; you can't pit your tax-free booze against our taxable stuff."

That left the deal still pending and put Diana in some doubt as to what value her own crew placed on her. A good ploy by Knut. As we said goodnight, Tøre gave me a souvenir — a whale's spinal disk with an inscription in Norwegian, saying, "Greetings from Caroline Mathilde."

It took a little longer than usual to clear the cobwebs the morning of Thursday, 29 July. Finally, around 1330 we were underway for the north, destination Ny Ålesund at Kongsfjorden (King's Bay). It was about sixty miles up the coast from the entrance to Isfjord, going inside beautiful Prins Karls Forland, which is a narrow island about forty miles long and only five miles off the Spitsbergen coast. The mountains on the Forland were glistening with new snow as the sun bathed them all night. The passage is shallow in places and one must pay special at-tention to the sailing directions in the *Arctic Pilot* and line up the proper peaks so as to avoid the two-meter shoals which occur in the northern part of Forlandsundet. I was conscious of a little colder weather; our breath vapor was pronounced and the wind had an increased chill factor.

King's Bay has historical significance, first in the ancient past as a favorite bay of the British explorers and whalers and then in this cen-tury as the place from which Roald Amundsen and the American Lin-coln Ellsworth took off in a dirigible, crossed the North Pole, and landed in Alaska. That was in 1925. Later Amundsen was to lose his life at-tempting to rescue the Italian explorer Nobile, both of whom took off from King's Bay. At Ny Ålesund there is an abandoned mining camp that ceased operations after a disastrous cave-in in 1962, which killed many miners and caused the overthrow of the Norwegian Labor Party. The Polar Institute maintains a radio station there in summertime, and the little post office draws attention because at 79° north latitude it is quite obviously the northernmost point in the world from which one can post a letter.

At breakfast time we glided into the dock at Ny Ålesund and tied up to the motor vessel *Sandsvalen*, which was under charter to the *National Geographic*. Lo and behold, Gordon Young of the *Geographic* was there with his photographer, Martin Rogers. Martin told us he had taken nearly ten thousand photographs between his winter and summer visits. What a file they must maintain in Washington! Per Johansen, owner of the rusty *Sandsvalen*, was an adventurer who had been all over Svalbard. Walter Levering had sought him for his trip across the top of Siberia, but Per did not fancy such a passage in a sailboat, which to him seemed but a toy. Maybe there were other considerations, but I kept quiet when Young editorialized in favor of power over sail for arctic exploits. Levering, of course, was totally right; no small power boat could carry enough fuel to cross Siberia, let alone Canada.

While the others were touring the decks of the rusty *Sandsvalen*, Young and I spoke briefly about Barentsburg. Young told me his visit there was red carpet all the way, except for the mines. They refused his request to see any part of the underground operation, making him suspicious that at least part of the mines' function was to store weapons. After all, if the Russians can smuggle missiles into Cuba, sending weapons to Barentsburg would be duck soup. On statistics alone, Young concluded that there was something quite fishy about the Russian mines. The housing and the accommodations of the Russians were far superior, according to Young, to that provided by Store Norsk, which alone suggests that Moscow attaches some significance to Barentsburg beyond that of an ordinary mining town. This theory was even more plausible to me because my friend Ted Leisenring, president of Westmoreland Coal Company, had once described his trip to Siberia to see a Soviet mining operation, and according to him it was vintage 1890 at best. The Siberian mines are far more productive than Barentsburg's, so why would the latter rate greenhouses, aviaries, and other earmarks of luxury?

Later, back home in 1977, when I heard that Young's article had been submitted for publication but mysteriously delayed (Young thought by the State Department), I could only conclude that my earlier surmise was accurate. The *National Geographic* is not an ordinary publication.

It is a tax-free institution, and its board of trustees includes many active and former members of the government in Washington. Spitsbergen had become a big chip in a game of high stakes. Too bad Ian Fleming was dead, I thought, for this was tailormade for James Bond, 007.

Before we left to send some postcards, Young warned us to watch out for attacks from terns. I thought he was pulling my leg when he said one had to carry a club to protect oneself. When we went ashore we must have disturbed a nesting ground, for all of a sudden we were dive-bombed by arctic terns. It was unbelievable how effectively they drove us away. We finally got to the little post office and sent cards to our friends, telling them they were receiving mail from the northernmost post office in the world.

Ny Ålesund looked like an abandoned mining outpost in Colorado that had seen better days, yet hikers and mountain climbers appeared out of the woodwork. On the dock an open shed contained several dozen sticks of dynamite, just sitting there for anyone to grab. I was told the dynamite was used to break up concentrations of ice around the wharf. How casual, I thought, as Orlin took a picture of Cromwell pretending to steal a stick or two.

After a pleasant lunch aboard *Reindeer* with Young and Rogers, who described their just-ended sortie to the North, we cast off and headed out of King's Bay just as a big cruise ship appeared at the entrance to the bay and slowly moved in toward the dock. Thinking she was a Swede, I called her captain on VHF, channel 16. We talked in English, but I could not understand him too well. Knut took over the mike and he and the captain had no trouble at all, speaking English! He was not a Swede but a Greek, no less, and his ship was the M.V. *Atlas* out of Athens, on a North Cape cruise. Her captain asked if she could dock in Ny Ålesund! Obviously they had never been there before. Knut told him he would have to anchor in the bay and send small boats ashore. Evidently this did not appeal to the captain, who then went on the P.A. to announce to the passengers they could not go ashore. On hearing the announcement, one of the passengers hurled out a package in a polyethylene wrapper attached to a small floating object. It appeared to be a message for *Reindeer*, which by this time was abreast of the cruise ship. We picked up the package, and inside was a letter addressed to a Madame Padopilous in Athens. I then signaled by hand that I would post the letter for him.

Little did he know that *Reindeer* would be away from civilization for a week! Later we mailed the letter in Longyearbyen.

We continued our voyage northward another forty miles to Magdalenafjorden, which is a particularly spectacular inlet in the part of northwest Spitsbergen known as King Albert I Land. We wanted to go to the head of the fjord but had to turn back because of the prevalence of loose pack ice off the Waggonway Glacier. Since I had been forewarned by the old whaling captain not to anchor off a glacier for fear of a calving berg, we anchored instead in front of a rocky moraine. It was open to the northwest and subject to sea swell, but that was the best we could do. All of us were too tired to row ashore to reconnoiter as Lord Dufferin had done, but that might well have been a lucky break. Since our return to the States I heard from Knut that an Austrian climber in 1977 was killed and eaten by a polar bear on the glacier behind Magdalenafjorden. This prompted the Sysselmann to order all visitors going ashore in Svalbard to be armed.

Also later in the summer of '77 I heard that the southern edge of the polar pack was all the way down to King's Bay, so a trip into the Arctic Ocean would not have been possible. Again this illustrates the variation in weather patterns that to a great extent control the ice floes. Incidentally, such floes must not have bothered the Russians, for in August 1977 they sent their nuclear-powered 25,000-ton icebreaker *Arktika* all the way to the pole. Pushing north from Murmansk, she became the first surface vessel in history to make it to the North Pole. Even in the nuclear age, this was an incredible feat, and no matter how sinister their intentions, the Soviets have demonstrated mastery of the arctic ice, for which they deserve respect.

Underway to the north again, it was definitely colder. We sailed close-hauled between Denmark and Amsterdam islands on the port hand and the Schmeerenburg glacier on the starboard. In the 1800s there had been thriving summer colonies of whalers and their families on both Denmark and Amsterdam islands. The right whale was apparently docile and was easily caught and slaughtered in the fjords of Spitsbergen. So profitable was this trade that the whales were fished to extinction. Since then the Norwegian authorities have adopted conservation measures, which also apply to the walrus and polar bear. The latter feeds principally on seals, so one wonders why sealing is still permitted in Norway and the arctic islands. We saw seals nearly every day, and later I was happy to learn that sealing was regulated.

I had wanted to stop at Bird Island or North Norway Island to see the large bird colonies Gordon Young had mentioned, but something told me to take advantage of the good weather and northwest wind to push right on through to the Arctic Ocean. It was 1630 on Saturday, 31 July, when *Reindeer* finally entered this most northern part of the sea. The top of Spitsbergen was bathed in the evening sun, a fantastic sight. We might have tried going around the island as Tilman had done, but the Sysselmann's report of ice in Hinlopen Strait sounded ominous. I wondered if I should sail northeastward to Nordaustlandet, the large uninhabited island next to Spitsbergen, and follow the course of a group of Germans on the yacht *Wappen von Bremen*. This might be the likeliest place to find a polar bear. Hell, I could even sail due north. Visibility was fine. But what would I prove? And what risk would I be taking? I was torn with decision-making. We were at 80° 02′ north, 598 miles from the Pole, and Moffen Island was ahead and a little to starboard.

This was the exact position of HMS *Racehorse* at this same time of year in 1773, with Captain Constantine Phipps, R.N., in command and Midshipman Horatio Nelson in the ship's company. Climactic conditions in 203 years could have changed, but by how much? Not far to the east of Moffen Island *Racehorse* and *Carcass* had encountered pack ice. In fact, they had become beset in the ice north of Nordaustlandet, not far from our present position. Only a sudden easterly gale had broken up the pack and obtained their release. Captain Phipps's book had left some indelible impressions on me. In tossing about in my mind the risk/reward ratio of further pursuit to the north and east, it was inevitable that I would compare our situation to his. I had an engine and I had radar. I had accurate charts and I had a radio. He had a heavily constructed ship capable of taking plenty of punishment from the pack. I had a pretty good incentive to get home safely; he had incentive for discovery and fame. These reflections and comparisons probably took three seconds, but they told me to cool it; this was far enough. I wasn't Nansen, Amundsen, or Sverdrup. How could I take the risk of getting beset in the ice?

Having decided that nothing was to be gained by standing farther north and a lot could be lost if we were to have bad luck, I announced the decision to look in at Moffen and make that the turning point. No one criticized the decision, and in fact Orlin agreed it was the wisest thing to do. He had read, as I had, many tales of sudden shifts of wind, weather, and ice, and by now I think he wanted to be sure his pictures got home to be developed. We all relaxed a little. So what if we didn't find a bear?

Besides, we were already three hundred miles north of the magnetic North Pole. Had we been at 100° west longitude instead of 20° east longitude we would have had to head south to get to the North Pole. Things take some funny twists when you are that far north. For instance, if we were right on the magnetic North Pole, every direction would be south on our compass, including true north. I got the feeling that when a fellow gets between north and north maybe it's time to get the hell south, no matter what the compass course.

Moffen, our last northern stop, was a flat sandy atoll occupied only by walruses. To see these three-thousand-pound critters wallowing on the beach is some sight! We managed to scare several of them into the water, where they bobbed up for air within ten yards of us.

Walrus-watching and photographing took an hour or so, and then we turned south and into Woodfjorden, which indents the north coast for thirty-five miles due south, between King Haakon VII Land and Andrée Land, the latter named after the Swedish explorer and balloonist who disappeared on his flight to the Pole. Jim Demarest, our resident geologist, was enthralled with Woodfjorden. On its eastern side the mountainous coast was rust-red sandstone with many folds which Jim said were formed at the beginning and not by glaciation. On the western shore the rock was igneous, a gray granite, completely different from the opposite shore. Snow fields set off the colors of the rock on both sides. We found a well-protected shallow anchorage at Mushamna, a bight on the eastern shore at 79° 40′ North Latitude, and at 0300 dropped our plow in fifteen feet of water.

Looking at the chart later, I noticed that the variation, which is the angle between true and magnetic north, was only one-half degree. What amazed me was that the variation just west of Prins Karls Forland was eight and one-half degrees and that was only one hundred miles away as the crow flies. That illustrates how close to the Pole we were. On that score, I will never forget Tom Watson's report of seventy-five degrees of

The welcoming committee at Moffen Island (Orlin Donaldson)

variation which he experienced north of Thule, Greenland. The difference is accounted for by the exact location of the magnetic pole, which was somewhere near the 100th meridian on the far side of the True Pole from our location. All of this is subject to error induced by magnetic aberrations, which was another one of my worries about going farther north in the Arctic Ocean. Had we been a larger vessel or an airplane with adequate source of electric power, we could have been equipped with a gyro compass, and that would have eliminated most navigational worries. A gyro works on the same principle as a spinning top. Once it's rotating fast enough, its axis will continue to point in the direction originally set. Thus when you are reasonably confident of your magnetic compass you can set the gyro to True North by adjusting for the variation that's shown on the chart. This could have been done before leaving Norway and before entering the polar region, where magnetic anomalies might throw the ordinary compasses into disarray.

Being lost on land is bad enough, but being lost on the ocean, especially a distant ocean with hazards galore, was not a scenario I had any wish to create. There are certain stable benchmarks a sailor has to go by: one is the horizon, another is land if any can be seen, another is the compass if it can be trusted, and last, celestial bodies if they can be observed. In one fell swoop each of those would be eliminated by bad weather and magnetic aberrations, and those are the sorts of things one must anticipate even though conditions may be A-OK at the moment. Any carelessness or cavalier attitude about danger, though seemingly remote at the time, could turn useful lives into statistics. It was my responsibility to see that that didn't happen.

The next day was a sunny and glorious Sunday, and after breakfast we headed southwest to the head of Bockfjorden, an offshoot of Woodfjorden. All hands except me rowed ashore and climbed up on the glacier, where they found a hot spring that protruded through the moraine in the foreground of the glacier, clear evidence of a volcanic intrusion. Jim took a few rock samples to take back to the lab. They also saw tracks, probably of reindeer, and brought back antlers and a hoof for souvenirs.

Along the water's edge, both at the head of Bockfjorden and also all over Woodfjorden, I noticed driftwood and wondered how it got there. Later, when checking with Store Norske people, I found it came from

Hot spring at Woodfjorden moraine (Stockton N. Smith)

Siberia along the Polar Current, which runs east to west before it joins the south-going current of east Greenland.

By prearranged plan I blew three blasts on the foghorn, signaling that we should soon get underway. The climbing party made their way down the rocky moraine parallel to a waterfall that was pouring the melted snow and ice into the bay. They rowed back to *Reindeer*, and then we started our journey back to Longyearbyen. Knut reached *Caroline Mathilde* on AM radio, and a rendezvous was planned.

Once we were underway, we didn't waste any time. It would have been fun to go bird-watching on Norway Island, where Young and Rogers said the birds were outstanding, but we all had similar thoughts about hanging around in the Arctic Ocean. Our luck had been good; why press it? As the weather got worse and the visibility lower, I was reminded that few of my fancy instruments were of any real use this far north. There were no RDF stations, no loran, and even the soundings on the charts were few and far between. The radar was still useful, however, and it was more than Nansen or Peary or Greely or Hall or Elisha Kent Kane had had. I thought of the experience of old Morten Isaksen and wondered what choice we would make if a late summer snowstorm and subsequent freeze were to trap us on the north coast. I didn't relish the idea of walking to Longyearbyen!

We passed Norway Island at 1100 and proceeded toward Denmark Island, where the *Caroline Mathilde* was anchored off the Schmeerenburg Glacier, as planned. Tøre and Alf had over a half-dozen fenders hung out on the port side, a sure sign of welcome. After a good lunch, we set sail again and that evening nipped into a tiny bight on the west coast that was protected from the wind but not the swells. Supper was delicious spaghetti and reindeer meatballs that we had acquired from Levering. Washed down with South African wine brought by Dicky Cromwell, this meal rated a good two and a half stars. The wine was a real surprise. No Romanée-Conti, I'll admit, but every bit as good as some Chambertins I've tasted. On the morrow we would be starting home with a pit stop at Longyearbyen to put Knut ashore and secure some fresh provisions.

Our luck couldn't last forever. The next day the wind was right out of the south, blowing forty to forty-five knots. We shortened to a double-reefed main and a number four jib. It took six hours to cover

Caroline Mathilde *awaiting* Reindeer *for
lunch off Denmark Island* (Stockton N. Smith)

Orlin, Dicky, Knut off Prins Karls Forland (Stockton N. Smith)

eighteen miles along the course, and to get some protection from the sea, which was pounding us hard, we had to go inside the foreland where the mountains gave us a welcome lee. By the time we made the narrows in Forlandsundet, the squall had abated and we broke out the reef. At 1430 the next day we rolled into Longyearbyen, and by prearrangement everyone split up to do his selected chores. My job was to launder the ship's linen, as well as my clothes and body. For this I chose the sauna bath in the basement of an apartment building where families of the miners lived. Orlin and Knut went to Store Norske to arrange a food requisition. Jim Demarest, Stocky, and Dicky cleaned the boat and got the cabinets and icebox ready for the fresh stores.

At one point in the course of coordinating all the errands that had to be done, I fell into conversation with the wife of a young engineer. She was curious about our trip, and I was equally interested in her life on the island. The thing that especially intrigued me was what they did in the cold and dark winter months. I couldn't have been more surprised at what she told me. First, I gathered that she and her husband were well educated. He was a mining engineer, and she worked in the company store. This was a tour of duty, more or less, but they were definitely not looking forward to leaving. That's how much they liked it. I wondered what on earth would one do in a remote company town, but she didn't seem to feel any deprivation of culture. She extolled the sports available: skiing, hiking, hunting, fishing, and even snowmobiling. She said the library was adequate and that grade-school education was as good as on the mainland. She felt free and in touch with nature. That was what came across. I had seen this at home — people reacting to the mechanics of modern life and wanting to get back to nature — go west, for instance, and live on a Montana ranch.

There was some tendency toward hibernation. She and her husband both worked eight hours a day, but in the winter they slept twelve hours, whereas in the summer only six. As the days lengthened in the spring, they planned more outdoor activity. It was not ideal for a bachelor, but it didn't look bad for married couples. We parted company on the happy note that she lived in such close proximity to Santa Claus. She went back to work, and I went back to *Reindeer* — mine, not Santa's.

Knut worked wonders with the young manager types at Store Norske. Not only did we get a whole side of beef and all the other food requested, but we were invited for supper as the coal company's guests. After supper one of the mining engineers gave us a very informative lecture on the coal operations, which were of great interest to me, since I was in that business in a small way. Other than overhead, their mining costs are quite competitive, but the support costs, such as the town, are prohibitive in American terms. They produce both steam coal for the utilities and metallurgical-grade coal for the steel industry. It seemed they were not a threat to American exports of steam coal, but I reckoned they could sell metallurgical coal in Europe on a competitive basis. It was a thoroughly enjoyable supper.

By noon the next day we were underway, homeward bound. At 1600 we left Kapp Linné at the western extremity of Isfjord to port and set sail for Jan Mayen, six hundred miles down the Greenland Sea. For three days and nights it was a pleasant reach, with southwest winds, force 5 or 6. At midnight on the third night, Diana took a sight of the sun at its lower transit and worked out our latitude, just as one would do a local apparent noon sight. This is the first time I had ever heard of a local apparent midnight sight! Local apparent noon sights are commonplace and quite convenient, because the sun hangs momentarily at its zenith. To compute latitude from such a sight of the sun, one simply takes the sextant altitude and applies corrections from the nautical almanac to get the true observed altitude. From the almanac one then applies declination and derives latitude directly.

Local apparent noon has been used by navigators for centuries to determine latitude without an accurate timepiece. All students of navigation are taught this simple technique. However, local apparent midnight is an unheard-of expression. It could be a useful technique only in high latitudes on a date and in a place that the sun never sets. The arithmetic is altered for the lower transit, but it is just as simple. Normally, of course, the sun is below the horizon during lower transit of the observer's meridian. Diana was thus able to produce our latitude with just one sight of the sun at noon and one at midnight. Owing to the non-existence of twilight at these high latitudes no star sights were possible; only sun and moon, until we got farther south and sufficient darkness took over the sky.

Meanwhile we had reentered the zone where loran lines were available, so Stocky pecked away at the dials on our little loran set and produced lines of position (LOP's) that gave us pinpoint fixes. How spoiled we were, compared with mariners as late as pre–World War II, who had no such sophisticated equipment available. We had to contend with the same weather and ice, but at least we knew where we were.

After three days and nights the wind veered to south southeast and gradually began to howl. We reduced to the number four jib and a double-reefed main. Visibility was fine, and we sighted the great volcanic peak of Beerenberg, which completely dominates Jan Mayen Island and occupies its entire northern half. This tiny dot in the Greenland Sea has only a radio and loran station manned by a team of some thirty men under an officer of the Royal Norwegian Signal Corps. There is no harbor at Jan Mayen, and owing to Tilman's loss of *Mischief* on the east coast in the ice and rock ledges, we were a little uneasy.

We were sixty miles away when Jan Mayen first appeared, and by the time we were within fifteen miles, the wind was howling out of the southeast at sixty knots. Jan Mayen would be the last Norwegian territory we were to see, and the radioman with whom we talked became quite excited about having us as guests when he learned that *Reindeer* was a sailboat, not a freighter or a trawler. The welcome mat was out.

9

Jan Mayen to Iceland

THERE IT WAS, Beerenberg — the biggest volcano in the Atlantic Basin — sprouting right out of the ocean to a height of 7,500 feet. My crew were snapping pictures, and no wonder; they were looking at one of the unique islands of the world — the first Americans aboard a private boat to have this privilege. Beerenberg is a tiny outcrop on the mid-Atlantic volcanic ridge, which includes Iceland, the Azores, and in the South Atlantic, Tristan da Cunha. Only a few men live on Jan Mayen Land; never in its history has it supported a permanent population. There is not a blade of grass, or any growth other than lichen and moss.

At this point, with the island some fifteen miles to the southwest, we had a hard beat to windward to get there. As we closed Jan Mayen, the gods seemed to be testing us. Our anemometer was still pinned at sixty knots, the maximum reading on the scale of the instrument. But we knew how hard it was blowing without even looking at the bloody gauge. Judging from the fresh chop of the sea, as opposed to rolling swells, this had to be a foehn wind, which we had experienced in Newfoundland and Labrador and about which we had been warned by Wright Britton. Of all living sailors I know, probably no one had been in the foehns more than Stu Hotchkiss, who commanded the schooner *Bowdoin* during World War II in Greenland. He gave me a full description of these blows. According to him, blow-me-downs and foehns are one and the same, essentially a local condition that sometimes exists

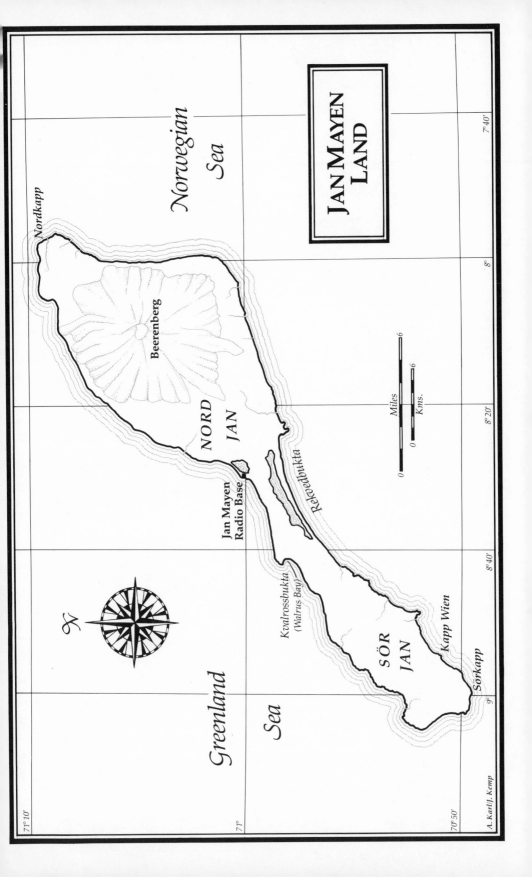

JAN MAYEN LAND

Nordkapp

Norwegian Sea

Beerenberg

NORD JAN

Jan Mayen Radio Base

Rekvedbukta

Kvalrossbukta (Walrus Bay)

SÖR JAN

Kapp Wien

Sörkapp

Greenland Sea

N

Miles

Kms.

0   6

0   6

71°10'

71°

70°50'

7°40'

8°

8°20'

8°40'

9°

A. Karl J. Kemp

around mountains or cliffs. I could go to MIT for a month's course in aerology and still not understand the true causes of this phenomenon. It has to do with expansion and cooling, updrafts and downdrafts. All I know is when the foehn wind hits, you become a believer quickly. More accurately, you become a little putz, and you hope the rabbinate has not consigned you to oblivion.

With only a number four jib, we slogged to weather, hoping to reach a lee on the western shore. Initially, I could not understand what was hitting us; it was so intensive from the southeast and yet the sea was not rough. That was the real clue that the wind was local. It swirled in gusts around the great mountain glacier, but finally, as we moved within the lee of the mountain, it diminished to more manageable proportions.

As I said, there are no harbors at Jan Mayen, none at all, only indentations in the coastline and few of those. But what a coastline! I have never seen one more inhospitable. No wonder Major Tilman lost his cutter *Mischief* on this coast. That would have been easy to do. Passing west to east around the south cape in limited visibility, she had bounced on the bricks and was later beached on the east coast, where ice entrapped her and sealed her fate.

Even on the leeward side of Beerenberg the wind was whistling. It was still no soldier's breeze! Working southwest along the coast, we came to what appeared to be a possible anchorage in a bight called Kvalrossbukta (Walrus Bay). As long as the wind remained east of south, this bight would offer reasonable protection. Its location in the middle of the island latitudinally, where land was relatively low, suggested a lower probability of blow-me-downs. This was corroborated by the British Admiralty *Arctic Pilot*, which noted that Kvalrossbukta is considered by Norwegians to afford the best summer anchorage in Jan Mayen. Summer anchorage! What, I wondered, would they recommend for a winter anchorage? The *Arctic Pilot* went on to say that in 1929 the Cambridge expedition in the *Heimland* anchored there and found at least six whale cookeries and a beach strewn with whalebone. Admiralty publications, like those of our own Hydrographic Office, are very useful, but sometimes they amuse me with their terseness and understatement. Whoever wrote the part about a summer anchorage must have been an armchair administrative assistant in London who had no idea that Jan Mayen was completely ice-locked in the winter!

The base radio people practically monitored our breathing as we sought a safe anchorage. After all, we were a visitor out of the blue and our being the first American yacht ever to visit probably struck them as an excuse to celebrate, that is, to the extent that celibates can celebrate. When they sighted Diana, I bet the testosterone count on Jan Mayen took a sudden jump.

We must have spent at least a half-hour nosing around the bay, recording the depths and trying to determine the safest place to drop the plow anchor. Meanwhile a detail from the base, which was located on the opposite side of the island, had driven down to the beach in a Land Rover to assist us. They had a radio in the jeep tuned to channel 16 so they could hear our conversation with the base. They must have wondered what was taking us so long to drop anchor. Our problem was that we didn't know the waters, and the written information was skimpy. When we did anchor, I wanted to make damn sure *Reindeer* stayed put. The bottom, judging from the surrounding beach, was probably basaltic sand, but we didn't know its true configuration or consistency. I had no cruising guide to the Jan Mayen coast.

When we dropped the hook, we made certain to have twenty-five feet of chain attached to the shank of the anchor and then about two hundred feet of one-inch nylon anchor line. On top of that, we slid a twenty-pound lead weight down the nylon rode to act as a cushion against a sudden sea surge and to lower the effective angle of the entire anchor line. This has the same effect as letting out more scope, which is not always possible in a tight anchorage or a place where the bottom drops off steeply.

By the time we completed the anchoring detail it was 2100, and we all were pooped. I radioed that we would eat supper aboard and get a good night's sleep, then come ashore in the morning. They understood and invited us for lunch the next day. Then we went below to enjoy steak Diana, she having insisted it was her turn to be chef.

What a tough, long day! It called for a drink but the best we could muster was three beers — the tastiest half-glass of lager that I had ever consumed — as we lay safely at anchor in Walrus Bay, the site of the earliest Dutch whaling settlement in the first part of the seventeenth century.

While Henry Hudson is said to have sighted Jan Mayen in 1607, a

Facing page: Reindeer *at solitary anchor in a bight on the west coast of Jan Mayen* (Stockton N. Smith)

Dutch whaling captain called Jan Jacobsz May landed on the island in 1614 and claimed territorial rights for his country. For thirty years or more, a summer whaling station flourished at Walrus Bay until the whales got wise and altered their pattern. Whaling then petered out, and to this day the whale fishery has been nonexistent around the island.

Before hitting the sack and while enjoying Cromwell's last bottle of South African wine, which had come all the way from latitude 34 S., we talked about whales. Orlin, who had secretly studied the cetacea, was obviously one up on the rest of us. However, Diana let slip out at a carefully controlled rate her fairly impressive knowledge of the subject, and Jim Demarest was so good he always used Latin terms to express himself. We were soon involved in a game of one-upmanship on the subject of whales.

There were only three I could positively identify: a pilot, a killer, and a humpback. Actually, I could probably also identify a gray from its mottled skin that looks like camouflage. The killer whale I will never forget from the sighting off Labrador. Also, I have been cruising right alongside a mother finback and her calf in Drake Passage in the Virgins, but I really could not tell the difference between a finback and a sei whale. I have also seen the tusk of a narwhal off Kap Ferrel, but that is about the limit of my knowledge. I have never cracked a book on the subject, and in that respect I knew I was at a disadvantage with Orlin and Jim and most probably also Diana.

The three of them played out their knowledge to the audience of the two boys. Late in the conversation I made my entry, making sure to begin only with questions for which I knew they had no answer, but about which I was certain they would argue. Very shortly my questions had the distinct ring of authenticity; so much so that I began to detect their yearning for some more information from me.

"I wonder if you can tell which of the baleens has two spouts," I asked studiously, not even knowing a baleen had dual spouts. That started an immediate argument between Diana and Orlin on the answer, which cast some doubt on both of them but put me in the unassailable position of seeming to know a baleen did have two spouts.

My follow-up was another ploy: "We all know about krill," I said, "but just how many species of planktonic crustacea do you suppose there are?" I put crustacean into the Latin form to sound more professorial, and I could see Stocky's eyes pop out. He hadn't studied Latin since prep school, so he cast no doubt at all on my mixed phraseology. Orlin stuttered and stammered; Jim immediately qualified himself as a non-scholar on other than the geology aspects of oceanography; and Diana merely said she had no idea.

Then, after an appropriate pause indicating the opposition had folded, I told them the one thing I did know (I had read it in the *National Geographic*), which was the migratory habit of the great humpback. There was utter silence as I described this. All I said, in fact, was that they went from the South Atlantic to the North Atlantic, passing within fifty miles of Bermuda. Then I suggested we'd better get to sleep, leaving the impression that humpback migratory patterns were only the tip of the iceberg of my knowledge of whales. Everyone needed sleep and no one questioned the idea to end the conversation on that note. Months later I was much amused when Diana asked me how I knew so much about whales!

The next day we did not arise 'til ten o'clock, and after a light break-fast I contacted our waiting hosts on the VHF. Stocky and Orlin rowed ashore in the dinghy, but as they got to the beach they were toppled over by a big wave, which drenched them. On seeing this, the local boys graciously launched their motor lifeboat, and we transferred from *Rein-deer* to the dinghy to the lifeboat. Because of the continued swells that rolled into Walrus Bay, we preferred not to have the lifeboat, which was high-sided and made of steel, come alongside the painted hull of *Reindeer*. We transferred to the dinghy first. When I plopped into the dinghy my cap fell into the water, but otherwise all went easily. We made it from the dinghy to the lifeboat to the beach. And what a beach! All black sand with plenty of remnants of the Dutch activity of the late 1500s, another reminder of the preservative qualities of the Arctic. We could see whalebones all over the beach and a mass grave with a cross (presumably the original cross has been renewed), marking remains of Dutch whaling men who had died there. It is not easy to dig in rock, so the grave consists of a pile of stones, and Orlin, impelled by his usual curiosity, later found human bones protruding from the rocks, which the garrison had moved up the beach to make room for a small oil storage tank.

Our hosts drove us to the base, where we were shown to the shower

Mass grave site on Jan Mayen beach (Orlin Donaldson)

Lifeboat on the rugged coast of Jan Mayen (Orlin Donaldson)

room and the sauna bath. While I was in the sauna I wore my cap so that it could also bake out after its dunking. Orlin later made a sketch of me, sitting in the sauna, bare but for a cap, and presented this to me at a dinner party in February.

After washing up, the crew were entertained in the recreation room prior to lunch. During this time the commandant, a lieutenant colonel in the Norwegian Signal Corps named Colonel Fure, told me how pleased they all were that an American pleasure boat, the first in their records, had stopped at this lonely outpost. He described his communications mission, and we exchanged stories of our respective backgrounds. The colonel offered me souvenirs, including a clip of .30 caliber ammunition that came from a Nazi warplane downed at Jan Mayen during the war. I appreciated his kindness, but turned down this gift because I knew it had much greater meaning to him. We discussed his life and that of his garrison of some thirty radio and loran people, whose pay was nontaxable and whose tour of duty was usually one or two years. Just recently they had been granted permission to have their wives visit for the grand total of four hours every six months, flying on the supply plane, which in good weather would return to the mainland at Trondheim on the same day.

Fure and I then turned to the subject of the Russians. I could tell that he knew a little bit about the cold war, enough to know that there was more to it than met the eye. Suddenly he leaned over and pulled out of his footlocker a board which had the name of an American town (near a military base) stenciled on it in English. He said he had found several pieces of a crate in the highlands near the South Cape while out hiking. He could tell that at least one man had landed there, and from the looks of the area it was no accident. Whoever the intruder was, he hadn't considered it desirable to inform the commanding officer. I recognized the markings immediately as the address of a current American military base to which the crate had been consigned by the manufacturer, but I didn't think it was my business to share this knowledge with him.

"How do you know it's not Russian?" I asked him.

"Because it's in English," he said.

I thought for a moment. "Look," I told him, "if the Russians wanted to cover their tracks, don't you think they might leave American markings to throw you off?"

While the young colonel had not thought of that, he immediately acknowledged the possibility, and I could see lines etched in his face. While he cogitated on that idea, I mulled over what our boys were up to. My guess was ASW (antisubmarine warfare), but I was in the dark too. Both of us emerged from his quarters like teenagers from a spy movie. The unknown is always bigger and more powerful than that which is visible. Hell, I know Russian subs have a signature that our side can detect by its sound. My guess — and it's only a guess — is that we have listening devices planted all over arctic waters. It wouldn't surprise me to find out that our boys had "wired" Jan Mayen. Again, only a conjecture, but I wasn't going to tell that to the colonel.

While I was talking with the C.O., other members of the crew were inspecting various parts of the base, including the desalinization plant, where fresh water is made from seawater. I joined them in time to see the radio and loran equipment. Most of their electronic equipment, if not all, was American. Certain areas were apparently off limits, but I didn't regard this as unusual.

After our tour we were ushered into the mess hall for a splendid luncheon of hors d'oeuvres, cold cuts, fruit and cheese, and almost anything one would want. A miniature American flag placed in the middle of the serving table added a nice touch and told us how they felt more than any words they could say. After lunch we relaxed in the recreation room and exchanged stories with those off-duty men who could speak English.

In the afternoon we took more tours. Especially interesting was the topography and texture of the landscape. We were told that at one point the U.S. Space Agency considered Jan Mayen as a training ground for the astronauts headed for the moon. Certainly the surface of the island bore a close resemblance to those pictures sent back from the moon by the astronauts. The cliffs were black basaltic rock, but in the higher parts the rock was covered by ice and snow year-round. We could see intrusions of granite on the cliffs, along with some moss and a great deal of lichen. From mid-November to mid-April the island is completely surrounded by ice and covered by snow. In winter it must be fierce. During those months polar bears are frequent visitors, along with arctic foxes. Both are protected under Norwegian law.

Jan Mayen can be divided into three separate parts: Beerenberg, by far the largest, occupies the northern part. The central part is the lowest and only inhabitable area. The southern part, where Colonel Fure had found evidence of uninvited visitors, is highland with lakes and very rough terrain. Beerenberg, which has a crater over one mile in diameter, dominates Jan Mayen. The base of the mountain has a circumference of thirty miles, and because it's completely covered by glacier looks from a distance like an enormous cumulus cloud. Geologists say that Jan Mayen Land is relatively young, perhaps twelve to fifteen thousand years old. In 1970, the volcano erupted and added three square kilometers of new land on the northeast side. Since eruption is always a potential occurrence, one of the functions at the base is to monitor the volcano seismologically, purely for safety purposes. During the last eruption all the men were safely evacuated from the island until everything quieted down. Since an earth tremor usually precedes an eruption, there has been ample time (so far, at least) to remove all hands from danger.

The island of Jan Mayen is without question the most remote, godforsaken piece of property I had ever seen. Its origin and history were largely a matter for conjecture, at least in geological terms, until the 1970 eruption. After that, scientists began to study its tectonic formation. There had been a description of volcanic activity on the island as early as 1558 in a treatise by two Venetians, Nicolo and Antonio Zeno. Scientists had completely discounted this book until the eruption of 1970, but subsequent investigations gave it credibility, along with reports of other volcanic activity in 1732 and 1818. The 1970 eruption was accompanied by an average of six hundred to eight hundred earthquakes between 20 September and 12 October of that year. This is an amazing level when compared with a maximum of ninety earthquakes in one day during a nonvolcanic earthquake swarm in January 1973.

According to several studies by scientists, the crustal structure and volcanic petrology of Jan Mayen is a close analog to that of the Westmann Islands, which we had visited, south of Iceland. Having seen what happened at Heimaey and also earlier the movies of the fiery birth of the island of Surtsey, both in the Westmann Islands, I could only wince at the thought of being on Jan Mayen during one of those earthquake swarms. Favorable tax treatment would be hardly sufficient inducement for me to be resident, even if they put a meter with a Richter scale outside my living room window.

After all our sight-seeing, it was nearly suppertime, and our hosts suggested we stay for supper and depart afterward. Thus we joined them for another meal, this one featuring whale meat for a main course. I thought it tasted something like deer; it certainly was not fishy. All the food is brought by plane from the Norwegian mainland, while mail is normally dropped by air from Iceland. At the conclusion of the meal our hosts insisted on giving us fresh fruit and other goodies to replenish our larder for the four-hundred-mile trip down to Iceland.

The Norwegians were perfect hosts. They drove us to the beach at Walrus Bay and cranked up the air-cooled engine in the motor whaleboat, which rested in her cradle atop a tractor-trailer combination. We all jumped into the lifeboat, including one of their pet huskies, who apparently was quite used to such rides. They launched us into the water and motored out to *Reindeer,* which we boarded while they stood by to see us off.

Cromwell went forward to winch in our plow anchor, which was solidly dug into the bottom, while the rest of our crew stood by, singing the "Song of the Volga Boatmen." When the anchor was aweigh, the songsters switched to "Ivan Skavinsky Skivar" and followed that with "The Whiffenpoof Song," although no Yalemen were present to give it authenticity. Meanwhile, as we hoisted our sails and *Reindeer* quickly accelerated toward open water, hard on the wind, all hands waved goodbye to our hosts. We all regretted leaving Jan Mayen Land. It had been a splendid visit, in fact one of the highlights of the whole trip and totally unanticipated.

Working our way out of the bay, we short-tacked along the shore and thus got a close look at the steep rock walls of the west coast. The colors were striking: rust and green against a black background, fringed on the top by patches of snow. The rust color came presumably from outcroppings of iron oxide, and the green was from lichen and moss. The cliffs were alive with birds, and the evening sun poured light on a scene that defies description. At the same time the massive glacier of Beerenberg looked like Fujiyama in the background.

Reindeer beat to windward until she weathered the last part of the South Cape and was well on her way to Iceland, some four hundred miles to the south. Only three hundred miles to the west was Scoresby

Farewell at Jan Mayen (Diana Russell)

Sound, the largest fjord in the world, located at the midpoint of Greenland's east coast. Tilman tried to get there but was frustrated in his attempt by the pack ice. No yachtsman I have ever heard of has put in there, although it could be done if a long spell of westerly wind broke up the pack long enough for a vessel to cut through. Ships have been there and lives have been lost, especially when a sudden shift in wind to the east pushed the pack on to the coast and trapped the unwary.

Scoresby Sound got its name in 1822 when the Scoresbys, father and son, arrived there in the ship *Baffin of Liverpool*. The Scoresbys were whalers, and they had decided to combine exploration with the whale fishery, subordinating the former to the latter for economic reasons. Their ships were constructed specially for the arctic ice, so it was not considered a tragedy or even a great inconvenience to become beset in the ice. They just furled their sails and waited for the wind to shift.

Our situation was quite different. I didn't dare risk a quick detour to Scoresby Sound. The structure of *Reindeer* did not give us the impunity of the old whalers. *Reindeer* was built to race, not wallow in the ice! Our course was down Denmark Strait, and that would be adventure enough. While the east Greenland pack had been known to extend all the way out to Jan Mayen, this year we were in luck. There was no sign of ice except on the glacier or in the south highlands.

The first night out of Jan Mayen I had Diana Russell on my watch, and she was a great shipmate. Naturally I would take an occasional sideways glance at her with no special nautical thoughts in mind, but she didn't know that, so everything proceeded without complication. Although Diana works in the man's world of marine architects, there is no doubt of her gender. Her mother is just as attractive, and both are brains from Bryn Mawr. Mrs. Russell is part Czarist Russian, a Brahmin so to speak, and Mr. Russell is the second son of an English peer. Both are great fun. Mr. Russell's older brother, Lord Ampthill, made history in the House of Lords by supposedly fathering a child during World War II that, according to *Time* magazine, took twelve months to gestate. In other words, he was in the Army in France for twelve months prior to the birth. *Time,* as well as the British press, played up the big controversy that ensued on the death of Lord Ampthill. The law lords decided the title went to the wartime child. Whenever I asked Diana about that phenomenon she told me to shut up. On the evening watch, after I extracted all the skeletons from the Russell closet, Diana decided to be a smartass and ask me about my criminal career.

"Tell me," she said, "what was it like when you were in jail?"

"Fair turnabout, Diana; you heard about that?"

"Of course I heard about it. Something about an ice cream cone?"

"Yeh, that's right," I said, "I stopped to buy a cone on my way home from work. That was back in nineteen-sixty. When I left the Dairy Queen I made a U-turn that a local cop decided was reckless. He then pursued me with his light flashing. Since I had no idea I had committed an offense, I kept on driving until he got abreast and waved me over in what appeared to be a rage. That led to a contretemps which ended in a blow to my nose by his blackjack, which broke my nose bone, and then a counterattack by me."

I then elaborated on all the details, including the trial judge's ruling that had barred me from introducing testimony of the FBI, which had entered the case because of my civil rights complaint. I then described the two days I spent in jail before I appealed my case all the way to the U.S. Supreme Court, where it was reversed and sent back to the Supreme Court of Pennsylvania. The latter upset my conviction for simple assault, and the case was closed. There were some very bizarre elements in this case, and needless to say it taught me a lot about what goes on in some of the seamier sides of life and how the police themselves can be criminal and about the cause of crime, especially in the ghettoes of the cities.

One of the ironies of the case was that the lawyer who argued my side successfully before the U.S. Supreme Court was William T. Coleman, the former Secretary of Transportation in Ford's cabinet and a black, and the issue was a white man's civil rights. I told Diana that not every ice cream cone costs a quarter. This one cost $25,000.

"The funny thing," I told Diana, "was the touch football game."

"What do you mean?" Diana asked.

"Well, we inmates were playing touch football, which was not all that touch, if you know what I mean. Anyhow, I was blocking, and I guess I knocked a couple of guys on their respective fannies, and that earned me a place in an otherwise all-black backfield. And, by the way, those blacks were a hell of a sight more interesting than the whites in the pokey. They had a great sense of humor. Being in jail was just cops-and-robbers to them. They called me 'Navy,' because they heard on the radio some stuff about my football-playing days. But, to get back to the game, which was choose-up, I will never forget catching a touchdown pass from the black quarterback. They all looked at me as though I was one of their own and cheered. I had made the first team. Our quarterback was a bank robber, the left halfback was a pickpocket, and the right halfback was a rapist. I was the fullback!"

"Wow!" said Diana. "I wonder if I'm safe?"

Just then a whole school of porpoises joined us and we knocked off the tales of the past.

Reindeer steadily moved south toward Iceland, sometimes beating, sometimes reaching. On 12 August, Orlin secretly baked a cake and Dicky and Orlin made a feathered headdress to present to Stocky on his twenty-first birthday. On the headband they printed with a magic marker: "CHIEF OF THE FUGAWI." Stocky had earned this by dominating the navigator's seat and twirling the loran dials constantly. He would mumble unintelligible remarks about sky waves, master traces, slave traces, and blips, all language of loran, which is an acronym for

Long Range Aid to Navigation. We ate the last of our halibut steak, and Dicky broke out another bottle of South African wine, which he had hidden for this special occasion.

During this hitch the crew gradually became aware of a putrid odor that emanated from the area of Orlin's bunk. Orlin seemed impervious to the smell, much in the manner of someone with bad breath. Living in close quarters, one's nose gets very discriminating to all types of smell: diesel oil, gasoline, alcohol, bilge, icebox, and of course the head. But this smell defied the senses, and its location was even more puzzling. Finally in desperation Stocky located the source. Orlin, in his passion for exotic food, had put some dried fish in a stowage pocket next to his bunk, where tools are usually kept. So, what had started as a whispering campaign about Orlin suddenly erupted into confrontation. He had forgotten the fish, and his claim that it was still edible met solid opposition. The delicacy went unceremoniously overboard.

After many hours of steady sailing, the wind went light and the engine was necessary. We had plenty of fuel, so that was no problem. From 250 miles north of Iceland we reached the New York high seas operator on thirteen megaHertz and talked as clearly as though we were talking to someone next door. It was of some comfort that we could confer with people at home and with such ease. So often did we avail ourselves of this privilege that the New York operator began to ask us jokingly, "Oh, is that you, *Reindeer?* How is it up there in the ice?"

To make a successful connection, it was necessary to select the right frequency band, which varies with the time of day. Normally daytime requires higher frequencies than night. When calling the high seas operator on single-side-band radio, which on my set includes frequency bands in the four-, eight-, thirteen-, and seventeen-megaHertz frequencies, we would first speak to a technician, who helped select the optimum frequency for clear transmission. These high-frequency transmissions bounce off the ionosphere, and if the wrong frequency is used, the wave may skip New York but be perfectly clear in Miami, for instance. The selection very much depends on the time of day. We raised New York and Miami fairly readily, but for some strange reason never could get Britain or Norway, which were relatively close by.

After Stocky's birthday celebration Diana sighted Grimsey and the mountains of north Iceland. We had covered twelve hundred miles in a south sou'west direction and were now down to the Arctic Circle once again. On Friday, the thirteenth of August, we glided into the harbor of Siglufjördhur one day ahead of schedule. The town looked a bit down at the heels because of the seeming demise of the herring fishery, upon which a lot of the business of this small port depended. Fisherfolk are apt to be set in their ways and therefore slow to respond to a change in conditions. Siglufjördhur will prosper again, because of all the north coast harbors it is located closest to the sea.

I had allowed two days for crew change and restocking the boat with food, water, and fuel. Diana and Jim gathered their belongings and took off for Akureyri, a north coast town sixty miles away, from which they flew to Reykjavik and thence to New York. The newcomers would be Salley Norwood from Halifax and young Michael Ponce and Courtenay Jenkins, whose respective parents were vacationing in Maine. I had talked by radiotelephone with Michael's father and knew that the two boys were somewhere in Iceland. Salley Norwood, however, had not been heard from, but my wife told me by radio that she had left Halifax for Reykjavik.

We cleared Customs and Immigration and went about the business of restocking the victuals, but there was no sign of the new crew members. I called Stefan Arndal at the Telecommunications Center in Reykjavik, and he assured me the boys were on their way but were low on cash. That didn't accord with what Michael's father told me on the phone, so I suspected the boys were up to something or had gone on a spree. Before leaving Jan Mayen, we had sent word to Arndal that we were on schedule, but the Norwegian radioman, unbeknown to us, had wired that we were arriving in Reykjavik, not Siglufjördhur, and when Stefan, our prearranged contact man, heard that, he told Salley to sit tight in Reykjavik. She was bewildered by the change in plans, but, after staying an extra day at the Loftleider, wisely decided to fly north anyway. Salley rolled up to the dock at 1100 on Sunday, leaving only the two boys unaccounted for.

My nerves were a little frayed by concern for the next hitch, which would put us in ice-infested waters. Both Orlin and I felt we had to leave no later than 1700, or five in the afternoon. Yet I could not leave Ponce and Jenkins in Iceland, possibly without money. Finally at four o'clock Michael arrived at the dock in a police car. The gendarmes, it seemed, had Courtenay in jail for stealing a rented car. I talked to the chief, who was one and the same as the Customs officer, and we managed to get it straightened out. Jenkins, in whose name the car was rented, had signed a rental contract to return the car to Akureyri. My information is somewhat conjecture, because the boys gave us only a very sketchy story. Michael and Cort were so shocked by the price for renting a car that when they got to Siglufjördhur, they called the rental company in Akureyri and told them they were leaving the car in Siglufjördhur because it had broken down. Of course the rental agent smelled a rat and called the cops in Siglufjördhur, who promptly arrested them. While Corty was in jail trying various explanations, Michael went back to the car and pulled a wire out of the distributor in order to make Corty's story hold up.

When Michael got back to the boat, somehow I assumed all hands were on board, and we cast off the docking lines and proceeded out of the harbor. We had almost cleared the harbor entrance when I casually counted heads and discovered to my horror that Corty was missing. We turned around and picked him up at the dock, which was filled with onlookers much amused by our error. This time we sailed out for good, set watches, and headed for Denmark Strait, about whose danger only Orlin and I had any full understanding.

10

Denmark Strait

WITH FULL MAINSAIL and a number two genoa jib, *Reindeer* glided slowly westward into Denmark Strait, which separates Iceland from Greenland. We soon passed Horn, the last bit of land to port. It was the northwest tip of Iceland, which jutted out into a body of water that had a worse reputation for storms than the waters around Cape Horn of South America. Unlike those at Cape Horn, however, these waters were burdened with ice, no friend to mariners over the centuries. The wind was light and northerly. The sea was strangely calm, almost ominous.

This was the moment we had been planning for many months, and now with Denmark Strait before us, I was overtaken by uncertainty.

Even with the advice of experts behind me, this part of the trip would be dangerous. We had attained Spitsbergen, our northern goal, but now the job was to get home, by a route that promised all the challenge we could handle. Spitsbergen was a geological gem, Jan Mayen Land an impressive sight, but east Greenland — this was where we might match ourselves against nature's toughest elements.

Newfoundland was another sixteen hundred miles away, a long stretch back to familiar territory. For the first time on this long journey I didn't know what to expect. There was no way to be completely prepared. Recent reports were so conflicting, and history was the least reassuring. Worst of all, I kept thinking of what Jack Parkinson had told

Southern Greenland from the air (Diana Russell)

me, but I could not show this concern to my crew, not even Orlin, who had a lot of faith in me.

It was late August. Having reached latitude 80° -02′, north of Spitsbergen, 598 miles from the Pole, our forty-three-foot sloop had been farther north than any American sailboat in history, although at that moment I didn't realize it. I had allowed myself, or so I thought, sufficient self-satisfaction for sailing so near the North Pole, compensation enough for someone who four years earlier had been lying on his back in a hospital bed, quadriplegic. What now lay ahead precluded any further sentimentality.

We were now at a point thirteen hundred miles southwest of our northernmost probe, and now in late August it would get dark at night despite the fact that we were astride the Arctic Circle. It would be great if we could get through the ice to the Eskimo village of Angmagssalik and King Oscar's Haven on Greenland's east coast, as Captain Toft had so blithely indicated was possible. This settlement was unknown to the Vikings and wasn't discovered by the rest of the world until the late 1800s! More important, we wanted to get into Prins Christians Sund, a fjord farther south that could lead us through inside passages to

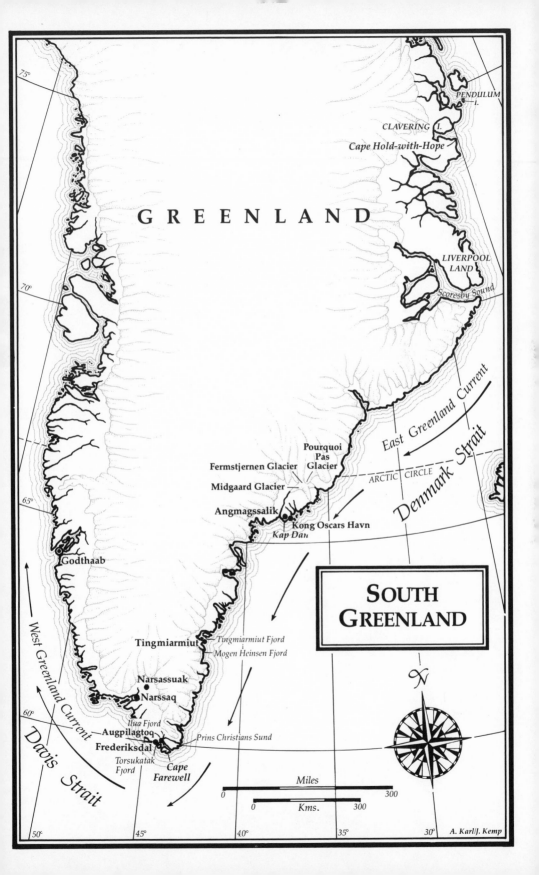

75°

PENDULUM I.

CLAVERING I.

Cape Hold-with-Hope

G R E E N L A N D

70°

LIVERPOOL LAND

Scoresby Sound

East Greenland Current

Pourquoi Pas Glacier

Fermstjernen Glacier

ARCTIC CIRCLE

Midgaard Glacier

Denmark Strait

65°

Angmagssalik

Kong Oscars Havn

Kap Dan

Godthaab

SOUTH GREENLAND

Tingmiarmiut

Tingmiarmiut Fjord

Mogen Heinsen Fjord

Narsassuak

N

Narssaq

West Greenland Current

60°

Ilua Fjord

Augpilagtoq

Prins Christians Sund

Frederiksdal

Torsukatak Fjord

Cape Farewell

Davis Strait

Miles

0   300

0   Kms.   300

50°   45°   40°   35°   30°

A. Karl/J. Kemp

*Sunset in Denmark Strait — East Greenland
pack ice (Orlin Donaldson)*
*Denmark Strait looking eastward from the
radio station at Prins Christians Sund,
showing the ice* Reindeer *has just
traversed (Stockton N. Smith)*

The Jan Mayen coast (Diana Russell)

The forbidding face of Mt. Beerenberg, Jan Mayer (Orlin Donaldson)

pursuers of the Royal Navy in that same war, before she was finally caught by the British fleet while trying to escape the trap?

I thought of the unfortunate fate of one of the founders of the Cruising Club of America, Bill Nutting, who in 1924 disappeared off Greenland; then Rockwell Kent's trip on *Direction* that was wrecked on the west coast of Greenland, and more recently Major Tilman's *Baroque*, wrecked and abandoned below Angmagssalik. The score for survival in Greenland of American yachts alone during the last fifty-two years had been three out of six. A dismal record. One would have expected better results, because they had approached from the west, where the coast is much less dangerous with less pack ice than that of the east. I felt like an Eighth Army tank commander throwing his men and equipment against Rommel, not knowing quite what was going to hit him but fairly certain that it would be something fierce. I not only had my son Stocky with me but also the son of one of my best friends, plus four other people for whom I was responsible. I worried for their sake as well as my own. Moreover, history was not on my side. No sailing yacht I had ever heard of made it through the east Greenland pack except for Major Tilman of Britain, and he was then promptly wrecked on uncharted rocks near Angmagssalik.

We were not, of course, bent on getting into the *Guinness Book*. But we knew that some of the greatest sights and experiences in the world were to be attained only at a certain risk. If we could do it, if we could get through to the ancient Viking settlements, we would have a hell of a thrill. If not, well, the trip was still worth it — assuming we could make it back with boat and crew intact, leaving the whole island well to starboard. They talk of leaving Cape Horn to port; I might talk of leaving Cape Farewell to starboard!

What we were up to was dicey, all right. Yet Tilman got through to Angmagssalik in 1974. Why couldn't we? Captain Toft in Copenhagen had said we might get through to Prins Christians Sund, although of course he thought we had a ninety-foot trawler! Anyway, Orlin had all that dope from NOAA. We could handle the ice, and what the hell, if it looked bad we could bag it and sail to St. Anthony, Newfoundland, thought I. Once more I began to hear the rhapsodies, not the dirges.

It was Orlin Donaldson's notion that we were retracing the Viking voyages of Erik the Red, his son Leif Erikson, and others. Thus we the Greenland settlements of the earliest Vikings on the southwest coast. That was the plan, but could we or should we execute it in view of the obvious hazards?

What lay ahead was ice, more ice than anyone could imagine — ice with wind, ice with fog, ice with night, ice with snow, ice above, ice below. We had already seen plenty of ice in and around Spitsbergen, but up there visibility had been good — no darkness at night at such high latitudes in midsummer — and the air and water temperatures had been well above freezing.

The Gulf Stream takes good care of Iceland, Norway, and Spitsbergen, but Greenland is less fortunate. It is the world's largest island, and it's nearly surrounded by ice in the summer (except well up on the west coast) and, indeed, encased by it in the winter. The East Greenland Current runs south, bearing with it ice from the polar pack and huge icebergs calved from immense glaciers on the east coast. This current rounds the southern tip of Greenland, Cape Farewell, and joins the north-going West Greenland Current. Those icebergs not blown out to sea in summer when the ice is moving make the full passage along both coasts before drifting westward into the Labrador Current, which then carries them south along the Labrador and Newfoundland coasts. The northern part of the west coast of Greenland is normally ice-free in summer, but that was a long way from our location. In all the world only Antarctica can match Greenland for heavy concentrations of ice.

Of course we knew this and were well equipped. We could handle storms, fog, and freezing temperatures. As long as our radar worked, we didn't even mind the big icebergs. But the low-lying pack ice was a horse of a different color. It could trap you; it could carry you; it could crush you. Despite all my research on ice conditions, I really had no concept of the extent of the ice off this coast.

It was late afternoon and the sky was gray. I took another apprehensive glance at the northwest coast of Iceland. Could this be the same spot that the English explorer Tilman described as being so vindictive to sailors such as he who ventured into these waters? Could this be the same Denmark Strait that Jack Parkinson had described as a bloody cauldron of storm, a place renowned for howling gales, heavy and confused seas, as well as ever-present ice in almost every dimension? And wasn't this exactly where the German battleship *Bismarck* eluded her

*Probing the East Greenland pack. Salley
Norwood on the foredeck (Orlin Donaldson)*

*Overleaf: Impenetrable pack close to East Greenland
coast. Mountains dimly visible in the
background (Orlin Donaldson)*

Sundog in East Greenland (Orlin Donaldson)

*Facing page: Pack ice drifting into Prins Christians
Sund, Greenland (Orlin Donaldson)*

*Danish radio/loran technician showing us
the ruins at Herjolfnes, Greenland
(Orlin Donaldson)*

would in our own private way upstage all the celebrants of America's two hundredth birthday by honoring the first millennium of the Viking discovery of North America.

I couldn't help thinking about the Vikings as we neared the path of their seaborne migration. What guts they had! Here I was, nearly a thousand years later, with all sorts of contraptions of modern man, yet full of fear. They must have been scared, too, even the toughest of them. The thought of those intrepid Norsemen quaking in their primitive boats prompted me to call the crew together in the cockpit for a pep talk.

"I hope you people realize where we are," I said. "Those releases you signed back home were designed for just this body of water. We can expect horrendous weather. I don't know about the ice. The reports are conflicting. As for satellite reports, forget 'em. Satellites can't see through cloud cover, and they say it's been raining for three weeks in Denmark Strait."

I had heard a report that the ice was light and scattered, so I didn't know whether to believe the Icelandic Coast Guard's warning about solid pack all the way to Cape Farewell. I added, "I guess we'll have to look for ourselves." Then there was a long silence. I wondered if I had scared them. I wanted them wary but not scared. It was an uncomfortable moment.

Orlin finally broke the silence. "Maybe we'll run into a fishing boat that will know," he said.

"Yeah, and maybe Angmagssalik Radio will tell us," I replied.

"In any event, I want everyone to wear a safety belt while on deck. I don't care what the wind is doing. The only way to survive in this cold water is to stay aboard."

On the chart, the fjords of southern Greenland looked fantastic, and they made one really fear ice slides, even though Captain Toft had assured me that these shouldn't occur at this time of year. What's more, Cape Farewell, the alternative route, was no bargain; as late as 1959 a brand new Danish passenger ship went down with all hands off Cape Farewell in a storm. So Prince or *Prins,* sound or *sund,* we were coming.

We had taken that terrific pounding in four gales in June on our way north to Iceland, so I felt sure we could survive the expected storms in the strait. If it were to blow like mad, we could shorten sail. Nothing is so short as bare poles, and if it came to that we could heave-to and go below, leaving a mate on watch. It was snug below with charcoal burning in the fireplace and plenty of kerosene for the stove. Our food supply was quite adequate, and we had an oversupply of cooks or gourmet chefs, as they preferred to be regarded. There were seven of us deployed on two watches.

On this segment my watchmates were Salley Norwood and young Michael Ponce. Salley was fifty-four, lived in Halifax, and came from a sailing family. I met her back in '57, the year my boat *Galliard* won the Halifax Race, but I never really got to know her until we met in 1971 in a Newfoundland fjord called Avirons Bay. Through mutual friends Salley became interested in this trip, which was lucky for me, for she was very able in all categories, including especially navigation. She and Orlin were the only two other than myself who had studied some history and thus were well prepared, or at least as prepared as one can get.

Salley came by her nautical skills quite naturally. Her late father, Colonel Jack MacKeen, was an avid sailor. Their home was on the lovely Northwest Arm, right opposite the headquarters of the Royal Nova Scotia Yacht Squadron. In recent years Salley had cruised in the Hebrides, Scotland, and even had navigated a boat to Bermuda and back. Sailing was second nature to her. Also she had a very pleasant way of getting people to do what they should be doing. If young Michael were not in his safety harness, Salley would say "Michael, darling, I'm fond of those omelettes you make. I don't want you to go overboard. Don't you think you better put on your safety belt?" Michael, who actually was a professional cook, would comply immediately. Salley had the same touch with all of us, but the kids were in the palms of her hands. What an asset she was!

Orlin had accumulated so many facts from his study of the Arctic that when he dropped names, the boys thought it was a pure snow job. None of the youngsters, for instance, knew much about the refraction anomalies so typical of the far north. Stocky and I, of course, remembered the inverted images seen at great distances off Labrador in 1974. We also remembered ice blink — the mirage that looked like a wall of ice very near us but turned out to be pack ice much farther away than it seemed.

Of course I remembered Scoresby's account. One evening during our passage toward Greenland, I saw huge mountains to the north and was not surprised that the chart showed these mountains to be 175 miles north of our position! We were seeing the mountains of ten, eleven, and twelve thousand feet in the central east coast, known to explorers as the Fjord Region. This is the highest part of the coast, characterized by the largest glaciers outside Antarctica and by the very largest fjords in the world, the largest being Scoresby Sund. The rock on that part of the coast that isn't covered by snow is mostly basaltic from prehistoric volcanic activity. In the far north the coastline is not as mountainous, consisting more of sedimentary formations all the way to Peary Land at the top. The southern part of the east coast is also starkly rugged. It is composed mostly of granite and granitic gneiss, believed by geologists to be the oldest on the earth's surface. Interior Greenland is entirely covered by the ice cap, which has an average thickness on the order of eleven thousand feet.

We had a ton of charts on *Reindeer*. Keeping them orderly and in a place where they could be quickly consulted was not easy, but the charts of Greenland were simple to identify. They were the ones without soundings! There were literally dozens of fjords and sounds that were uncharted.

Prins Christians Sund had one line of soundings down the middle and Ilua Fjord and Torsurkatak Fjord, both of which we had to pass through, had none. These were the first charts we had ever seen where whole areas were blank — no soundings at all. That meant no surveys. It dawned on us you couldn't survey waters impossible to reach by vessel. Soundings aren't made from air. Very few, if any, of the fjords of the coast of east Greenland have been surveyed, yet we were trying to sail into them.

Likewise, no anchorages were indicated on these charts. Stocky tried to imply that the Navy had their own charts for their purposes, which he declined to specify. Who was he trying to kid? I knew he meant submarines, but I also knew they hadn't turned over any classified documents on these waters to a tyro in the NROTC like him. The paucity of anchorages was characteristic of all of Greenland.

This just wasn't anchoring country. Come to think of it, Sam Allen and Rockwell Kent had smashed up the sloop *Direction* on the rocks of the west coast during a storm when their anchor wouldn't hold. In his account of his trip, Sam Allen mentioned that his Danish host at Narsak described a trip he made to the east coast as thrilling — "thrilling because only half the ships that go ever come back." Later I had reason to regard that as one of the more Delphic utterances I had ever heard! If Stocky's purpose in pointing out such hazards was to put me on edge, he needn't have bothered. I'd been on edge since the coast of Iceland had gone down over the horizon.

The smoothness of the sea and the light wind just didn't add up; I was mystified. While standing in the cockpit I started to hear Jack Parkinson's words: "You'll have your head handed to you" and "You'll have ice water at your crotch in no time flat." Instinctively I asked someone to pump the bilge and I riveted my attention to the jagged ice in the distance ahead. Jack was right there in the cockpit in spirit and was getting a big kick out of being there.

Back in 1972, Parkinson had called me on the phone when I was in the hospital to ask me to ride a new jumper he had bought in England. I couldn't believe it; he was asking an oaf like me to be his jockey at Cheltenham or some place like that. It wasn't very considerate of his horse, and it was surely no way to win a race, but it was pure Parkinson. He was a sentimental guy. After I told him over the phone that I was temporarily incapacitated (actually a nurse had to hold the damn phone to my ear because they hadn't yet operated and I was still a mess), he sent me as a present a copy of a book he had written called *Yarns for Davey Jones*. On the inside flap he wrote: "To Newbold Smith-Reindeer from Jack-Winnie of Bourne" (his yawl).

Jack was killed in an accident not long after I got out of the hospital. I was unable to attend his funeral on Long Island, but my friends who were there told me the recessional hymn was "Roll Out the Barrel." That couldn't have been a more fitting choice. The clergyman probably gagged, but Jack must have loved it.

Anyway, while Jack's spirit was with me we both relished the beauty of the scene, pinching ourselves for just being there. But I still wondered why in hell it was so calm. This wasn't how he described it in USS *Bainbridge* when she was looking for *Bismarck* or running before gigantic seas and a 110-knot wind trying to survive convoy duty. Before I could ascribe this weather to clean living on my part I heard a voice whispering, "Just you wait, my boy."

We kept working westward and a little to the south, hoping to get to Angmagssalik, which now numbered some 750 citizens. Stocky and I both talked to Angmagssalik Radio on the AM band and were given an

Enormous East Greenland icebergs. The 11,000-foot mountains in the background are 175 miles distant (Orlin Donaldson)

ice report that was very discouraging. According to their information, the pack ice strung all the way down the coast. They knew of no open leads. This report was hard to believe at first. It certainly differed from what Icelandic Coast Guard had said, so I was skeptical, but of course it proved to be accurate. Our radarscope showed bergs at the exact spots where they were reported. Only a fool would push farther west at that latitude. We were now starting to encounter scattered drift ice, and with darkness coming I decided to abandon our attempt that day to get through the pack. Angmagssalik Radio suggested we try Tingmiarmiut, which was a radio outpost down the coast but north of Prins Christians Sund. For the second time since leaving the States, we hove-to.

Before darkness we sighted on our starboard hand the biggest icebergs I had ever seen. Some of them were well over a mile long and 300 feet high. Beyond them were the huge mountains of Schweizer Land and Mt. Forel — 11,200 feet — and 175 miles from our position as obtained by loran! We were looking at glaciers with names like *Pourquoi Pas*, *Fermstjernen*, and *Midgaard*. They dwarfed anything I'd ever seen from the water in my life. To the west was a barrier of ice with many tempting traps, culs-de-sac galore. We were just south of Cape Dan. One mistaken notion that governed my thinking that day was that if we could somehow break through the pack, we would have smooth going the rest of the way down the inside passage to Prins Christians Sund. This was my inland waterway syndrome! In retrospect I'm sure I got that idea from Toft, and on this occasion it was a mistake. Fortunately, Stocky plotted all the ice that was reported on the radio, and he prevailed on me to give up this false notion. We decided to alter course to the south and go for Tingmiarmiut Fjord.

Before turning in that evening, Michael called me on deck for a look at the aurora. What a sight! Never had I seen such lights dancing in the sky. I knew it was another arctic phenomenon, but I had had no idea of its beauty. No wonder the heathens worshipped the gods of nature over the centuries.

The next day we ran into three big Russian trawlers, and I managed to speak on VHF to the radioman on one. His English was limited, and I could get no useful information out of him. Soon the wind veered to northwest. Visibility was good, but again the pack ice forced us to alter course to the southeast into open water. We were making a sawtooth course to the south as we tried unsuccessfully to get into the coast, while at night and back out at sea we would heave-to and wait for dawn. Our course from Cape Dan to Tingmiarmiut was strikingly similar to that of Nansen in his drift on the floes. Soon the wind hauled to northeast and we set a chute for a while. Imagine, I thought to myself, setting a chute in Denmark Strait! I know guys who just wouldn't believe that, but out in open water, as long as visibility was good, it was safe.

Then for the first time the wind started to pick up. I was on watch with Michael, but Stocky and Courtenay were also on deck admiring their handiwork — getting the chute set and pulling. We were up to eight knots, just slicing through the sea. All hands, at least those awake, must have had a feeling of power. It wasn't their power, of course, but they had harnessed it, so they had a stake in it. I looked back, and whitecaps began to appear all over the water. The sky had darkened. That was enough for me.

"Okay," I shouted, "let's douse the chute."

"Aw, Dad, we're going great. Nothing to worry about," said Stocky.

"Get it down," I responded; "this is no race."

I was a bit impatient, but then, I knew more about the Strait of Denmark than he did, and that wasn't saying much. Cort and Stocky got the spinnaker down with Michael's help. They brought it in under the blanket of the mainsail and quickly bagged it and stowed it in the forepeak. All the while the wind was piping up and the sea was building. I was quite prepared to tack downwind to keep up speed, but the knotmeter was now reading 8.5 knots even without any headsail. Ordinarily, when the wind direction is dead astern without a spinnaker, it is obligatory to steer up to a broad reach to get decent boat speed. That's because downwind the mainsail tends to blanket the jib, whereas with a spinnaker you hold its tack out on the boom so it gets clear air. At this point, however, this was all academic; we were now doing nine knots with just the main. Again I became concerned and ordered a double reef be put in the main. We altered course closer to the wind and tied in the reef quickly and easily. Then Stocky and Jenkins went below for a rest. It was darker both from cloud cover and the lateness of the afternoon. Michael had the helm and steered pretty well under difficult conditions. The boat had a natural tendency to round up, so he had to concentrate. The wind was about force 8 and we were still doing nine knots.

I was cold and a little hungry, so Michael went down to brew up some tea, while I took over the wheel. Suddenly, a huge dark object loomed directly ahead. It looked like an island. Could my navigation be that far off? Were the compasses screwy? We were on the starboard jibe and I swerved left to miss the rock, in so doing almost jibing. We had rigged a preventer on the boom and that saved me from possible damage or wild jibe. We just missed the rock, but it wasn't a rock; it was a huge basking shark lolling on the surface! That dumb fish didn't know what a bellyache he just escaped. Likewise, I don't know what sort of damage he might have done to our hull. He must have been thirty feet long, although the guys below wouldn't believe me. The shark woke up and submerged before anyone got up on deck to see him.

We continued the downwind roller coaster, but along about 1800, seven hours after it had piped up, the wind died down. After the squall, we again edged into the coast toward Tingmiarmiut, which was then only thirty-five miles to the west. Visibility was erratic, but before dark we were only ten miles offshore and could see the awesome mountains and glaciers beyond the pack ice in the foreground.

Thinking back, one of my many impressions of the east Greenland coast that day was the formation of birds sitting on flat-topped or tabular icebergs. In one instance, I saw two lines of murres standing stark still like the corps de ballet in *La Bayadère,* while one murre in the middle, perhaps named Nureyev or Baryshnikov, danced a solo number. Then, suddenly, as *Reindeer* neared the scene, the whole colony rose off the iceberg in perfect synchronism. The angles and distance between dancers didn't vary an inch, both in the ballet on the berg and in the flight thereafter. Also, the multivaried ice formations and the mountain peaks in the distance had a symmetry that is hard to imagine. The many shapes, even when asymmetrical, had artistic asymmetry. In the fleeting minutes when east Greenland was visible, I saw enough to know of no equal in grandeur in the world, at least that I had ever seen or heard of, but boy, what work to see it! Then Orlin spotted a sun dog, which is a phenomenal elliptical image around a small berg, and he was quick to get a snapshot of it. I was below at the time, but he assured me we would see it later on film, and we did. It was like a giant halo. I had never even heard of it, but old Orlin knew it right away. Another example of his keen preparation.

We worked our way westward in a narrow lead, using the main and motor. The wind was almost dead calm. Jagged rock, four thousand feet high, was clearly visible beyond the ice ahead. For some reason I was still obsessed by the theory that open water was just ahead, that the coast had an "inland waterway." My theory was based on prevailing wind and the configuration of the rugged coastline. I was wrong, dead wrong. Soon we were in a cul-de-sac and night was rapidly approaching. Ice was all around us, some of it higher than our mast. For the first time I was really uptight. I grabbed the wheel from Dicky and did a 180° turn. It was so narrow I had to back down in order to turn around without bumping solid ice. I sent Jenkins to the pulpit to watch for bergy bits and powered back out of the pack as fast as possible. We threw out a sea anchor and hove-to in open water as soon as we got there.

At 0500 we awoke to the sound of a Minke whale swooshing through the surface of the water in an otherwise totally silent universe. It was eerie; we could see the rugged coast but the pack ice was unbroken, although full of false leads. This was now 61° 28′ north and 41° 55′ west. Again that afternoon we were trapped in another cul-de-sac. This time for a few minutes I thought it was curtains. I had been paying too much attention to seals and birds on the ice and not minding my *p*'s and *q*'s. We retreated eastward and out into clear water, where a Canadian trawler suddenly hove into view. I had a long talk with the captain, who said the ice was solid all the way to Cape Farewell. He said it was impossible to break through the pack.

"Better go around Cape Farewell," he said in a nice way, not wanting to see us take chances, "but give it wide berth."

By then I reckoned we knew the ice environment as well as anybody, and since it was not blowing I resolved to give it one more go the next day. It seemed that the solid pack was running in lines from northwest to southeast, like massive rock jetties jutting out obliquely from the shore. This was approximately the area where both Nansen and Holm had recorded unusual current patterns, possibly with eddies in different directions. Strange, I thought to myself, the never-ending way of nature. I must be seeing the exact same conditions that confronted Nansen and Holm a century ago, not to mention the Norse, Danes, Dutch, and British of three and four centuries earlier.

For the third straight night, and the fourth night in Denmark Strait, we hove-to. Before securing for the evening, we took bearings on various bergs, for which we wrote descriptions. To the southwest was a Chinese Wall, some parts of which were yellow, as though dogs had urinated on the snow. It had been cold ever since entering this current, which bears so much polar ice. Both air and water were below freezing at all times, except in the direct rays of the sun. Icicles had formed on our rigging and tell tales. Courtenay Jenkins, whose bizarre garb earned him the nickname of "Elvis," had an icicle hanging from his earmuff! Keeping warm was a continual concern, and one of our better devices for that was the chicken-wire basket that Orlin rigged in the engine box, where we put our gloves and mittens to warm when off-watch. The deck was often wet from spray or fog that condensed, and this would form a sheet of ice, making it slippery to move about. Down below, however, it was snug as a bug, with heat radiating from our charcoal fireplace. When the engine was running, the baseboard radiator also put out Btu's for our comfort. Fortunately the night was calm, and we didn't need to post a watch.

At 0530 on Saturday, 21 August, Corty woke us. Stocky twirled the loran dials, which put us thirty miles southeast of the entrance of Prins

Christians Sund. We had drifted a lot during the hours of dark, and our neighbors of the night, including the Chinese Wall, had disappeared. Considering the calmness of the night, this was a mystery. We had to believe our loran fix, of course, so we lost no time getting underway to the northwest, twisting and turning in all directions to avoid the pan ice and blocks, which covered approximately seven-tenths of the surface.

Then the visibility dropped, as fog rolled in. As we approached the coast the loran became useless. Our only remaining aid to navigation was radar, but Stocky and I found it difficult to match the radar trace with the coastline on the chart. Still we twisted and turned and plowed forward, sometimes actually pushing the ice away. We kept a man at the pulpit at all times, giving steering signals to the helmsman. It was tedious, but we were committed now; no going back. If we got beset here, I figured the current would carry us south and the ice would eventually release us in the vicinity of the skerries off Cape Farewell. Not inviting, but not hopeless.

After fruit and hot cocoa for breakfast, all hands stayed on deck. They didn't have to be told this was their finest hour. They knew it. It was amazing how everyone concentrated. No jokes, no small talk. Stocky kept at the radar. Salley and Courtenay alternated on the bow watch. Both looked more like skiers or mountaineers than sailors. All of us had on mittens and earmuffs. We kept steering for better leads and in so doing we really couldn't keep an accurate track of the course made good. I was hoping that Stocky could match up the picture on the radarscope with what we had on the chart, but he couldn't do it.

Cromwell, whose curly hair looked like a frosted Christmas tree, kept a vigilant eye on the pan ice. We sure as hell wanted to avoid submerged ledges of ice, and Dicky watched to port and starboard like a hawk. On several occasions we had to back down; the lead would close. Progress was slow, but we kept going. Lunch was crackers dipped in peanut butter. Who cared? We had come a long way down Denmark Strait, and at least it wasn't blowing. However, visibility was stinko, at times ten yards. It was eerie. There were no sounds. We were alone, but that at least meant we didn't have to worry about other fools out there. The foghorn was forgotten.

According to Stocky we were getting close to the mountainous coast, but he couldn't be sure where. It all looked the same on his scope. The limited visibility and the stillness surely fine-tuned the senses of everyone on deck. They could have heard a twig crack at a thousand yards.

Finally, at 1500 Stocky, constantly operating the radar for eight hours and looking at the cathode-ray oscilloscope, guided us into a bay with huge granite walls that were almost impossible to see through the fog. We couldn't identify where we were. It wasn't Prins Christians Sund. That we knew; it was too small. Our first guess was that the current had pushed us south of the sound during our twisting passage, so we worked along the rocks northward. This produced nothing resembling the chart's rendition of the coast south of the sound. We then turned southward. Stocky raised the radio station on VHF, but we had no means of getting a directional bearing.

It was of some comfort to be on the coast, but then the thought of sunken ledges occurred to me. I sent Corty to the spreaders to get better depth perception of the water. If there were any sunkers in those coves, we wouldn't have known about them because of the lack of soundings on the charts. I would bet the only humans that had been in those coves were hunters and trappers in the wintertime, when they could walk or go by dogsled on the ice. At no time did the fathometer register any soundings (it covers thirty fathoms, or 180 feet), even though we were often within ten feet of the cliffs! Up on the spreaders Corty was seeing over the low-lying fog better than we on deck, and he called some good turns from that post. At last we came to open water in a bay where the fog had lifted. Clearly this was the entrance to the sound we had sought all day.

Finally at eight that evening, 2000 on the dot, we powered into the dock at Prins Christians Sund Radio Station to the welcome of the men who were stationed there. Half of the station crew was on the dock to meet us. Already a welcoming dinner party was being prepared at the mess hall in the building complex atop the rocky mount of the station. Since the purpose of the station was communications with regular trans-Atlantic air flights and weather forecasts, most of the men spoke English, and even before arriving I had talked with the station chief and asked if I could buy diesel oil. He said I couldn't buy it; he would give it to me. It was Saturday night and just the right time to have a Danish-American party in their recreation room with its well-stocked bar.

What an ideal place! To get to the site of this impromptu bash we had to climb five hundred feet of stairs from the dock up to the base's buildings. It was easier going up than coming down, as things turned out, but that was no fault of gravity.

All of our hosts wondered how we got through the ice. They said we were the first sailing yacht in history to enter Prins Christians Sund from the east, but how they knew that is in itself a question. I find it hard to believe we were the first. Surely some Icelander must have wandered in there years ago. At any rate, they proceeded to fete us in grand style, though whether for our accomplishment or the mere excuse for a party it was difficult to say.

First, they offered us any amount of Scotch whisky our bladders could hold. Coming ashore from a week at sea, none of us was too steady after two drinks, but what saved us was a good hot meal, which Jergen, the chef, prepared especially for us. Our hosts had already eaten, so when the party resumed after dinner, the visiting team had the advantage. The home team had not interrupted their celebrating during our meal. Some of us switched to Tuborg, which isn't half-bad beer, and I think perhaps that was the turning point. Before I was enfeebled by my hosts' hospitality, I had a very interesting conversation with two or three of the technicians at the station. All were Danes, except one Greenlander, who didn't appear to have much Eskimo blood but who nevertheless was proud of being a Greenlander. One of the men had read Farley Mowat's story about the famed controversy that ensued after Peary reached the North Pole. Dr. Frederick Cook claimed to have reached the Pole a year earlier, in April of 1908, and told such a convincing story in Copenhagen that their distinguished Royal Society of something-or-other gave him their coveted medal, like the Nobel Prize in exploration. Peter Freuchen, an early twentieth-century Greenland explorer who happened to be in Copenhagen when Cook came in from the "Pole," was absolutely sure of his being a fraud. The nice Danes were taken in by the hoax. People in the States took sides, and the newspapers fanned the controversy. After prolonged debate and much challenging and so forth, most everyone came to realize that Cook's claims were questionable. In my opinion, Farley Mowat does not do credit to himself by "coming out" for Cook, who, it should be recalled, more or less admitted he had exaggerated. Whether Peary was one thousand yards from the Pole or even five thousand yards, I'm convinced he was there. What's more, he had four Etah

Eskimos and his aide, Matthew Henson, with him as witnesses. I often wondered how he could get a horizon for sights, but he used accepted methods to cope with that problem. Peary's attack on the Pole was unbelievably well organized, and I thought I defended him pretty well. The Dane who backed Cook agreed to "have another look."

By midnight it was time to call it quits. Hardly anyone was making much sense. Measured by body count, it was a close contest, at least at the time we visitors filed out. When last seen, the home team were draped over the furniture in artistic angles of repose.

The visitors then had a tough downhill course to the boat, during which there were a few casualties. Orlin, Dicky, and I buckled up in an alpine fashion and managed to stay on the ladder, or stairs, if one prefers. Stocky meandered into the dog compound, and Salley unfortunately took a few spills, which produced some coloration around her nose and eyes. As so often is the case, the Good Lord took care of the worst amongst us: Corty and Michael. The latter had the nerve later to recite a story that exaggerated my perfectly normal need to visit the head in the middle of the evening. He claimed I did this overboard in full view of Salley and others who had made it to the cockpit. In any event, it was a good party and no doubt a good muscle relaxer for what lay ahead.

The thought reverberated in my head that we had made it through Denmark Strait. While not home yet, we sure as hell were around the Tattenham Corner, as they might say at Epsom.

11

Bounding Home

SUNDAY MORNING WAS BRIGHT and blue overhead. Orlin and Stocky had already climbed to the top of the hill for pictures. The wind had piped up. It was whistling in from the east and had already pushed a lot of the pack ice into the fjord, where only the previous night it had been clear.

As we were having breakfast a small motor vessel came in and tied to our outboard side. We switched positions so she could unload the supplies she had brought from Narssaq, a town to the west. This little boat was run by a Dane and his Greenlander son. The boy, who was part Eskimo and looked more Eskimo than white, was about twelve and could handle firearms, as demonstrated by a few potshots he took off the stern with his old man's rifle. They delivered their cargo and quickly got underway to the west.

I began to sense some urgency about leaving, because the sound was getting clogged with east Greenland pack ice pushed in by the easterly wind and flood tide. Per Pedersen, a seven-foot-tall weatherman at the station, rolled out a barrel of diesel, and we transferred enough to fill our two regular tanks. Pedersen told me we should expect a cold winter in 1977.

"Why do you say that?" I asked.

"Because we have observed an unusual switch in the upper air current. It's blowing from northwest," he said. He said it so matter-of-

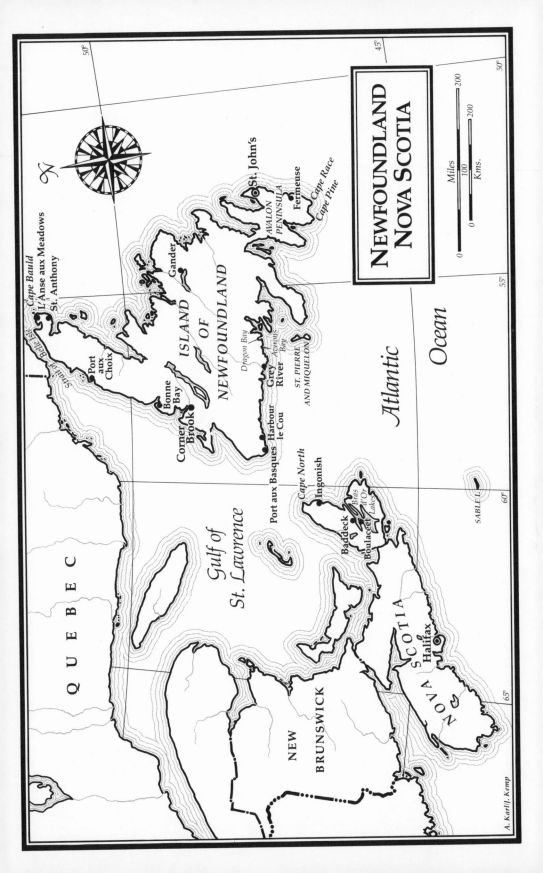

factly that I just put it down as something to remember. What I should have done was buy orange juice futures on the Commodity Exchange on the theory that the orange groves in Florida would freeze. He was so right! That winter the eastern half of the United States was in a deep freeze. January, 1977, was the coldest month in my lifetime.

After expressing our gratitude to the station manager, Arne Martens, I gave him a New York Yacht Club burgee as a souvenir, and he gave me a Danish courtesy flag, which, to be proper, I should have had at our starboard spreader since entering Danish territory. While all this transpired, a rather substantial bergy bit floated in and trapped us at the dock. Pedersen jumped into a work boat and nudged the ice out of the way, using his boat like a push tug. Then off we went to the west.

The ice again had become tricky and I steered into at least two culs-de-sac before finding an open lead down the sound. All afternoon the wind picked up in intensity. We were heading for the village of Augpilagtoq, but around 1800 I noticed off to starboard a little cove with what looked like a beach. The beach was a small gravel moraine with a glacier in the valley behind it. There were two small icebergs that appeared to be at anchor off the beach. It looked as if it might be a good anchorage. I put the helm over and slowed down a little as we headed into the cove. The chart had only one string of depth recordings in the middle of the sound, and that showed over two hundred fathoms. My fathometer was still off soundings.

Suddenly Salley shouted, "It looks shallow ahead, skipper!" I started to put the helm over, but a berg prevented me from turning. We then crunched aground. The difference between two hundred fathoms and five feet had been no more than two or three boat-lengths.

What a mess! We couldn't get her off by backing down the engine, and she wouldn't turn an inch in forward gear. The only thing to do was get out an anchor and try to kedge off, which meant taking time to blow up the rubber dinghy to carry out the anchor. Meanwhile the tide was running out! I sent Stocky out in the dinghy with the plow and chain and plenty of line. We finally got the anchor set and managed to kedge the bow around so that it was pointing back in the direction from which we had come. But still no luck getting loose, and the boat was starting to heel as the tide went still lower. We were stuck.

While Stocky was out in the dinghy, we handed him a lead line to take soundings. There was plenty of water where the anchor was, so we had to inch our way eastward. By now it was hopeless to get off before the next flood tide, which meant at least another six hours. I resigned myself to that, but I worried that when the tide came back perhaps the wind would drive us farther up on the gravel shelf. Knowing we would need one anchor to kedge, I had Stocky put out another forty-five-pound plow anchor to the east, with lots of scope — two hundred feet, to be exact.

We were now heeling to a point where water was over the lee rail. I turned the rudder in the opposite direction from the heeling, so it wouldn't be wrenched off. Then we went below for supper. It was blowing over thirty-five knots in our little cove and at least forty-five to fifty in the middle of the sound, which was a perfect funnel for an east wind. On deck you couldn't hear for the howling of the wind. I couldn't help thinking of the irony of getting through the dangers of the pack, only to fetch up on a beach in Prins Christians Sund. My mind raced through all the bad things that could happen, including abandoning ship. This was exactly what happened to Sam Allen and Rockwell Kent and the others. Thank God there were no boulders around, but being hit by a wind-driven berg was surely not out of the realm of possibility if the wind were to shift direction. That could destroy us. This was no fun. Here we were past nearly all the hurdles, and yet now our boat was in serious trouble. Would the hull hold together? Would some through-hull fitting break and let water fill up the boat? How about the rig? Would all tangs hold or would our upper shroud let go and the mast go over the side? These were all possibilities, but there wasn't anything any of us could do about the situation. We just had to wait for the tide, and each tide takes six hours. The ebb tide, as best I could calculate, had over three more hours. If that were correct, then we had a chance, because it meant we didn't go aground at exactly high tide. It meant that after three hours of further ebb and three of the incoming flood we would be back to where we were now. Then, with another three hours of flood, we should have enough tide to refloat. We would have to be damn careful not to allow the boat to slip farther up on the shore on the incoming tide. Careful attention would be paid to the two anchors after the tide change. Meanwhile, we could only go below, keep warm, try to cook supper, and get some rest.

Aground in Prins Christians Sund. Salley Norwood and Courtenay Jenkins measure the angle of heel with an orange (Orlin Donaldson)

Orlin cooked and served supper at the unhappy angle of heel of 45°. It was a strain just to get the plates back up to the sink. Salley lay on the mast, which was wrapped in an Orlon blanket to put insulation around the highly conductive and cold aluminum. She soon went to sleep on the mast! After supper, I found myself resting on the shelf over the port quarter-berth while the boat lay at 65° heel. I had assured everyone the boat would hold together and that a little mud and gravel wouldn't hurt us. The gravel was less than three-quarters of an inch from my body and I could feel it grind. Back in that quarter-berth I felt as though I were packed in a steamer trunk with the Devil himself as the baggage master. There wasn't much sleep that evening as we waited for the turn of the tide. However, the situation was far from hopeless and the longer we lay there the better were our chances.

The tide finally started to flood in the early morning, and the boat gradually righted. We pulled her off by putting the kedge anchor line to a winch and cranking. At 0345 in the morning we were afloat. What a relief! It was an early start to Augpilagtoq, a small native village in Ilua Fjord, which was only a few miles to the west. We had never seen such canyons! The mountains around us rose to five, six, and even seven thousand feet, mostly straight up for the first four thousand feet. It was exhilarating to be off the bottom, but the canyons in the wee hours of the morning were intimidating. The passage was a third the width of the East River of Manhattan, and the wind whistled right down the path of the fjord, while chunks of ice dotted the surface and snow and ice rimmed the dark rock visible in the early hours. But we were free, by God, we were free!

Augpilagtoq was nestled in the rocks, and the entrance to its harbor was invisible until we got there. It was a tiny slit in what looked like the side of a mountain. We poked our way in and tied up so that we wouldn't swing in the wind. The harbor was entirely too small for anchoring. A red hospital boat came in later and tied up behind us. She was making the rounds with a Danish dentist who fixed toothaches and repaired cavities. Later I noticed the native crew on the hospital boat eating a lunch of dried uncooked fish, which I later learned was a delicacy.

We went ashore to the government store to buy some staples. While in the store I was assisted by a blonde Eskimo, a Greenlander whose genes must have favored her Nordic father. She didn't have much personality, but I was fascinated by her looks. Her eyes were blue and her skin was fair, but her forehead was flat and her eyes had an almond shape and thus a hint of the Oriental. To my overture of a smile, she couldn't have been less interested, not that I was any bargain. Clearly she was telling me she had no interest in white men, which is just as well, for had it been otherwise I might have offered her a berth in *Reindeer*. How could I explain a blonde Eskimo to American Immigration, let alone my wife? This girl reminded me of the controversy between Stefansson and Amundsen. The latter was highly critical of the Icelandic explorer Stefansson, who claimed there were blonde Eskimos. Amundsen must have studied genetics, for he carefully pointed out that Mendel's Law stated that the second generation of one half-breed parent mixed with a full-breed could produce a full-breed of one race or the other. This was just one of many criticisms that Amundsen fired off after the publication of Vilhjalmur Stefansson's book entitled *The Friendly Arctic* in 1921. Gilbert Grosvenor of *National Geographic* gave Stefansson the idea for that title, because much of Stefansson's theme concerned the livableness of the Arctic. No one had ever explored more of the Canadian Arctic than Stefansson. He lived with the Eskimos and beyond the Eskimos, and he proved that animal and sea life was abundant all the way to the polar regions. Amundsen, who had traversed the Northwest Passage and the Northeast Passage and had discovered the South Pole, had some credentials, of course, and he bristled at what he thought was an implication that life up there was easy. As in the famous North Pole controversy between Peary and Cook, scientists chose sides and the press ate it up. Explorers were not always the most tolerant chaps! Amundsen's railings unwittingly insured smashing success for Stefansson's book.

Augpilagtoq was a real Eskimo village. The arrival of a modern American sailboat caused a stir. School let out, and the kids came down to the dock to gawk at us. We gave out souvenir flags and coins, and those who received such items were immediately mobbed, so we had to avoid showing any preference. We invited a few boys aboard, and they looked at everything the way we might look at things on the moon. Orlin, Stocky, and Michael scouted the whole village, taking pictures all over. I don't know who looked more fascinated, our guys or theirs. We didn't get beyond sign language, but that was quite sufficient, except in one case: I thought I had bought a bottle of peanut butter, which turned out to be mustard.

We departed around ten o'clock, sailed westward in Ilua Fjord, and then turned the corner south in Torsukatak Fjord. In late afternoon we emerged on the southwest coast at Frederiksdal. Again we had to be very careful, for the waters off the town were dotted with skerries, not all of which were on the chart. It was noticeably warmer and the topography was much less stark. We even saw occasional fields of green against a brownish backdrop and a few sheep grazing in the tiny fields! This was Greenland as the first Vikings saw it almost a thousand years ago.

Greenland is the world's largest island (Australia being a continent). From north to south it is 1,650 miles in length, and at its widest part 750 miles. The most westerly part of Greenland is west of Boston and its most easterly is on the same meridian as the east coast of Ireland. While the island is enormous in size, the population is only around 45,000, of whom some 7,000 are Danes, the rest Greenlanders, which means Eskimo or Eskimo/Dane combination. Greenlanders thus com-

School lets out to see us at Augpilagtoq. Orlin Donaldson with teacher and class
(Courtenay Jenkins)

prise more than half the Eskimo population of the world, which numbers only 60,000.

The earliest Eskimo inhabitants are said to have come across from Canada around 500 B.C. Being nomadic, they followed the game. Their primary migration was down the west coast, which is milder and more habitable. There has been some evidence that one group followed the reindeer and musk-ox across the top and down the northeast coast but not past the barriers of the great fjords of the central east coast. Eskimos found on the southeast coast were believed to have migrated there from the west coast, around or inside Cape Farewell. This group lived in isolation for so many centuries that even at present they have difficulty understanding the language of the west coast Eskimos, while the latter speak the same language as those of Labrador, Baffin Land, Ellesmere Island, and even the Yukon — the Inuit language, albeit with widely varying dialects.

At no time in my research did I find the slightest hint of the ancient Vikings on the real east coast. Whether Henry Hudson, who sighted this coast at Cape Hold-with-Hope in 1607, was the first white man to see it is moot, but the Scoresbys, senior and junior, in 1820 were certainly the first to do any serious exploration thereof. They were a cut above the average whaler, and they spent the better part of a summer cruising around what's now called Liverpool Land, charting it and describing it for future mariners.

Dutch, English, and Danish whalers had long fished the area, and some of them must surely have made it ashore. In 1777, for instance, fifty whaling vessels were caught in a storm and crushed by the ice in the Liverpool area of the coast. Out of 500 men, 400 lives were lost, and the rest drifted south on the floes to Cape Farewell. Some of them made it all the way to Godthaab on the west coast. Eskimo graves in the Scoresby Sund district have been found to contain iron artifacts, which suggests that some of these men, or other white men, made it ashore and possibly joined the settlements on this part of the coast. Scoresby mentioned, as did Nansen later in the nineteenth century, the natives' fascination with iron objects and other accouterments of Western man. Thus, the discovery by later expeditions of such items found in graves seems to confirm the earlier presence of the white man.

Scoresby also observed plenty of driftwood from trees known to be Siberian, an observation that encouraged the great Fridtjof Nansen to make his nearly successful attempt in 1893 to reach the North Pole by drifting across with the Siberian ice.

Another explorer who reached east Greenland well to the north was Captain D. C. Clavering, RN, who was taking Captain Sabine to the High Arctic to measure the force of gravity in the area. He sailed into Pendulum Island in 1823. From there he took a small boat to what is now called Clavering Island, where he found a family of twelve Eskimos. This was an important discovery, because these were the first Eskimos actually known to be living on the east coast north of the Arctic Circle.

The only other settlement on the whole coast was discovered by the Dane Gustav Holm in 1884. He made it to King Oscar's Haven and found the village of Angmagssalik, which we had chosen as our first Greenland destination in 1976. Holm found a thriving town of 413 natives, which must have startled the world, particularly the Danes and Norwegians, who had sent out scores of expeditions for over three centuries to look for the missing eastern settlement, or Osterbygden, as it was called. Not one of these expeditions made it through the east Greenland ice. Of course, Angmagssalik was not what they were looking for; they were looking for the "lost" Vikings, not Eskimos.

The Holm expedition gave Nansen the coastal knowledge he needed for his famous sledge journey, the first ever made across the Greenland ice cap in 1888. Nansen and Sverdrup and their two Lapps, Balto and Ravna (like the Sherpas of this century) were put ashore on the ice near Kap Dan from the steam barkentine *Jason,* only to find out they were on the drifting pack ice, separated from the shore. They drifted southwest some 150 miles before they were able to get ashore at Mogen Heinsen Fjord just south of Tingmiarmiut. From here they trudged back north almost to Angmagssalik before setting off across the ice cap to the west coast on their famous journey.

In 1925, the Danes moved ninety Eskimos from Angmagssalik to a good hunting and fishing location in Scoresby Sund. It was this group and offshoots thereof that the American explorer Louise Boyd came across in her seven sorties to arctic east Greenland from the midtwenties to 1938. Employing a Norwegian sealer, like *Nordkap II,* Miss Boyd mapped and photographed nearly the entire coast from Franz Josef Fjord all the way north. Her studies were so unique and useful that the U.S. Navy and Coast Guard put great reliance on them in World War II. She was awarded special citations by the U.S. government, and the Danes named an entire area of east Greenland Miss Boyd Land.

It was easy to see what fascinated Louise Boyd. Now that we had arrived in the very bay into which nearly one thousand years ago the Vikings had sailed or drifted from the sea, there was excitement in just being there. We were helped to an anchorage in the harbor by a young Eskimo in a kayak. Chunks of small icebergs were scattered about to remind us that the West Greenland Current flowed north, bearing the pack with it. Going ashore, our photographers found a fairly primitive-looking place but happy people. There were clothes hanging on clotheslines and fish and a few seals also hanging out to dry on the luckier fishermen's homes. Trash disposal was not very modern or esthetic, as it had been strewn out on the rocks and only partially carried away by the tide.

Near Frederiksdal was a loran station manned by Danes. One radio technician, named Anderssen, kindly offered to escort us across the inlet to the site of the first Viking settlement, that of Herjolf, which was a treat of the first magnitude. Imagine! Here we were at Herjolfnes, looking at the ruins of the original barn and the first church. Still standing was a stone baptismal font where no doubt the first Christians of Greenland gathered to sanctify the newborn. Apparently many artifacts discovered on this site had been sent to Copenhagen's museum, but those left there made us all feel small and a bit awed.

This led to a discussion of the physical nature of Greenland. First, only 5 percent of the country is unhabitable, and that's mostly on the fringe of the west coast. The rest is primarily ice cap, mountains, and permafrost. If all the ice in Greenland were melted, say by thermonuclear devices, the world's oceans would rise by twenty-three feet! Anderssen told me that in some of the fjords on the west coast, such as Jakobshavn for instance, as much as twenty million tons of ice are discharged into the water per day. The glacier moves at an enormously fast rate, some sixty-five to one hundred feet per day. When the bergs are calved into the water they move farther north along the coast, then across Baffin Bay to join the Labrador Current. Some of these bergs live several years and travel thousands of miles, while periodically grounding, floating, and regrounding. Were it not for the tremendous movement of ice in all forms between Greenland and Labrador, geologists believe that this area would dwarf the Baltimore Canyon and perhaps even equal the North Slope as a source of hydrocarbons, particularly natural gas. One hopes that technology will somehow solve the problem of lifting this gas but not at the risk of damage to the environment, which would be catastrophic.

The sociological problems that Anderssen discussed were even more challenging than the physical ones. Big changes were brought about by World War II, when airport construction and military necessities put white men into Greenland at a time when the natives numbered only about twenty thousand. Western health standards increased life expectancy from around thirty-five years to sixty-one years and even more. More recently birth control has been introduced, and this has tended to control overpopulation. Perhaps the worst measure taken by the Danes was moving so many natives into the towns like Godthaab. In one fell swoop whole villages moved from semi–Stone Age structures to apart-

Dicky Cromwell scoops up ice for the icebox before we leave Greenland for Newfoundland (Stockton N. Smith)

ment dwellings, and they had no idea how to cope with such a change. Suddenly Denmark had a major social problem on its hands in its Greenland territory, and as in the rest of the Western World the response to such a problem was welfare. As a corollary of this, alcoholism became rampant and the suicide rate soared. If there is any one clear-cut answer to these problems, it has as yet not emerged. Some of the natives themselves have opted for going back to their own culture, hunting and fishing and self-reliance, but by far the majority have become in a sense wards of the state. Approximately forty-one thousand Greenlanders are subsidized by five million Danes to the tune of $130 million per year. There was a touch of déjà vu to all this, but nothing we could say or do would make any difference or add anything, and I was getting itchy to get on the move.

After absorbing all these lessons in history, we finally departed for the northern tip of Newfoundland, some 750 miles to the southwest and across the Labrador Sea. That evening we met the pack ice of the west coast, and it was no patsy. Again we had to slow down and twist, turn, and shove. Some of us wondered what we had done to anger the gods again, but at least it wasn't cold. A remarkable change in temperature. We kept moving, even in the dark, and by 2200 we finally poked through to the ice-free water of the Labrador Sea, some forty to forty-five miles offshore. We celebrated with a late supper and afterwards called Peggy, the Ponces, and others at home through our friend the New York high seas operator. On 25 August the wind hauled to the northeast and came in gale force. We went to the number three genoa alone, furling the main, and then the number four, roaring downwind at nine knots for eight hours. By 1645, the wind diminished and, happily, came in from the northwest. Up went more canvas, and we still flew along.

Michael had a head cold and, reaching in the medicine cabinet for a pill for him, I dropped the bottle in the toilet. What a predicament! Orlin and I worked three hours taking the damn thing apart. We found the inside of the pump full of calcified deposits, which we had to chip out with a hammer and chisel. After that dirty and sweaty job, Orlin and I went topside and treated ourselves to the strongest drink we had left — tea. It went down well, and we chatted about our trip. We figured there had been about twenty-seven people, all told, involved in one or more stages of the trip. Places where the crew changed totaled eleven. These ports and the dates for arrival were part of the plan laid out in January. We took no small pride in the fact we had made it to every single port at or before the date planned six or seven months earlier. The optional part of the trip, namely Greenland, had been negotiated, and what we had seen there far surpassed our expectations. The whole crew seemed to smile with satisfaction, not of having achieved any record but of having added immeasurably to our knowledge and having shared an undertaking none of us would forget. It was not yet the end of the trip but maybe, just maybe, it was the end of the toughest part.

All the next day we rode like a roller coaster, and in the sun it was warm and comfortable. On the twenty-seventh the wind lightened; it was "Elvis's" (Courtenay's) birthday, so we prepared a special meal in his honor. It came out of cans, but it was delicious. On 29 August, a Sunday, we glided into the government wharf at St. Anthony, Newfoundland. We had crossed and recrossed the North Atlantic, and it was appropriate for three of us, who were members of St. Anthony Hall, to land at a town named after our patron saint.

St. Anthony, nearly at the northern tip of Newfoundland, is the head-quarters of the Grenfell Mission. Dr. Peter Roberts, on the Mission's staff, lent us his car and his laundromat, and we worked like mad, getting stores and supplies and fixing the stove, which once more was on the blink. Gary Madeira, son of one of my oldest friends, and Andy Harris, both from Philadelphia, flew in to St. Anthony in a float plane from Gander. The same plane took Stocky and Dicky back so they could get to opening sessions of their senior year at Virginia or see their girl friends, whichever came first.

By late afternoon the next day we were again underway, this time north to weather Cape Bauld and turn the corner down the Strait of Belle Isle and into the Gulf of St. Lawrence. We bombed it all the way to Port aux Choix, where we put in to see the museum on the spot where the earliest tribe of prehistoric maritime Indians had once lived, around 2500 B.C. The visit was marked by a rather solid jolt on the rocks, this time charted. I had apparently learned no lesson in Greenland!

The next day we found ourselves in a stiff wind in the Gulf, some seventy knots to be exact. This storm was so tiring that I decided to stop for a rest at Bonne Bay, our old stamping ground in 1974. Just for fun I called Gander Radio for a weather report. In the manner of his Albion ancestors, the Newfie weatherman told me there was a local disturbance in the Gulf. I thanked him for telling me about it, and we carried on.

The rest was anticlimax. We went straight for the Bras d'Or Lakes of Cape Breton, leaving Cape North to starboard, along with the bold cliffs of Ingonish. At Baddeck we stopped to let off Salley and Gary, then dropped in at the Russells' at Boulaceet. From there it was on the wind to Halifax and the hospitality of the Royal Nova Scotia Yacht Squadron. After a short break, we left for New York with favoring northwest winds and a touch of fall in the air. All seemed right with the world; even the Russians, I decided, were nice guys after all. Orlin, I conceded, was right about Shurbitov. Nothing conspiratorial about him, just a good fellow, so I dropped the idea of reporting his visit to the ONI (Office of Naval Intelligence) or the CIA.

We arrived at the Gulf Dock at Twenty-third Street in New York on Sunday, 12 September, three and a half months from the time we had sailed out of Chesapeake Bay. The Big Apple never looked better, and we made a generous contribution to the East Side restaurant business.

Later, after returning home, when news of the trip had spread around, I began to receive congratulatory mail and telegrams, mostly from the cognoscenti. Of all the communications that came my way, nothing was more warming and eye-popping than the following message on a plain postcard:

> Congratulations,
> Shurbitov
> Commander, United States Navy

Bibliography

The following books were consulted or read in full in the preparation of the voyages and the material for the book.

Amedeo Luigi of Savoy, Duke of the Abruzzi, *On the Polar Star in the Arctic Sea* (London: Hutchinson & Co., 1903).

Boyd, Louise, *The Coast of Northeast Greenland* (New York: American Geographical Society, 1948).

—— *The Fjord Region in East Greenland* (New York: American Geographical Society, 1935).

Chapman, Frederick Trench, *Voyages to Vinland* (New York: Alfred A. Knopf, 1942).

Dole, Nathan Haskell, *American in Spitsbergen* (Boston: Marshall Jones Co., 1922).

Ellsberg, Edward, *Hell on Ice* (New York: Dodd, Mead & Co., 1938).

Enterline, James Robert, *Viking America* (Garden City, N.Y.: Doubleday & Co., 1972).

Forbes, Alexander, *Northernmost Labrador Mapped from the Air* (New York: American Geographical Society, 1938).

—— *Quest for a Northern Air Route* (Cambridge, Mass.: Harvard University Press, 1953).

Freuchen, Peter, *Arctic Adventure* (London: William Heinemann, Ltd., 1936).

Gad, Finn, *History of Greenland*. Volume I, *Earliest Times to 1700*, translated by Ernst Dupont (London: C. Hurst & Co., 1970).

Gleason, Robert J., *Icebound in the Siberian Arctic* (Anchorage, Alaska: Alaska Northwest Publishing Co., 1977).

Greely, A. W., *Three Years of Arctic Service* (New York: Charles Scribner & Sons, 1886).

Greve, Tim, *Svalbard: Norway in the Arctic Ocean* (Trykkeri, Norway: Grøndahl & Sons, 1975).

H. M. Admiralty, *The Arctic Pilot* (London: Her Majesty's Stationers, 1975).

Hall, Charles Francis, *Arctic Researches* (New York: Harper Brothers, 1865).
Hyde, Alexander, *The Frozen Zone* (Hartford, Conn.: Columbian Book Co., 1875).
Ingstad, Helge, *Westward to Vinland* (New York: St. Martin's Press, 1969).
Jones, Gwyn, *Eirik the Red* (London: Oxford University Press, 1961).
Journals of the Royal Cruising Club, *Roving Commissions* (London: Royal Cruising Club Press, 1951–1976).
Kane, Elisha Kent, *Arctic Explorations* (Philadelphia: Childs & Peterson, 1856).
Kent, Rockwell, *N by E* (New York: Brewer & Warren, 1930).
Lansing, Alfred, *Endurance* (New York: McGraw-Hill, 1959).
MacMillan, Donald B., *Four Years in the White North* (New York: Harper Brothers, 1918).
Magnusson, Magnus, and Hermann Palsson, *The Vinland Sagas* (Harmsworth, England: Penguin Books, 1965).
Moody, T. W., and F. X. Martin, *The Course of Irish History* (Cork: Mercier Press, 1967).
Morison, Samuel Eliot, *The European Discovery of America: The Northern and Southern Voyages* (New York: Oxford Universtiy Press, 1974).
Mowat, Farley, *The Polar Passion* (Toronto: McClelland & Stewart, Ltd., 1967).
Nansen, Fridtjof, *Farthest North* (New York: Harper Brothers, 1897).
The Arctic Voyages of Adolf Erik Nordenskiold 1858–1879 (London: Macmillan & Co., 1879).
Nyborg, Anders, *Førøyar* (Rungsted Kyst, Denmark: International Publishers, Ltd., 1975).
Peary, Robert E., *Northward over the Great Ice* (New York: Frederick A. Stokes Co., 1898).
Phipps, Constantine John, *A Voyage toward the North Pole* (Dublin: Sleater, Williams, Wilson, Husband, Walker & Jenkin, 1775).
Scherman, Katherine, *Daughter of Fire* (Boston: Little, Brown & Co., 1976).
Scoresby, William, Jr., *Journal of a Voyage to the Northern Whale Fishery* (Edinburgh: Archibald Constable & Co., 1823).
Severin, Tim, *The Brendan Voyage* (New York: McGraw-Hill, 1978).
Sheldon, Paul B., *Lure of the Labrador* (New York: Seven Seas Press, 1973).
Stefansson, Vilhjalmur, *The Friendly Arctic* (New York: Macmillan, 1943).
Talcott, Dudley, *Report of the Company* (New York: Random House, 1936).
Tilman, H. W., *Ice with Everything* (Sydney, B.C.: Gray's Publishing, Ltd., 1974).
Thördarson, Matthias, *The Vinland Voyages* (New York: American Geographical Society, Research Series No. 18).

In addition to the above, the author consulted many publications of the U.S. Hydrographic Office (now the National Oceanographic and Atmospheric Administration), the British Admiralty, the Norsk Polarinstitutt, and Canadian, Danish, and Icelandic publications.

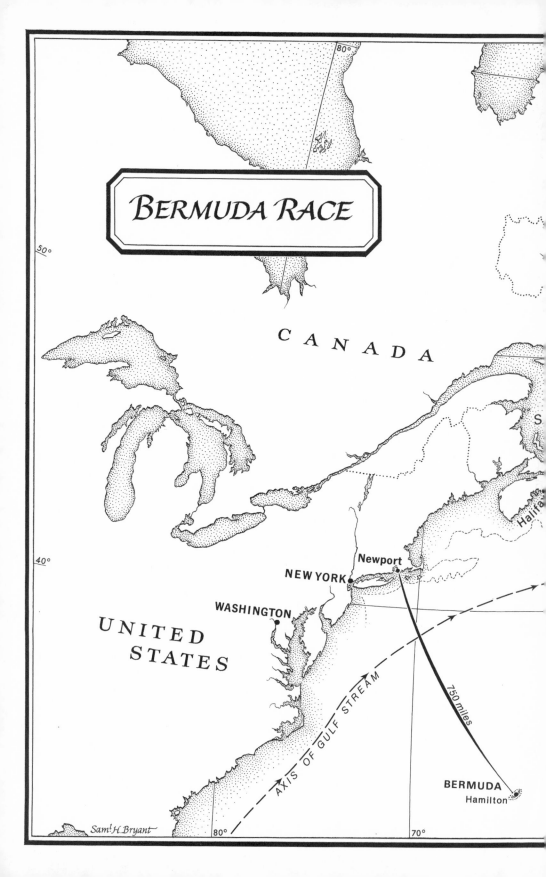

BERMUDA RACE

50°

80°

C A N A D A

S.

Halifa[x]

40°

Newport

NEW YORK

WASHINGTON

U N I T E D
S T A T E S

AXIS OF GULF STREAM

750 miles

BERMUDA
Hamilton

Sam! H. Bryant

80°

70°